Expository Notes on Ezekiel

by

H.A. Ironside

www.solidchristianbooks.com

www.harryironsidebooks.com

2014

This was written in 1949

Contents

Preface

For many years it has been on my heart to try to produce a running commentary on the book of Ezekiel, but until the present, circumstances have not permitted this. During the last few months it has brought great blessing to my own soul as I have given many hours daily to meditation upon and study of this remarkable book, of which the present work is the result.

No one can be more conscious than I of its many imperfections, and yet it is my hope that there may be enough in it of a truly spiritual character that it will prove a means of blessing and edification to those who take the time to read it thoughtfully and prayerfully.

H. A. Ironside

Introduction

Of all the prophetic books Ezekiel is the one that has been neglected most. Many persons are repelled by the marvelous vision of the opening chapter and, finding it too difficult to understand, proceed no further; and so they lose the blessing they would gain otherwise by a careful study of this entire book in dependence upon the Holy Spirit as teacher, who inspired the prophet to write it (2 Peter 1:21). Yet to the reverent student the book presents no real difficulties that may not be overcome by a careful comparison of scripture with scripture. Thus one may be preserved from a private interpretation which would not harmonize with the rest of God's revealed Word.

Dr. Andrew Bonar, one of Scotland's illustrious Bible teachers in days gone by, in order to stir his hearers up to a careful study of every book of the Scriptures, would suggest the possibility of meeting a glorious being in the golden city who would be recognized as the prophet Ezekiel. Dr. Bonar imagined he heard the newcomer to paradise exclaim, "Ezekiel, how glad I am to meet you! This is a wonderful privilege!" To this he made the prophet reply, "I am pleased indeed to see you. I see you know my name. How did you like the book I wrote?" Then, because of never having given that portion of Holy Scripture serious consideration, the confusion of the newcomer would be dwelt upon in such a way as to create in the minds and hearts of his hearers the desire to become thoroughly acquainted with the great work in question.

Ezekiel is primarily the exponent of the divine government. Throughout his book he dwells upon the fact that God is over all, working out His plans and carrying out His own decisions, in spite of Satanic efforts to thwart His purpose. The devil may be, and is, the god and prince of this present world system, but over and above all is the throne of the Eternal Majesty, whose ways are past finding out, but who controls the destinies of Israel and the nations, "working all things according to the counsel of His own will."

The book divides naturally into four parts. Division 1 includes chapters 1 to 24: prophecies relating to Israel, calling to repentance in view of threatened judgment, all of which were uttered before the fall of Jerusalem; division 2, chapters 25 to 32: prophecies relating to seven nations with whom Israel had close relationship or providential dealings; division 3, chapters 33 to 39: the moral condition of Israel exposed, and the promise of a future restoration to God and to their land; division 4, chapters 40 to 48: a grand apocalyptic picture of the coming glory, when once more it shall be said of Jerusalem, "The Lord is there."

Ezekiel was of priestly ancestry, but was probably carried into captivity (in the reign of Jehoiachin) before he began to enter on his duties as priest. He was contemporary with Daniel who was carried into captivity earlier, in the reign of Jehoiakim. His ministry covers a period of some twenty-one years, from B.C. 595 to 574. We know nothing whatever as to his early life, and only such incidents of his life as a captive as are given us in his book. The account of the death of his wife is most affecting. His whole demeanor bespeaks a man subject to the will of God, and yet of resolute spirit, so that he was able to stand firmly for the truth and to witness against the iniquities of his people without flinching, no matter how great the opposition became.

There is a very definite and intimate connection between this book and that of The Revelation. The living creatures of Ezekiel's visions and those of the Apocalypse are clearly one and the same; and the closing vision of the restored earthly city and temple corresponds to that of John's concerning the heavenly city, in which no temple is seen, because the whole is one vast sanctuary where the redeemed will dwell in unclouded light in the presence of God and the Lamb. Many other similarities and contrasts will be observed by the careful student who reads with reverence and dependence upon the Holy Spirit.

The subject of the divine government is often lost sight of by those who fail to realize that grace does not annul or set aside government. God has not vacated His throne as the supreme Ruler over the nations, and it still remains as true of nations as of individuals that whatsoever is sown must be reaped. This is the background for a true philosophy of history, and explains much that is going on among the nations in our own times. To all this Ezekiel gives us the key.

Part I, Prophecies Relating To Israel (chapters 1-8)

Chapter One The Vision Of The Chariot Of God

"Now it came to pass in the thirtieth year, in the fourth month, in the fifth day of the month, as I was among the captives by the river Chebar, that the heavens were opened, and I saw visions of God. In the fifth day of the month, which was the fifth year of king Jehoiachin's captivity, the word of Jehovah came expressly unto Ezekiel the priest, the son of Buzi, in the land of the Chaldeans by the river Chebar; and the hand of Jehovah was there upon him"—vers. 1-3.

The book opens very abruptly by the declaration that in the thirtieth year the prophet saw visions of God. Scholars are not united as to what thirtieth year is referred to. Some consider it the thirtieth year of the dynasty of Nabopolassar, the father of Nebuchadnezzar, who founded the Babylonian empire. Others take it as the thirtieth year of Ezekiel's life, the year when, had things been in order and he in the land of Israel, he would have entered upon his responsibilities as priest. In either case, the fact of his call to the prophetic office is not invalidated. He was divinely appointed to be a witness to Israel and Judah after the first victories of Nebuchadnezzar and the second deportation of captives to Chaldea. He dwelt among these by the River Chebar. To him the heavens were opened and visions of God were vouchsafed. While there is a very close link between the prophecy of Daniel, who wrote of the times of the Gentiles, and Ezekiel who dwelt on the government of God among or over the nations, it was to him, particularly, that the heavens were opened. He was enabled to look into the throne room, as it were, of the Almighty and to understand how the affairs of men and of nations were overruled by Him who sat upon that throne in awful and sublime majesty.

It was five years after the carrying away of the ungodly king Jehoiachin, and in the fifth month of that year, that Ezekiel was called to his high office as a prophet of the Lord to the people of the captivity. He was the son of Buzi, a priest, but of which course we are not told. His ordination is expressed in the words, "The hand of the Lord was upon me." How blessed when His hands are laid on any man, and thus one is divinely called to represent God in a world that has turned away from Him. Happy is he who today can say in truth,

> "Christ, the Son of God, hath sent me
>
> Through the midnight lands;
>
> Mine the mighty ordination
>
> Of the pierced hands."

Whether or not one is officially commended of his brethren or of some authoritative body in the professing church, the great thing is to be ordained of God to minister in holy things.

"And I looked, and, behold, a stormy wind came out of the north, a great cloud, with a fire infolding itself, and a brightness round about it, and out of the midst thereof as it were glowing metal, out of the midst of the fire. And out of the midst thereof came the likeness of four living creatures. And this was their appearance: They had the likeness of a man; and every one had four faces, and every one of them had four wings. And their feet were straight feet; and the sole of their feet was like the sole of a calf's foot; and they sparkled like burnished brass. And they had the hands of a man under their wings on their four sides; and they four had their faces and their wings thus: their wings were joined one to another; they turned not when they went; they went every one straight forward. As for the likeness of their faces, they had the face of a man; and they four had the face of a lion on the right side; and they four had the face of an ox on the left side; they four had also the face of an eagle. And their faces and their wings were separate above; two wings of every one were joined one to another, and two covered their bodies. And they went every one straight forward: whither the spirit was to go, they went; they turned not when they went. As for the likeness of the living creatures, their appearance was like burning coals of fire, like the appearance of torches: the fire went up and down among the living creatures; and the fire was bright, and out of the fire went forth lightning. And the living creatures ran and returned as the appearance of a flash of lightning"—vers. 4-14.

Artists have attempted to picture this majestic vision of the Eternal One riding through the universe on His chariot of glory, but no human mind can visualize the description in its intricate details. As we read the words of the prophet we are reminded anew that as the heavens are high above the earth, so are God's thoughts beyond our thoughts and His ways above our ways. But even though the vision may be, as a whole, beyond our comprehension, there is much in it that becomes clear as we study it attentively.

As Ezekiel looked heavenward he beheld a stormy wind, evidently a whirlwind, coming from the north, which to an Israelite was the place of mystery, of darkness and of distress. The biting north wind brought with it blight and desolation. Babylon's legions entered the land from the north, spreading desolation wherever they went. Though false prophets cried, "Peace, peace," endeavoring to quiet the fears of the people, there would be no peace but rather destruction, because of the waywardness and disobedience of the leaders and people alike. A storm was coming. It was God Himself who had decreed it in His righteous government.

As the prophet gazed upon the enfolding cloud, he discerned the form of a great chariot with wheels of enormous height, the attendants of the divine majesty surrounding it, and one in the form of a man riding in triumph through the heavens.

The living creatures are identical with those of The Revelation, and yet the description is somewhat different. There each individual cherub has but one face, though there are four, as here; and they bear respectively the faces of a man, signifying intelligence; a lion, speaking of majesty and power; an ox, telling of patient service; and an eagle, the symbol of swiftness in execution of judgment and acute discernment from afar. Here each cherub has the four faces. These are the heads of the four orders of creation, the human, the wild beasts, the cattle of the farm, and the bird kingdom. There were two cherubim over the ark, attached to the mercy-seat, speaking of judgment (discernment), and justice (righteousness), the habitation of God's throne. The four here in Ezekiel and in The Revelation tell of these powers in connection with the government of the world. Four is the number of the world powers, as in Daniel 2 and 7 and elsewhere.

The cherubim here are seen in connection with divine activity in the affairs of the nations. They are the expression of the divine attributes. Whether they are actually created beings, like or akin to angels, or whether they are symbolic representations of these attributes, is a moot question. At any rate, we see in them the manifestation of the divine nature acting in righteous government over the nations. From the days of the Early Church fathers these cherubim have been linked with the manner in which Christ is presented in the four Gospels, and sometimes very fancifully, and apparently with no real grasp of their significance. For instance, "the lion of St. Mark" is well known and implies that Mark presents Jesus as the Lion of the tribe of Judah. But this is surely incorrect. It was Matthew to whom it was given so to portray Him; whereas Mark's record is symbolized better by the patient ox, the servant of God and man. Luke gives us pre-eminently the face of a Man—the Humanity of our Lord in all its perfection. John completes the story by setting Him forth as the heavenly One— the Eternal Son become flesh, aptly pictured by the eagle. In Christ all fulness dwells. He is the complete manifestation of all the divine attributes.

There are details that one who is more spiritually-minded might understand better, but which forbid more careful attempt at exposition as far as the present writer is concerned. The wings connect the cherubim with the heavens, and by these they are covered in the presence of the Throne Occupant. Under their wings are hands as of a man—hands ready to succor and help when needed, or to strike in judgment, if necessary. Nothing here is arbitrary; all is under the control of Him whose heart is concerned about all His creatures.

"They went every one straight forward." Nothing can turn aside the undeviating principles of the divine government. No schemes of men, no flaunting of God's Word, no studied attempts to thwart His righteous rule, can avail. Steadily the chariot of the Lord rolls on, accomplishing the ends He has in view.

Every one of the cherubs had the face of a man. This seems to be the predominant face. The others, archetypal heads of creation, occupy a secondary place. The face of a man tells us that heaven truly understands and enters into our problems. The Lord is mindful of His own, and His heart goes out to every creature He has made. These cherubim are the executors of His judgments as the seraphim are the agents of His grace (Isa. 6). But judgment is His strange work and is executed only when grace has been ignored or rejected.

The wings of the living creatures are used for worship and for service. Like the seraphim, with twain they cover their faces as they bow in adoration before the Majesty of the heavens. The other two are used to speed them on His errands. We may learn a lesson from this for ourselves: worship comes first, then service.

"They went every one straight forward: whither the spirit was to go, they went." There is no vain repetition in God's Word. The fact that this statement is repeated only helps to impress upon us the immutability of God's counsels. No power, either human or diabolic, can turn them aside. All are directed by the Spirit who is the expression of the divine activity and is ever working throughout the universe.

The appearance of the living creatures was ethereal, like flaming torches, even as we read, He "maketh His angels spirits; His ministers a flaming fire" (Ps. 104:4; Heb. 1:7). The angels are the ministers of God's providence through whom He rules the present creation. "But unto the angels hath He not put into subjection the age to come" (Heb. 2:5). That age will be ruled through His redeemed ones, associated with Christ on His throne, according as it is written, "The time came that the saints possessed the kingdom" (Dan. 7:22). The fire that went up and down among the living creatures is the Shekinah glory, the manifest presence of the God of Israel, the uncreated light that once abode over the mercy-seat and between the cherubim, in the Holiest of all, of the tabernacle in the wilderness and the temple built by Solomon. This glory Ezekiel saw leaving the temple and returning to heaven. Some day it will come back to earth again and hover above the holy city, and the glory shall be a defence over all (Isa. 4:5). During all the long period of the times of the nations, while the Jews are scattered and the temple-site is occupied by a mosque of the false prophet of Islam, the glory is departed from the earth. "Ichabod" is written over all this scene. So one has to look up to see it by faith in that place where Christ sits exalted at God's right hand.

The living creatures come and go—swift messengers bent on the King's business—as the appearance of lightning. Limitations of time are not theirs. Instantly they dart from one end of the universe to another as they carry out the bidding of their Imperial Lord. Even so shall His coming be when He returns to earth the second time, for "as the lightning, that lighteneth out of the one part under heaven, shineth unto the other part under heaven; so shall also the Son of Man be in His day" (Luke 17:24).

We turn to consider next the wheels with their terrible rotations as the chariot of the Almighty moves on in majesty.

"Now as I beheld the living creatures, behold, one wheel upon the earth beside the living creatures, for each of the four faces thereof. The appearance of the wheels and their work was like unto a beryl: and they four had one likeness; and their appearance and their work was as it were a wheel within a wheel. When they went, they went in their four directions: they turned not when they went. As for their rims, they were high and dreadful; and they four had their rims full of eyes round about. And when the living creatures went, the wheels went beside them; and when the living creatures were lifted up from the earth, the wheels were lifted up. Whithersoever the spirit was to go, they went; thither was the spirit to go: and the wheels were lifted up beside them; for the spirit of the living creature was in the wheels. When those went, these went; and when those stood, these stood; and when those were lifted up from the earth, the wheels were lifted up beside them: for the spirit of the living creature was in the wheels"—vers. 15-21.

These wheels connect the chariot with the earth. There are wings above and wheels below, and both are in perfect harmony, for the Lord hath His way in the sanctuary and in the sea (Ps. 77:13, 19). He is both the God of heaven and the Lord of the whole earth. All things serve His might. There is no one who can say unto Him, "What doest Thou?" or hope to resist His power. He makes the very wrath of man to praise Him, and that which would not contribute to His glory He restrains (Ps. 76:10).

Wheels, with their ever-recurring revolutions as they move on through the ages, suggest the great changes to which men and nations are subject. Nothing is at a standstill; everything is in constant motion. This is as true in nature, the material universe, as in the moral and spiritual realms. Solomon marvelled as he watched the great wheel of the world go round. He exclaimed, "One generation goeth, and another generation cometh; but the earth abideth forever. The sun also ariseth, and the sun goeth down, and hasteth to the place where he ariseth. The wind goeth toward the south, and turneth about unto the north; it turneth about continually in its course, and the wind returneth again to its circuits. All the rivers run into the sea, yet the sea is not full; unto the place whither the rivers go, thither they go again" (Eccl. 1:4-7). We say that history repeats itself. This is but another way of saying that the wheels are continually revolving.

And there are wheels within wheels, so arranged that we cannot follow their intricacies. But we see them everywhere, different principles working at one and the same time, in the world, in politics, in the church, in all phases of human society. So true is this that the mind becomes bewildered trying to keep all the different movements in mind, until we are tempted to think that all is utter confusion, and there is neither order nor sanity in the universe. But the spirit of the living creature is in the wheels and all are controlled by a higher power than the merely human, or blind chance, or what men call *fate*. Moreover, there are eyes in the wheels, and these speak of intelligence and careful discernment and discrimination. "The eyes of the Lord are in every

15

place, beholding the evil and the good" (Prov. 15:3) ; and, "The eyes of the Lord run to and fro throughout the whole earth, to show Himself strong in the behalf of them whose heart is perfect toward Him" (2 Chron. 16:9). Those eyes are ever over the righteous, and His ear is open to their cry (Ps. 34:15). And so as the wheels move on, though so high that we are unable to comprehend fully what God is doing, we may rest in this precious truth, that nothing moves but at His command or by His permission. In the days of the voice of the seventh angel, when he shall begin to sound, the mystery of God's long toleration of evils— His apparent indifference to the cruelties practised against His people and the wicked behavior of those who seemed to triumph for a time while the righteous suffered in silence— frill all be made clear, and we shall see that though the wheels were high and the mysteries of the divine government beyond our present ability to comprehend, yet all were under His control who was working according to plan in a way that puny man little realized. The wheels have never been separated from the living creatures. Nothing is left to chance. All movements among men are under divine control, and even Satan can act only as God gives permission, as we see in the account of His dealings with the patriarch Job.

"And over the head of the living creature there was the likeness of a firmament, like the terrible crystal to look upon, stretched forth over their heads above. And under the firmament were their wings straight, the one toward the other: every one had two which covered on this side, and every one had two which covered on that side, their bodies. And when they went, I heard the noise of their wings like the noise of great waters, like the voice of the Almighty, a noise of tumult like the noise of a host: when they stood, they let down their wings. And there was a voice above the firmament that was over their heads: when they stood, they let down their wings. And above the firmament that was over their heads was the likeness of a throne, as the appearance of a sapphire stone; and upon the likeness of the throne was a likeness as the appearance of a man upon it above. And I saw as it were glowing metal, as the appearance of fire within it round about, from the appearance of his loins and upward; and from the appearance of his loins and downward I saw as it were the appearance of fire, and there was brightness round about him. As the appearance of the bow that is in the cloud in the day of rain, so was the appearance of the brightness round about. This was the appearance of the likeness of the glory of Jehovah. And when I saw it, I fell upon my face, and I heard a voice of one that spake"— vers. 22-28.

The firmament, the heavenly dome, is over the living creatures, for it is under the heavens that the divine government is exercised. Nor is there ever any conflict between the various divine agencies or the divine counsels. What seems to man's finite mind to be intricate and confused is clear to the spiritual one, who sees God behind all His works and ways. So the cherubim act in perfect harmony and are thus joined to one another. All act in obedience to the voice above their heads, the voice of Him who sits unmoved upon His throne, undisturbed by all the storms of earth that rage below.

As Ezekiel looked up he saw the likeness of a Man upon that throne. This is a clear intimation that the Man of God's counsels, the Lord Jesus Christ, is ever to occupy that place of power and majesty. It was the preincarnate Christ that the prophet beheld, "the likeness of a Man." Now, since redemption is accomplished, the Man Christ Jesus sits in His glorified human body on that throne of the Eternal. Consider the description of the Son of Man walking amid the lampstands in The Revelation, and note how intimately that links with this.

The rainbow about the throne, also seen again in the Apocalypse, speaks of the unchanging covenant God made with Noah, and gives assurance that no matter what catastrophes prevail for the moment, God's watchful eye is ever upon this earth, and while it remains, summer and winter, seedtime and harvest shall not cease. The storm may rage and the very sun may seem to be blotted out of the heavens, but the Word of our God shall stand forever. His covenant He will not break, nor alter the thing that has gone out of His lips. Faith can rest on this and so be quiet and peaceful in the day of trouble.

Chapter Two The Prophet's Commission

"And He said unto me, Son of man, stand upon thy feet, and I will speak with thee. And the Spirit entered into me when He spake unto me, and set me upon my feet; and I heard Him that spake unto me. And He said unto me, Son of man, I send thee to the children of Israel, to nations that are rebellious, which have rebelled against Me: they and their fathers have transgressed against Me even unto this very day. And the children are impudent and stiff-hearted: I do send thee unto them; and thou shalt say unto them, Thus saith the Lord Jehovah. And they, whether they will hear, or whether they will forbear (for they are a rebellious house), yet shall know that there hath been a prophet among them. And thou, son of man, be not afraid of them, neither be afraid of their words, though briers and thorns are with thee, and thou dost dwell among scorpions: be not afraid of their words, nor be dismayed at their looks, though they are a rebellious house. And thou shalt speak My words unto them, whether they will hear, or whether they will forbear; for they are most rebellious. But thou, son of man, hear what I say unto thee; be not thou rebellious like that rebellious house: open thy mouth, and eat that which I give thee. And when I looked, behold, a hand was put forth unto me; and, lo, a roll of a book was therein; and He spread it before me: and it was written within and without; and there were written therein lamentations, and mourning, and woe"—vers. 1-10.

When God calls a man to act for Him in some particular capacity, He fits him for the service he is to undertake. Augustine well said, "God's commandings are God's enablings." The flesh may shrink from the great task, but he who counts on God will be able to say, "I am full of power by the Spirit of the Lord" (Micah 3:8). God never sends anyone at his own charges or to act in his own strength, much less to be guided by his own wisdom. This was clearly manifested in the case of Moses (Exod. 4:10-15), and of Jeremiah (Jer. 1:4-19); and it comes out very definitely here in the call of Ezekiel to the prophetic office. Already he had seen visions of God. Now he was commissioned to be God's mouthpiece to Israel and the nations. Jehovah still speaks in power and clarity after the lapse of two-and-a-half millennia.

The opening words of this chapter are most challenging. The Lord said to Ezekiel, "Son of man, stand upon thy feet, and I will speak unto thee." The expression "Son of man" is distinctive. In the Old Testament it is used of mankind generally (Job 25:6; 35:8; Psalms 144:3; 146:3), as also in several passages in the prophets (Isa. 51:12; 56:2; Jer. 49:18, 33; 50:40). It is used prophetically of Christ Himself in Psalm 144:3, and Daniel 7:13, and we know from the Epistle to the Hebrews that the "Son of Man" of Psalm 8:4 is actually our blessed Lord. But it is a characteristic title of Ezekiel, being found eighty-five times in this book. Once Daniel is so addressed, but it is never applied to any other prophet. It was our Lord's favorite title for Himself as recognizing His link with that lost world which He had come to save (Luke 19:10). It emphasized the reality of His Manhood, even as the title "Son of God" stressed His Deity.

As son of man, Ezekiel was to realize that although divinely called and supernaturally inspired, in himself he was but a man as others to whom he was to proclaim the words given him by God. He was commanded to stand on his feet, at attention, as it were, while the Lord commissioned him for his high and holy office. He was a priest already, and now was to become a prophet—one who was to speak for God to His people the word which had been spoken to him.

Moved and strengthened by the Spirit, undoubtedly the Holy Spirit who had entered into him, Ezekiel stood reverently before the Lord, listening in awe to the voice that spoke to him.

It was no easy service to which he was called. The Lord made it plain that he was to go to a nation of rebels, a people who had failed down through the centuries. The fathers had turned from God to idols, and the children had followed in their steps. Nor was there any likelihood that the children of the captivity, or those remaining in the land, would be any more ready to listen and to obey than their progenitors had been. They were all "impudent children and stiff-hearted." Ezekiel was to go to them, nevertheless, and give them another opportunity to repent that more dire calamities might be averted.

He was not to speak as from himself, but he was to declare with authority, "Thus saith the Lord God!" It is this that gives dignity and force to the messenger of Jehovah. He who goes before his fellows to declare the thoughts of his own mind, or the imaginations of his own heart, is not the messenger of the Lord. It is not for His ambassadors to delight men with eloquent phrases magnifying the achievements of others or glorifying their own labors. The one business of the servants of God is to proclaim the word of the Lord in faithfulness and yet with grace and humility. "Where the word of a king is, there is power" (Eccl. 8:4), and God is a great King whose Word shall never return to Him void, but shall accomplish that for which He sends it (Isa. 55:11).

Ezekiel did not have to "get up" sermons or compose learned discourses. He simply had to receive the word from the Lord his God and then to give it out in the power of the Spirit to those to whom he was called to minister. The same is true of every anointed servant of God today. Such have been called of the Lord to preach the Word, not human philosophy, specious reasoning or vain imaginations, which, after all, are only evil, and that continually (Gen. 6:5). This may often involve self-denial on the part of the preacher. Like Paul, he may have to be careful not to depend on the wisdom of words, lest the cross of Christ, the real message, be made of none effect. Dr. Harry Emerson Fosdick, the well-known liberal orator, has decried expository preaching as the poorest type of pulpit ministry, "because it leaves so little scope for the imagination." But this is the very reason the man of God should glory in unfolding the precious truths of the Scriptures instead of weaving a web of oratory out of himself, as a spider makes its lacy snare to entrap its prey.

Irrespective of the people's attitude toward his message, Ezekiel was to give out what God had given him. And whether they should hear or whether they should forbear—that is, refuse to heed, they would know that a prophet had been among them, when the words he proclaimed had been fulfilled.

He was not to be afraid of any who might threaten bodily harm. His confidence was to be in the One who sent him. Even though suffering resulted, as suggested by briers and thorns, and dwelling among scorpions, he was not to shrink from the task committed to him, nor be dismayed by the angry countenances of the rebellious house of Israel. It always means suffering to stand for God under adverse conditions. But grace will be supplied according as it is needed, that one may be enabled to endure as seeing Him who is invisible.

In ver. 7 the Lord reiterates and epitomizes all that had gone before. "Thou shalt speak My words unto them, whether they will hear, or whether they will forbear; for they are most rebellious." The apparent failure of the prophet's mission would not invalidate his authority as the spokesman for Jehovah. It is not necessary that one should be what the world calls successful: it is all-important that one should be faithful to the trust committed to him.

The real danger was that Ezekiel might grow weary of the struggle and become discouraged and fainthearted because of the opposition and the lack of response to his testimony. So the Lord warned him, "Be not thou rebellious like this rebellious house." And then He gave the strange command, "Open thy mouth, and eat that which I give thee."

As Ezekiel looked he beheld the form of a hand, reaching down from the cherubim, and in it a scroll, the roll of a book. This was the prophetic message he was to give to the people. Opening it up, there was revealed the terrible prophecies of lamentations and mourning and woe which were to be the burden of his message. To eat this roll was to take God's word into his very being, to make it part of himself, as it were, and so to be prepared to give it out to the remnant of the captivity.

Chapter Three Eating The Roll

"And He said unto me, Son of man, eat that which thou findest; eat this roll, and go, speak unto the house of Israel. So I opened my mouth, and He caused me to eat the roll. And He said unto me, Son of man, cause thy belly to eat, and fill thy bowels with this roll that I give thee. Then did I eat it; and it was in my mouth as honey for sweetness."—vers. 1-3.

In vision the prophet heard the command of the attendant messenger of the Lord of hosts, bidding him eat the scroll on which the word of the Lord was written. John had a similar vision on Patmos. Both he and Ezekiel are depicted as literally devouring the book. One is reminded of the declaration of Jeremiah, "Thy words were found, and I did eat them; and Thy Word was unto me the joy and rejoicing of mine heart" (Jer. 15:16). And again, the asseveration of the patriarch Job, "I have esteemed the words of His mouth more than my necessary food" (Job 23:12). In meeting the temptation of the devil to act without a command from the Father and so to make bread from stones, our blessed Lord quoted from Deut. 8:3 when He said, "Man shall not live by bread alone, but by every word that proceedeth out of the mouth of God" (Matt. 4:4). Only as we feed on the Word can we become strong in the Lord and the power of His might. Before Ezekiel went forth to give the word of God to others, he must eat the roll—that is, feed upon that word himself. The testimony of the Lord must become a part of his very being, so to speak, if he would so declare it that those to whom he ministered would feel the force of it in convicting power.

At first the prophet took the roll into his mouth, but did not seem to swallow it. In this he was like many who have a certain head knowledge of or intellectual acquaintance with the truth of Scripture, but have never really made it their own. So to Ezekiel the word came imperatively, "Son of man cause thy belly to eat." God desires truth in the inward parts. David could say, "Thy word have I hid in mine heart, that I might not sin against Thee" (Ps. 119:11). The truth must possess the very reins of our being. We must not only taste its sweetness, but also feed upon it, receive it into our inmost being, that it may completely dominate our lives.

Then, and then only are we prepared to give it forth to others. The minister of God must enjoy the Word himself by meditating upon it, inwardly digesting it, and so making it a part of himself. Then he is ready to declare the whole counsel of God to those who are famishing for want of it.

"And He said unto me, Son of man, go, get thee unto the house of Israel, and speak with My words unto them. For thou art not sent to a people of a strange speech and of a hard language, but to the house of Israel; not to many peoples of a strange speech and of a hard language, whose words thou canst not understand. Surely, if I sent thee to them, they would hearken unto thee. But the house of Israel will not hearken unto thee; for they will not hearken unto Me: for all the house of Israel are of a hard forehead and of a stiff heart"—vers. 4-7.

God would not have His servant under any illusions as to the possible effect of his message or of the attitude of those to whom he was sent to proclaim the Word of the Lord. He was not to go to the heathen, or to some nation of strange language and barbarous behavior. He was sent to his own people, the nation that had the law of God and had failed to obey it. As they had refused to heed the word spoken from Sinai, so they would refuse to heed that which the prophet was to put before them. But it was his business to proclaim the message. Results could be left to God. It is even so today. Those to whom it is given to preach the gospel are not responsible for its acceptance by their hearers. If men do receive the Word in faith, it becomes to them a savor of life unto life; if they refuse to obey, it is of death unto death. But God is honored as His servants speak for Him according to the illumination given by the Holy Spirit, and He has promised that His word shall not return unto Him void, but it shall accomplish that for which He sent it. The hearers of the message become the more responsible because of added light. The Word itself will be their judge in the day when the secrets of all hearts shall be revealed.

"Behold, I have made thy face hard against their faces, and thy forehead hard against their foreheads. As an adamant harder than flint have I made thy forehead: fear them not, neither be dismayed at their looks, though they are a rebellious house.

23

Moreover He said unto me, Son of man, all My words that I shall speak unto thee receive in thy heart, and hear with thine ears. And go, get thee to them of the captivity, unto the children of thy people, and speak unto them, and tell them, Thus saith the Lord Jehovah; whether they will hear, or whether they will forbear"—vers. 8-11.

Ezekiel was sent of God, not so much to the remnant remaining in the land of Palestine, but to those who had been carried away already as captives. One might have supposed that their afflictions would have made their hearts soft and their consciences tender, and that in their distress there would have been a great turning to the Lord. But it was quite the contrary. They became all the harder as they resented the suf- fering that had come upon them. They despised the chastening of the Almighty, and so profited nothing by what they had been called upon to pass through. It was, therefore, a thankless errand on which Ezekiel was sent, as far as man's estimation of his message was concerned. Naturally, he might be inclined to faint under all this and to become discouraged when there was no response to his words; but He who commissioned him was behind His servant, and He undertook to strengthen him for the task and to make him as strong for God as the people were strong against Him. The prophet was to stand as adamant against all the circumstances he would be called upon to meet. His strength lay in the realization that he had been divinely appointed to proclaim the truth of God without fear or favor. If the captives refused to hearken and obey the voice of the Lord, that was their responsibility, not Ezekiel's. It is well for every man of God to understand this. Nothing else can so lift him above all that he may be called upon to experience in the way of contempt or open opposition of those whom he labors to help.

"Then the Spirit lifted me up, and I heard behind me the voice of a great rushing, saying, Blessed he the glory of Jehovah from his place. And I heard the noise of the wings of the living creatures as they touched one another, and the noise of the wheels beside them, even the noise of a great rushing. So the Spirit lifted me up, and took me away; and I went in bitterness, in the heat of my spirit; and the hand of Jehovah was strong upon me. Then I came to them of the captivity at Tel-abib, that dwelt by the river Chebar, and to where they dwelt; and I sat there overwhelmed among them seven days"—vers. 12-15.

This was a fresh revelation of the power of God as Governor among the nations, given to encourage the prophet as he was about to begin his ministry. He had to learn that there was no might in himself; he could not carry on in what was merely human energy. The Spirit of God proceeding from the throne, took him up and placed him under divine control. This was ever true of our blessed Lord in the years of His humiliation. He ever chose to act, not in His inherent omnipotence as God the Son become flesh, but He put Himself under the guidance and control of the Holy Spirit. It was the Spirit who "drove Him into the wilderness," and it was by the Spirit of God that He cast out demons and accomplished all His mighty works.

His servants, too, are to be under the same authority as they go forth to witness. The "noise of a great rushing" that stirred Ezekiel's soul, reminds us of the sound as of a rushing, mighty wind at Pentecost, when the promised Comforter descended upon the one hundred and twenty disciples, baptizing them into one Body (1 Cor. 12:12, 13) and empowering them for service. The book of the Acts is far more truly designated as the Acts of the Holy Spirit than the Acts of the Apostles. It was the Spirit who empowered Peter and John and the rest for witness-bearing. The Spirit of the Lord caught away Philip when his work with the Ethiopian treasurer was done. The same Spirit opened and closed doors for Paul and his companions; and by the Spirit all testimony for Christ has been maintained throughout the centuries since.

It is evident that Ezekiel did not seek the position of being the mouthpiece of God. As a result of the book of "lamentations and mourning" which he had eaten, his own spirit was filled with bitterness. He was keenly conscious of the sadness of the burden of the Lord which he must proclaim. Borne along by the Spirit, however, he found himself among the captives at Tel-abib by the River Chebar. To them he was to give forth what God had given him. But so great was his inward exercise that for a full week he sat looking on, dumb with grief, as he considered their present condition and realized the hardness of their hearts and their unwillingness to heed what he was sent to declare unto them. At the end of the seven days God spoke again.

"And it came to pass at the end of seven days, that the word of Jehovah came unto me, saying, Son of man, I have made thee a watchman unto the house of Israel: therefore hear the word at My mouth, and give them warning from Me. When I say unto the wicked, Thou shalt surely die; and thou givest him not warning, nor speakest to warn the wicked from his wicked way, to save his life; the same wicked man shall die in his iniquity; but his blood will I require at thy hand. Yet if thou warn the wicked, and he turn not from his wickedness, nor from his wicked way, he shall die in his iniquity; but thou hast delivered thy soul. Again, when a righteous man doth turn from his righteousness, and commit iniquity, and I lay a stumblingblock before him, he shall die: because thou hast not given him warning, he shall die in his sin, and his righteous deeds which he hath done shall not be remembered; but his blood will I require at thy hand. Nevertheless if thou warn the righteous man, that the righteous sin not, and he doth not sin, he shall surely live, because he took warning; and thou hast delivered thy soul"—vers. 16-21.

Solemn are the responsibilities put by God Himself upon one whom He calls to be a watchman and to speak for Him to His people. It was undoubtedly this and the kindred passage in chapter 33, that the Apostle Paul had in mind when he declared to the Ephesian elders, "I take you to witness that I am free from the blood of all men." While among them, he had borne his testimony night and day with tears, and had not shunned to declare the whole counsel of God.

Though in an earlier dispensation, it was the same burden that was laid upon the heart of Ezekiel. Set apart by God and appointed to be a watchman in Judah, a tremendous responsibility devolved upon him. He was to warn the wicked of the judgments coming if they continued to live in defiance of God's holy law; and, likewise, he was responsible to stress the importance of continuing in the way of righteousness when addressing those who were

26

endeavoring to act in obedience to the commandments of God. If he failed to do this, and the wicked persisted in their evil ways until overtaken by judgment, and the unwarned who had walked in righteousness turned aside to commit iniquity, they should die in their sins, but their blood would be required at the watchman's hand. He would have to answer to God for leaving the people unwarned. It was a terrible responsibility, but the same responsibility rests on every chosen servant of Christ today.

In considering these verses, we need to remember that it is righteousness according to the law of Moses that is in question. We do not have before us here the gospel of the grace of God. The time had not come for that glorious revelation. The law said, "Which if a man do, he shall live in them" (Lev. 18:5). This, we are told distinctly in the Epistle to the Galatians, is the very opposite of the gospel.

In the Old Testament dispensation, where there was real faith in God, it would be manifested by delight in His Word and obedience to His law. But there might be outward conformity to the law without any true work of grace in the soul.

Israel was under the government of God as His covenant people, and hence responsible to walk before Him in righteousness. If they did this, they would be blessed in temporal things. If they became wilful and disobedient they would come under judgment.

The ministry of the prophets was to call the people back to righteousness and to warn them of the folly of going on in any evil way. It was this which the Lord stressed as He sent Ezekiel to proclaim His Word to the captivity. If faithful in declaring the Word of God, he would deliver his own soul at least, even though his preaching seemed to fall upon deaf ears; but if he failed to give the warning he would have to answer before God for the blood of those who were destroyed for lack of knowledge.

The chapter closes by telling us of another vision of God in His governmental ways, given to prepare the prophet further for the great task set before him. He says:

"And the hand of Jehovah was there upon me; and He said unto me, Arise, go forth into the plain, and I will there talk with thee. Then I arose, and went forth into the plain: and, behold, the glory of Jehovah stood there, as the glory which I saw by the river Chebar; and I fell on my face. Then the Spirit entered into me, and set me upon my feet; and He spake with me, and said unto me, Go, shut thyself within thy house. But thou, son of man, behold, they shall lay bands upon thee, and shall bind thee with them, and thou shalt not go out among them: and I will make thy tongue cleave to the roof of thy mouth, that thou shalt be dumb, and shalt not be to them a reprover; for they are a rebellious house. But when I speak with thee, I will open thy mouth, and thou shalt say unto them, Thus saith the Lord Jehovah: He that heareth, let him hear; and he that forbeareth, let him forbear: for they are a rebellious house"—vers. 22-27.

We have here an oft-repeated story in the Holy Scriptures. No man is fit to go forth to represent God to other men if he himself has not been in the presence of God. Nor will one experience of the divine manifestation fortify one for all that is to come. One must needs be given new revelations from time to time of the glory, power, love, and wisdom of God, so that in freshness of spirit and vigor of soul he may stand before his fellows as one sent forth by divine command.

To know God and to be consciously in His presence always produces humiliation of soul and a sense of utter worthlessness, but it also leads to worship and adoration. It was so with Ezekiel. Overwhelmed by the vision of the glory of Jehovah, he fell prostrate on his face. Strengthened by the Spirit he was lifted to his feet, and his commission given its final form. In the power of the flesh he was to do nothing; he was not to speak except as the words were given him of the Lord. But when he received the message from the Lord, his mouth would be opened and he would declare unfalteringly, "Thus saith the Lord Jehovah." This ever gives authority to the Word preached when, instead of speaking as from oneself and in the wisdom of words, the servant of God gives forth that which has been communicated to him through the Spirit and the Word. Then, whether people hear or forbear, it is all one. The message is delivered: God is honored; and the messenger can be at peace, knowing he has discharged the obligation put upon him.

It was thus with our Lord Himself, who spake as never man spoke, with authority and not as the scribes; and it was so with His chosen representatives. as they declared the Word, not in their own wisdom or might but as c f the ability which God gave.

Chapter Four Teaching By Object Lessons

In this and the first part of the next chapter we find God telling the prophet to use what We might think of as the kindergarten method of compelling attention to the word he was to make known. In a series of object lessons he was to illustrate God's dealings with the city of Jerusalem and the houses of Israel and Judah. First we have the pictured siege of Jerusalem.

"Thou also, son of man, take thee a tile, and lay it before thee, and portray upon it a city, even Jerusalem: and lay siege against it, and build forts against it, and cast up a mound against it; set camps also against it, and plant battering rams against it round about. And take thou unto thee an iron pan, and set it for a wall of iron between thee and the city: and set thy face toward it, and it shall be besieged, and thou shalt lay siege against it. This shall be a sign to the house of Israel"—vers. 1-3.

All this was in order to draw the attention of the captives and to lead them to inquire as to the meaning of the sign or symbol. At the very time that the prophet was in this way illustrating the siege of Jerusalem, the armies of the Chaldeans had thrown a cordon around the doomed city and were pressing for its complete surrender, or failing in that its exposure to all the horrors of an Oriental sack. False prophets were endeavoring to persuade those of the captivity that God would never permit His holy city and His beautiful sanctuary to be overrun and destroyed by the idolatrous armies of Nebuchadnezzar. But these optimists spoke out of their own hearts, not by divine revelation or inspiration, and the falsity of their utterances was soon to be made manifest. The solemn facts that needed to be considered were these: the city was denied already by the vicious practices of the people of Judah, and the sanctuary had been contaminated for years by the setting up of images of heathen gods and goddesses within its sacred precincts. Therefore, He who is a jealous God and will not give His glory to another, could not in righteousness defend the place where His name had been so terribly profaned. God had been very patient and had waited long upon a rebellious and gainsaying people. Now His long-suffering mercy had come to an end, and He was to be toward His people as an enemy, taking as it were the part of their cruel foes in order that Judah might be chastened for her sins and manifold transgressions. It was not that His heart was changed toward His people, but His holiness demanded that their sins be dealt with. Their wickedness had left them helpless before their foes, and there was no power to resist the oppressor.

The next sign was of a different character and yet connected intimately with that which had preceded it.

"Moreover lie thou upon thy left side, and lay the iniquity of the house of Israel upon it; according to the number of the days that thou shalt lie upon it, thou shalt bear their iniquity. For I have appointed the years of their iniquity to be unto thee a number of days, even three hundred and ninety days: so shalt thou bear the iniquity of the house of Israel. And again, when thou hast accomplished these, thou shalt lie on thy right side, and shalt bear the iniquity of the house of Judah: forty days, each day for a year, have I appointed it unto thee. And thou shalt set thy face toward the siege of Jerusalem, with thine arm uncovered; and thou shalt prophesy against it. And, behold, I lay bands upon thee, and thou shalt not turn thee from one side to the other, till thou hast accomplished the days of thy siege"—vers. 4-8.

It is not easy to understand the exact meaning of the times recorded here. J. N. Darby says, "It is certain that these days do not refer to the duration of the kingdom of Israel apart from Judah, nor to that of Judah, because the kingdom of Israel lasted only about 254 years, while that of Judah continued about 134 years after the fall of Samaria." He suggests, therefore, that "the longer period mentioned is reckoned from the separation of the ten tribes under Rehoboam, counting the years as those of Israel, because from that moment Israel had a separate existence and comprised the great body of the nation; while Judah was everything during the reign of Solomon, which lasted forty years. After his reign Judah would be comprised in the general name of Israel according to Ezekiel's usual habit, although on certain occasions he distinguishes them on account of the position of Zedekiah and of God's future dealings" (*Synopsis of the Books of the Bible*, p. 413, new ed.). This is perhaps as good an explanation as any of the day-for-a-year periods during which Ezekiel was to lie first on one side and then on the other, as the people of the captivity looked on. He was to be their sign, telling of God's long-drawn-out patience to their fathers and intimating that this day of His mercy was now coming rapidly to a close. The hand of Jehovah was to be upon him, enabling him to fulfil these weary vigils, which otherwise would have been almost impossible for flesh and blood.

The third sign was designed to express Jehovah's disgust at the vile abominations connected with the idolatrous practices into which His people had fallen from time to time.

"Take thou also unto thee wheat, and barley, and beans, and lentils, and millet, and spelt, and put them in one vessel, and make thee bread thereof; according to the number of the days that thou shalt lie upon thy side, even three hundred and ninety days, shalt thou eat thereof. And thy food which thou shalt eat shall be by weight, twenty shekels a day: from time to time shalt thou eat it. And thou shalt drink water by measure, the sixth part of a hin: from time to time shalt thou drink. And thou shalt eat it as barley cakes, and thou shalt bake it in their sight with dung that cometh out of man. And Jehovah said, Even thus shall the children of Israel eat their bread unclean, among the nations whither I will drive them. Then said I, Ah Lord Jehovah! behold, my soul hath not been polluted; for from my youth up even till now have I not eaten of that which dieth of itself, or is torn of beasts; neither came there abominable flesh into my mouth. Then He said unto me, See, I have given thee cow's dung for man's dung, and thou shalt prepare thy bread thereon. Moreover He said unto me, Son of man, behold, I will break the staff of bread in Jerusalem: and they shall eat bread by weight, and with fearfulness; and they shall drink water by measure, and in dismay: that they may want bread and water, and be dismayed one with another, and pine away in their iniquity"—vers. 9-17.

To a pious Jew, the manner in which the prophet's food was to be prepared, according to the first command of the Lord, would be unspeakably abhorrent. Ungodly men have misread these directions and have inveighed against the supposition that a holy God could ever have given such instruction. Misreading the command to prepare the food with human excrement as though it meant to mix unclean filth with the vegetables the prophet was to eat, has given ground for this. But the offal was to be used in the fuel, not in the food. And when Ezekiel (like Peter at Caesarea) protested that nothing unclean had ever entered his mouth, God, in pity for His servant, ordered that the dung of cattle be used instead. Anyone who has made a fire of buffalo chips on our western plains will understand at once what is meant. The food itself would not actually be contaminated, but the method of its preparation was meant to impress the captivity with God's detestation of everything connected with the worship of the false gods of the nations. Idolatry is ever unclean and so exceedingly vile that nothing could be too filthy to picture its abominable character in the sight of Jehovah.

In times of famine men have resorted to the most detestable things for food in their efforts to satisfy the cravings of their hunger. To such straits Jerusalem was reduced, and as the siege progressed, conditions would become worse and worse. There could be no mitigation of Judah's sufferings so long as they refused to heed the voice of God speaking through His servants the prophets. At this very time Jeremiah, in the holy city, was giving a similar testimony to that of Ezekiel among the captives in Chaldea, yet the people refused to hearken, so judgment had to take its course.

Chapter Five Threatenings Of Providential Judgments

A fourth object lesson opens the present chapter, the illustration of the sharp sword used as a barber's razor.

"And thou, son of man, take thee a sharp sword; as a barber's razor shalt thou take it unto thee, and shalt cause it to pass upon thy head and upon thy beard: then take thee balances to weigh, and divide the hair. A third part shalt thou burn in the fire in the midst of the city, when the days of the siege are fulfilled; and thou shalt take a third part, and smite with the sword round about it; and a third part thou shalt scatter to the wind, and I will draw out a sword after them. And thou shalt take thereof a few in number, and bind them in thy skirts. And of these again shalt thou take, and cast them into the midst of the fire, and burn them in the fire; therefrom shall a fire come forth into all the house of Israel"—vers. 1-4.

The sharp sword was a readily understood symbol of bloody warfare and told of the ruthless and victorious Chaldean armies which God in His providential judgment had permitted to overrun the land of Judah, and against which the people of Israel had no power to stand because of their apostate condition.

Using this keen-edged sword as one would use a barber's razor, the prophet was to shave off the hair of his head and his beard, and he was then instructed to divide the hairs into three parts, one part to be burned in fire, another to be smitten by the sword, and the third part to be scattered to the wind, thus typify- ing or illustrating what should befall the Jews because of their rebellion against God. One third were to be destroyed in the siege of Jerusalem, another third mercilessly cut down by Nebuchadnezzar's cohorts, and the rest to be scattered over the earth among all nations, according as they had been warned many times before. But a small remnant would be preserved even in the hour of Jehovah's indignation, because they sought His face and kept His testimonies. These were pictured by the few hairs reserved and bound in the skirt of the prophet's mantle, but even these were cast into the midst of the fire afterwards, for the righteous in Israel have had to suffer with the unrighteous during the long years of their exile from the land. All this is made clear in the verses that follow:

"Thus saith the Lord Jehovah: This is Jerusalem; I have set her in the midst of the nations, and countries that are round about her. And she hath rebelled against Mine ordinances in doing wickedness more than the nations, and against My statutes more than the countries that are round about her; for they have rejected Mine ordinances, and as for My statutes, they have not walked in them. Therefore thus saith the Lord Jehovah: Because ye are turbulent more than the nations that are round about you, and have not walked in My statutes, neither have kept Mine ordinances, neither have done after the ordinances of the nations that are round about you; therefore thus saith the Lord Jehovah: Behold, I, even I, am against thee; and I will execute judgments in the midst of thee in the sight of the nations. And I will do in thee that which I have not done, and whereunto I will not do any more the like, because of all thine abominations. Therefore the fathers shall eat the sons in the midst of thee, and the sons shall eat their fathers; and I will execute judgments on thee; and the whole remnant of thee will I scatter unto all the winds. Wherefore, as I live, saith the Lord Jehovah, surely, because thou hast defiled My sanctuary with all thy detestable things, and with all thine abominations, therefore will I also diminish thee; neither shall Mine eye spare, and I also will have no pity. A third part of thee shall die with the pestilence, and with famine shall they be consumed in the midst of thee; and a third part shall fall by the sword round about thee; and a third part I will scatter unto all the winds, and will draw out a sword after them"—vers. 5-12.

Jerusalem, the city where Jehovah had set His name and which was designated the holy city, had gone so far from God, following the ways of the heathen who knew Him not, that she had become as a stench in His nostrils and an abhorrence instead of a delight. Jerusalem was guiltier far than those nations, because they had never been favored with such knowledge as Israel. They worshipped idols because they knew not the one true and living God. Israel knew Him but forsook Him, spurned the holy law He had given, and ignored the entreaties of His prophets; consequently, He whom they had repudiated could deal with them only in judgment. He who loved them so tenderly had to become as their enemy. They must learn in suffering and anguish the bitterness of departure from His testimonies and from obedience to Him who had redeemed them from bondage and had borne with their manners for so long. Now his patience was at an end, and judgment must take its course. His eye would no longer spare nor His heart pity. They must eat the bitter fruit of the seed they had sown. It is a solemn instance of the principle that runs all through Scripture, which shows that whatsoever is sown must be reaped.

"Thus shall Mine anger be accomplished, and I will cause My wrath toward them to rest, and I shall be comforted: and they shall know that I, Jehovah, have spoken in My zeal, when I have accomplished My wrath upon them. Moreover I will make thee a desolation and a reproach among the nations that are round about thee, in the sight of all that pass by. So it shall be a reproach and a taunt, an instruction and an astonishment, unto the nations that are round about thee, when I shall execute judgments on thee in anger and in wrath, and in wrathful rebukes (I, Jehovah, have spoken it); when I shall send upon them the evil arrows of famine, that are for destruction, which I will send to destroy you. And I will increase the famine upon you, and will break your staff of bread; and I will send upon you famine and evil beasts, and they shall bereave thee; and pestilence and blood shall pass through thee; and I will bring the sword upon thee: I, Jehovah, have spoken it"—vers. 13-17.

Thus Jerusalem not only would be punished for her own sins, but also she would become an object lesson to the nations roundabout, giving them to see that sin always brings trouble and sorrow, and that only as nations walk before God in righteousness will they have His approval and blessing. Israel is today such an object lesson to the whole world if men but have eyes to see and hearts to understand.

Though God must deal with sin in His people, He never gives them up. Israel is still His by covenant, and in a coming day He will draw the remnant back to Himself and comfort them in their affliction. He will not keep His anger forever, but when they turn to Him in repentance He will own them once more as His elect and bring them again into blessing even greater than they have known in the past. Meantime, they are destined to be a desolation and a reproach among the nations as they have been for some twenty-five centuries of sad and awful affliction.

Chapter Six Judgment Pronounced On Israel

After long patience and many warnings God at last had come to the place where He could not, in righteousness, any longer recognize Israel as His own. They were to be henceforth, and until the time of their future restoration, as Hosea declared, "Lo-ammi"—that is, "Not My people." Such has been their condition during the past twenty-five hundred years, and such it will be until that great day when they shall look upon Him whom they have pierced, and mourn for Him as one mourneth for his only son, and shall be in bitterness for Him as one that is in bitterness for his firstborn (Zechariah 12:10).

In the first seven verses we get Jehovah's message of repudiation because of Israel's persistence in sin.

"And the word of Jehovah came unto me, saying, Son of man, set thy face toward the mountains of Israel, and prophesy unto them, and say, Ye mountains of Israel, hear the word of the Lord Jehovah: Thus saith the Lord Jehovah to the mountains and to the hills, to the water-courses and to the valleys: Behold, I, even I, will bring a sword upon you, and I will destroy your high places. And your altars shall become desolate, and your sun-images shall be broken; and I will cast down your slain men before your idols. And I will lay the dead bodies of the children of Israel before their idols; and I will scatter your bones round about your altars. In all your dwelling-places the cities shall be laid waste, and the high places shall be desolate; that your altars may be laid waste and made desolate, and your idols may be broken and cease, and your sun-images may be hewn down, and your works may be abolished. And the slain shall fall in the midst of you. and ye shall know that I am Jehovah"—vers. 1-7.

When the twelve tribes first entered the land of Canaan God promised temporal blessings of every kind so long as they walked in obedience to His Word. The land itself was to give every evidence of His good pleasure. It would be fruitful, abundantly so, and as a result their flocks and herds would multiply; and they, themselves, would be preserved in health. They would be strong so that no enemy would be able to stand against them. But now all was changed. They had sinned until there was no remedy, and so God commanded Ezekiel to set his face toward the mountains of Israel and prophesy unto or against them. He addresses Himself directly to the mountains and the hills, the water-courses, and the valleys. The land itself was to be the object of Jehovah's displeasure; it has been down through the centuries since. The people were to be scattered, and the country left desolate. God declared He would Himself bring a sword upon them—in this case the sword of Nebuchadnezzar and his Chaldean army. He declared He would destroy the places where they worshipped their idols, and would overthrow their altars and images; and those who had served them would be cast down, slain before these representations of their false gods. For many there would not be even burial, but their bones would be scattered roundabout the altars on which they had sacrificed to demons. Their cities would be laid waste; their sanctuaries given up to desolation, and the idols in which they trusted would be utterly demolished and thus proven to be powerless to help. No arm would be outstretched to save Israel from their cruel foes, but the slain should fall everywhere in the land.

Though judgment was thus to be meted out. God could not forget His covenant with Abraham no matter how wicked the people had become or how utterly degenerate and ungrateful. He had promised that Abraham's seed should inherit the land, and His Word must stand; therefore, He speaks next of a remnant which would eventually be brought back from the sword.

"Yet will I leave a remnant, in that ye shall have some that escape the sword among the nations, when ye shall be scattered through the countries. And those of you that escape shall remember Me among the nations whither they shall be carried captive, how that I have been broken with their lewd heart, which hath departed from Me, and with their eyes, which play the harlot after their idols: and they shall loathe themselves in their own sight for the evils which they have committed in all their abominations. And they shall know that I am Jehovah: I have not said in vain that I would do this evil unto them"—vers. 8-10.

This remnant appears in many places in the prophetic Scriptures. Even at the present time, Paul tells us, "There is a remnant according to the election of grace" (Romans 11:5)—that is, all down through the Christian dispensation there have been many Jews who have accepted the Lord Jesus Christ and borne witness to their faith by godly and devoted lives. It is true that so far as the great mass is concerned, blindness in part has happened to Israel until the fulness of the Gentiles be come in. But when God's present work of grace among the nations is consummated, and the Church has finished its testimony in this scene then God will turn again to Israel, and out of them will save a remnant who shall become the nucleus of the new regenerated Israel in the kingdom days.

The remnant referred to here, however, has to do with those in Israel who, during the years between the dispersion and the crucifixion of our Lord Jesus Christ, turned to God in repentance and sought to honor and glorify Him, even during the time that His judgment was being meted out to the nation. Of such God said, "Yet will I leave a remnant, that ye may have some that shall escape the sword among the nations, when ye shall be scattered through the countries." These hidden ones—"the quiet in the land," as David calls them—would still maintain a testimony for God. This remnant would be among the nations where they should be carried captive, and they would realize that judgment had fallen upon Israel because of their departure from God and because of their idolatry. They would loathe themselves in their own sight for the evils which had been committed, taking the place of repentance toward God on behalf of themselves and their people. Of such we read, "They shall know that I am Jehovah." And they shall know that He had not said in vain that He would bring evil upon the nation.

Conditions were such that no one taught of God could look on supinely or with careless indifference. Ezekiel himself was called to take an active stand in opposition to the evil.

"Thus saith the Lord Jehovah: Smite with thy hand, and stamp with thy foot, and say, Alas because of all the evil abominations of the house of Israel, For they shall fall by the sword, by the famine, and by the pestilence. He that is far off shall die of the pestilence; and he that is near shall fall by the sword; and he that remaineth and is besieged shall die by the famine: thus will I accomplish My wrath upon them. And ye shall know that I am Jehovah, when their slain men shall be among their idols round about their altars, upon every high hill, on all the tops of the mountains, and under every green tree, and under every thick oak, the places where they offered sweet savor to all their idols. And I will stretch out My hand upon them, and make the land desolate and waste, from the wilderness toward Diblah, throughout all their habitations; and they shall know that I am Jehovah"—vers. 11-14.

Notice the striking way in which the Lord speaks to His servant, commanding him to smite with his hand and stamp with his foot, as he cried aloud against the abominations of the house of Israel. The conditions of the times demanded vigorous denunciations with a view to awakening sleeping consciences. Because of their sin and their refusal to repent God declared they should fall by the sword, by famine, and by pestilence. Whether far or near there would be no escape from the avenging hand of the God whose commands they had spurned, and whose loving-kindness they had trampled under foot. No matter what they did they could not escape the providential judgments which were decreed. When all these dire prophecies were fulfilled they would recognize that He whose testimonies they had refused to heed was indeed the One true and living God. They had turned from Him to idols that could neither see, nor hear, nor speak, nor yet help them in any way when desolation came upon the land. They who had enjoyed so many evidences of divine favor should see their land become as a wilderness. They should know indeed that He who dwelt with them was Jehovah, the self-existing, Eternal One.

Chapter Seven The End Is Come

With this chapter the prophet's message, directed expressly against the land of Palestine, though of course including its sinful people, comes to an end. All God's pleadings and remonstrances had proven to be in vain: the people were insistent on taking their own way. Ezekiel, as we have seen, was already among those who were in captivity. Nebuchadnezzar's armies were once more threatening the land, and the false prophets were assuring Israel that God would intervene and save the nation. They utterly minimized the guilt of the people and declared that inasmuch as they were Jehovah's chosen, He would intervene on their behalf. But all such prophecies were soon to be proven utterly false. The end of God's patience had been reached, as we have seen. In wrath and indignation He was about to give them over to the power of the enemy to be destroyed by death or sold into slavery.

"Moreover the word of Jehovah came unto me, saying, And thou, son of man, thus saith the Lord Jehovah unto the land of Israel: An end, the end is come upon the four corners of the land. Now is the end upon thee, and I will send Mine anger upon thee, and will judge thee according to thy ways; and I will bring upon thee all thine abominations. And Mine eye shall not spare thee, neither will I have pity; but I will bring thy ways upon thee, and thine abominations shall be in the midst of thee: and ye shall know that I am Jehovah"—vers. 1-4.

Note the words, "The end is come upon the four corners of the land." There was no longer any hope. Their consciences had become utterly hardened; there was not the slightest evidence of repentance; therefore, God would judge Israel according to their ways, and recompense upon them their own abominations because they had not heeded the words of His prophets, nor turned from their idolatry. His eye would not spare, neither would He have pity upon them. It was not that His heart was hardened against them; He loved them still, but His holiness forbade His going on with them in their wickedness. When His judgments were poured out upon them they should know that it was indeed Jehovah with whom they had to do, and who had given them up to affliction and despair.

"Thus saith the Lord Jehovah: An evil, an only evil; toehold, it cometh. An end is come, the end is come; it awaketh against thee; toehold, it cometh. Thy doom is come upon thee, O inhabitant in the land: the time is come, the day is near, a day of tumult, and not of joyful shouting, upon the mountains. Now will I shortly pour out My wrath upon thee, and accomplish mine anger against thee, and will judge thee according to thy ways; and I will toring upon thee all thine abominations. And Mine eye shall not spare, neither will I have pity: I will toring upon thee according to thy ways; and thine abominations shall toe in the midst of thee; and ye shall know that I, Jehovah, do smite"—vers. 5-9.

The people had looked for good but looked in vain. An evil, an only evil, was coming upon them. Once more the prophet repeats the word, "An end is come, the end is come." It is a solemn thing indeed when God's patience is exhausted and His wrath falls without restraint upon those whom He would so gladly have delivered had they but given any evidence of repentance. Even when things had been at very low ebb in the past, the slightest proof of self-judgment was sufficient to avert threatened punishment; but now the people were wholly given to iniquity. They had cast God's law behind their backs, and even though there were, as we know, some godly ones among them, yet the state of the nation was such that these who had concern about their ways could only suffer with the rest of the people. When destruction falls, whether by natural calamity, such as earthquake, tornado, or pestilences, the righteous suffer with the wicked. It is true also when bloody warfare rages in a land. And so even the faithful remnant had to go through this time of terrible trial with the apostate part of the nation; though we see that afterwards, when Nebuchadnezzar had taken the city, provision was made for certain ones to remain in the land, and those that feared God were given opportunity to dwell quietly in the desolated region.

Instead of reading, "The morning is come unto thee," a better translation, we are told, would be, "The turn of the wheel is come"—that is, the great wheel of the divine government is rolling on, and nothing can turn it aside. The time had come when the day of trouble, which many prophets had foretold, should actually take place. The storm nearing, they had heard the divine thunder, not merely an echo from the mountains.

Verses 8 and 9 are extremely stirring. God was about to pour out His fury upon Israel and accomplish His anger upon them. He would judge them according to their ways. There should be no pity. It was too late for mercy: judgment must take its course. And when all these dire predictions came to pass, Israel should know that He who thus dealt with them was the Lord that smiteth.

This last expression might be looked upon as a compound: *Jehovah-Mekkadeschem*ₜ "Jehovah the Smiter." Those who refuse to recognize God as *Jeho-vah-Rahi* ("Jehovah the Shepherd"), or as *Jehovah-Jireh* ("Jehovah the Provider"), will have to know Him as "Jehovah the Smiter."

"Behold the day, behold, it cometh: thy doom is gone forth; the rod hath blossomed, pride hath budded. Violence is risen up into a rod of wickedness; none of them shall remain, nor of their multitude, nor of their wealth: neither shall there be eminency among them. The time is come, the day draweth near: let not the buyer rejoice, nor the seller mourn; for wrath is upon all the multitude thereof. For the seller shall not return to that which is sold, although they be yet alive: for the vision is touching the whole multitude thereof, none shall return; neither shall any strengthen himself in the iniquity of his life"—vers. 10-13.

There was to be no longer delay. The day of doom had already come. Israel's cup of iniquity was full; the tree of her pride had blossomed and budded; the hour when God would deal with her because of all her manifold iniquities had arrived. The armies of the Chaldeans had swept down upon the land. Jerusalem was already besieged. Because, on the part of Israel, violence had developed into a rod of wickedness, they should be dealt with in violence. The time had arrived; the day had drawn near. It was too late for buyer to rejoice or seller to mourn: the wrath of God was already being poured out upon the multitude. Commerce would be at an end; buying and selling would no longer have any place, and the whole land was to be given up to desolation.

Graphically the prophet describes the siege of Jerusalem in the verses that follow:

"They have blown the trumpet, and have made all ready; but none goeth to the battle; for My wrath is upon all the multitude thereof. The sword is without, and the pestilence and the famine within: he that is in the field shall die with the sword; and he that is in the city, famine and pestilence shall devour him. But those of them that escape shall escape, and shall be on the mountains like doves of the valleys, all of them moaning, every one in his iniquity. All hands shall be feeble, and all knees shall be weak as water. They shall also gird themselves with sackcloth, and horror shall cover them; and shame shall be upon all faces, and baldness upon all their heads. They shall cast their silver in the streets, and their gold shall be as an unclean thing; their silver and their gold shall not be able to deliver them in the day of the wrath of Jehovah: they shall not satisfy their souls, neither fill their bowels; because it hath been the stumblingblock of their iniquity"—vers. 14-19.

The trumpets had sounded for the defense of the city. All had been called to make ready, but none dared go forth to the battle. Everywhere outside the walls were seen the forces of the enemy. Because of the rigor of the siege, pestilence and famine prevailed within the city. Those in the field were given up to death by the sword; those in the city faced death by the conditions prevailing there. A few, indeed, might escape, but they should be like mourning doves looking down upon the ruined city. All hands should be feeble; all knees weak as water. There would be no strength whatever to enable Judah to stand against her cruel foes. Though they mourned and girded themselves with sackcloth, and horror possessed their souls, there was no hope. They had sinned until God would no longer hear their cry. Their silver and their gold which had been hoarded up could not deliver them in the day of divine wrath. All was at an end. Jerusalem was doomed; Palestine was to be given into the hand of the enemy.

"As for the beauty of his ornament, He set it in majesty; but they made the images of their abominations and their detestable things therein: therefore have I made it unto them as an unclean thing. And I will give it into the hands of the strangers for a prey, and to the wicked of the earth for a spoil; and they shall profane it. My face will I turn also from them, and they shall profane My secret place; and robbers shall enter into it, and profane it. Make the chain; for the land is full of bloody crimes, and the city is full of violence. Wherefore I will bring the worst of the nations, and they shall possess their houses: I will also make the pride of the strong to cease; and their holy places shall be profaned. Destruction cometh; and they shall seek peace, and there shall be none. Mischief shall come upon mischief, and rumor shall be upon rumor; and they shall seek a vision of the prophet; but the law shall perish from the priest, and counsel from the elders. The king shall mourn, and the prince shall be clothed with desolation, and the hands of the people of the land shall be troubled: I will do unto them after their way, and according to their deserts will I judge them; and they shall know that I am Jehovah"—vers. 20-27.

Even as we read these words we can feel in our souls the sadness and the hopelessness which they depict. Because of the many idolatries and the detestable things connected with them, Jehovah had set His face against His people and given their cities and their land into the hands of strangers for a prey. True, these were the wicked of the earth and possibly as vile or viler than Judah had become, but the difference was this: the Chaldeans were a heathen people who had never been in covenant relationship with God; the people of Judah had been separated to Himself. He had given them His law; He had given them His Word, but they had rebelled against Him; therefore, He would use even the most wicked of the nations to chasten them. He would set His face against them and permit the robbers to enter into the land and defile it.

The expression in verse 23, "Make a chain," suggests the captivity into which thousands were to go, bound with chains of their own sins. They were to be delivered in material chains into the hand of the enemy. Eventually the worst of the heathen would possess that land and all its holy places be defiled.

Some have seen in verse 24 a prophecy of the possession of Palestine by the Mohammedan powers who controlled and dominated it for some twelve centuries, until Allenby's entrance into Jerusalem, and the ousting of the Turks.

In vain should they seek peace, for they had turned away from the only One who could give peace. Therefore, mischief should come upon them; one distracting rumor after another should trouble them. In their distress they should seek a vision of the prophet, but there would be no answer. The law was to perish from the priest, and counsel from the elders. King Zedekiah, unstable, tricky, and hypocritical, should mourn; the leaders be clothed with desolation, and the hands of the people be troubled. God declared, "I will do unto them after their way, and according to their deserts will I judge them." They should know it was Jehovah who was afflicting them when all these things were fulfilled.

There is, of course, a sense in which we may look beyond the days of Nebuchadnezzar and see in this chapter a depiction of the horrors of the great tribulation, but while this is a lawful application it is really secondary, for the actual fulfilment had to do with the siege and taking of the city by the Chaldean armies.

Let not us of the Gentiles look with contempt upon the Jews because of their forgetfulness of God and the dire results that followed. Let us remember that we also, as a people, have proved utterly unworthy of the privileges bestowed upon us; and in due time Christendom, too, will be rejected of the Lord because of its apostasy and rebellion.

Chapter Eight Idolatrous Abominations

With this chapter Ezekiel begins a new series of messages which continue through chapter 11, but which are intimately linked with those that have preceded them. The date given is one year later than that of the visions and prophecies of chapters 1 to 7. Throughout this section God is still calling the people to repentance, as the judgment had not yet fallen. Ezekiel himself, as we know, was among the captives by the River Chebar; but in this eighth chapter he finds himself, in spirit, in the city of Jerusalem, in the temple of the Lord.

"And it came to pass in the sixth year, in the sixth month, in the fifth day of the month, as I sat in my house, and the elders of Judah sat before me, that the hand of the Lord Jehovah fell there upon me. Then I beheld, and, lo, a likeness as the appearance of fire; from the appearance of his loins and downward, fire; and from his loins and upward, as the appearance of brightness, as it were glowing metal. And he put forth the form of a hand, and took me by a lock of my head; and the Spirit lifted me up between earth and heaven, and brought me in the visions of God to Jerusalem, to the door of the gate of the inner court that looketh toward the north; where was the seat of the image of jealousy, which provoketh to jealousy. And, behold, the glory of the God of Israel was there, according to the appearance that I saw in the plain"— vers. 1-4.

While in the midst of a group of elders of Judah, it is evident that the prophet became unconscious of all about him. During this ecstatic state he beheld a glorious personage, evidently an angel, who appeared in the form of a man but in the likeness of fire, reminding us again of the words of the Psalmist, "Who maketh His angels spirits (or winds), and His ministers a flame of fire" (Ps. 104:4; Heb. 1:7). This glorious being put forth the form of a hand and took hold of the prophet by a lock of his hair. Ezekiel immediately found himself, in spirit, lifted up between earth and heaven; and, in the visions of God, he was brought to Jerusalem to the door of the gate of the inner court of the temple, the door toward the north. There he beheld a great idol, designated "the image of jealousy," because it was written in the law, "I the Lord thy God am a jealous God" (Exodus 20:5).

When we think of jealousy in connection with God we are not to confound it with the ignoble passion that so often works havoc in the hearts of carnal men. God is jealous because He knows that it is to our own hurt if we turn from Him to any other object of adoration. Even as the Apostle Paul wrote to the Corinthians, "I am jealous over you with a godly jealousy: for I have espoused you to one husband, that I may present you as a chaste virgin to Christ" (2 Corinthians 11:2). James says that the spirit that dwelleth in us enviously desireth. God yearns to see us wholly occupied with the Lord Himself.

God had revealed Himself to Israel as to no other people: gracious, merciful, a covenant-keeping God; yet One whose holiness demanded that sin be dealt with in judgment. He had told them distinctly, "Thou shalt have no other gods before Me" (Exodus 20:3); and had forbidden the making of any graven image before which they might fall down in worship. But they had cast His words behind their backs, and had turned to the idolatry of the nations surrounding Pales- tine, setting up their idols even in the very sanctuary of Jehovah.

As the prophet beheld, he saw again the glory of the God of Israel— that is, the vision of the chariot of the divine government which he had seen, as described in chapter 1. Nothing could be in greater contrast than the image of jealousy and the glory of Jehovah as here presented. The Lord spoke directly to the prophet, fixing his attention upon the idol thus set up in the temple.

"Then said he unto me, Son of man, lift up thine eyes now the way toward the north. So I lifted up mine eyes the way toward the north, and behold, northward of the gate of the altar this image of jealousy in the entry. And he said unto me, Son of man, seest thou what they do? even the great abominations that the house of Israel do commit here, that I should go far off from My sanctuary? But thou shalt again see yet other great abominations"—vers. 5, 6.

As Ezekiel gazed upon the idol, his own heart must have been stirred to its depth. He heard the voice of Jehovah say, "Son of man, seest thou what they do? even the great abominations that the house of Israel do commit here, that I should go far off from My sanctuary?" One can sense the pathos of this. God had been as a Father unto Israel: He had brought them out of Egypt and cared for them all through the centuries since. And now this was the return they gave Him: they spurned His Word, and followed after other gods, even worshipping stocks, stones, and metallic images which could neither see, nor hear, nor in any way deliver them in the hour of trial.

But this, in itself, was not all. The prophet was to behold other great abominations.

"And he brought me to the door of the court; and when I looked, behold, a hole in the wall. Then said he unto me, Son of man, dig now in the wall: and when I had digged in the wall, behold, a door. And he said unto me, Go in, and see the wicked abominations that they do here. So I went in and saw; and behold, every form of creeping things, and abominable beasts, and all the idols of the house of Israel, portrayed upon the wall round about. And there stood before them seventy men of the elders of the house of Israel; and in the midst of them stood Jaazaniah the son of Shaphan, every man with his censer in his hand; and the odor of the cloud of incense went up. Then said he unto me, Son of man, hast thou seen what the elders of the house of Israel do in the dark, every man in his chambers of imagery? for they say, Jehovah seeth us not; Jehovah hath forsaken the land. He said also unto me, Thou Shalt again see yet other great abominations which they do"—vers. 7-13.

The guiding angel brought Ezekiel to the door of the temple court, and there he beheld a hole in the wall, leading to a hidden door which opened into a secret room, which would not ordinarily be discovered by passers-by. Through this door Ezekiel was commanded to enter, and when he did so he beheld portrayed upon the walls roundabout, all kinds of creeping things, abominable beasts, and idols, such as one still finds upon the walls of Egyptian temples. Before these evidences of corrupt superstition and idolatrous wickedness there stood seventy venerable elders of the house of Israel, led by Jaazaniah, the son of Shaphan. These were evidently priests, for each one held a censer in his hand, from which clouds of incense ascended before the delineations of false gods.

The angel spoke to Ezekiel, saying, "Son of man, hast thou seen what the elders of the house of Israel do in the dark, every man in his chambers of imagery?" Men love darkness rather than light when their deeds are evil; and so these elders were carrying on unholy worship in this dark room as they adored the picture images upon the walls. They imagined that they were so hidden that the eye of Jehovah could not see them; in fact, they told themselves He had forsaken their land. In reality, it was they who had forsaken Him. They had turned to these senseless idols only to learn, eventually, the folly of trusting in any other than the living God.

But this was not all. There were greater depths of iniquity still to be manifested, and so the guiding angel said, "Thou shalt again see yet other great abominations which they do."

"Then he brought me to the door of the gate of Jehovah's house which was toward the north; and behold, there sat the women weeping for Tammuz. Then said he unto me, Hast thou seen this, O son of man? thou shalt again see yet greater abominations than these"—vers. 14, 15.

Christ is the Seed of the woman in this passage

Tammuz was a Babylonian god. He was considered by his followers to be the seed of the woman, spoken of in the book of Genesis (3:15). In the myths which were recited in connection with the Babylonian mysteries he was said to have been put to death in conflict with a giant bull; or, as others said, with a great dragon. But after some time he was supposed to have risen from the dead and to have power to free his subjects from their enemies. As the story of his death was recited in connection with the worship of Tammuz, priestesses sat about for the purpose of lifting up their voices in weird lamentations. It must have been a great shock to Ezekiel's feelings to find the same thing close to the door of the gate of Jehovah's house where Jewish women sat weeping because of the tribulation of this heathen god.

Again the word came, "Thou shalt again see yet greater abominations than these."

"And he brought me into the inner court of Jehovah's house; and behold, at the door of the temple of Jehovah, between the porch and the altar, were about five and twenty men, with their backs toward the temple of Jehovah, and their faces toward the east; and they were worshipping the sun toward the east. Then he said unto me, Hast thou seen this, O son of man? Is it a light thing to the house of Judah that they commit the abominations which they commit here? for they have filled the land with violence, and have turned again to provoke me to anger: and, lo, they put the branch to their nose. Therefore will I also deal in wrath; Mine eye shall not spare, neither will I have pity; and though they cry in Mine ears with a loud voice, yet will I not hear them"—vers. 16-18.

Still following his guide, Ezekiel was led into the inner court of Jehovah's house, to the door of the holy place itself; and there he saw, between the porch and the altar, twenty-five men who had turned their backs upon the temple of Jehovah, and were prostrating themselves upon the ground as they faced the east, worshipping the rising sun. Thus they put the creature in the place of the Creator. It might seem almost unthinkable that a people who had been taught the fear of the Lord in the way that Israel had, and who had learned of the true God who created the heavens in which the sun has its place and the earth which is illumined with its glory, that they would ever for one moment think of adoring the heavenly luminary, and would turn their backs upon the temple where the Shekinah glory shone above the mercy-seat between the Cherubim. Yet to such depth of iniquity had they fallen; and as a result the land was filled with violence, and when the people refused subjection to God it seems that every corrupt passion of the heart was turned loose. They had provoked the Lord to anger. Even though He yearned over them and longed to deliver them, He could not do other than deal in judgment with those who had thus spurned His Word and broken His holy law.

Derisively, we are told, they put the branch to their nose—an expression which has occasioned not a little questioning among commentators, but clearly seems to refer to a gesture of contempt, and manifests their attitude toward the Holy One to whom they owed their fullest allegiance.

Because of their perversity God could deal with them only in His wrath, and He declared, "Mine eye shall not spare, neither will I have pity; and though they cry in mine ears with a loud voice, yet will I not hear them."

It is well to remember that if men despise the grace of God, they must know the fierceness of His indignation. They bring this upon themselves when they turn from the path of obedience and deliberately walk contrary to His revealed will.

There is a solemn lesson in all this for us as well as for Israel. God would have us learn from their wretched failure what an evil and bitter thing it is to depart from Him and to take the path of self-will. Blessing is found in obedience; disobedience brings its own judgment with it. This is a lesson we are often slow to learn; but if we will not profit by the experiences of others, or by the direct declarations of the Word of God, we shall have to learn by bitter sufferings and disappointments, the folly of refusing subjection to His will.

Part I, Prophecies Relating To Israel (chapters 9-16)

Chapter Nine The Man With The Inkhorn

It is a mark of grace working in the soul when one is characterized by a holy horror of surrounding sin and uncleanness. By this is not meant a "Stand by thyself, for I am holier than thou," attitude, but a recognition of the fact that one is himself part of an iniquitous and gainsaying people; one who, like Daniel, Nehemiah, and Ezra, bears the sins of his people upon his own heart and takes his place with them in confession before God.

As the Lord looked upon the people of Judah in Ezekiel's day He saw very little evidence of this spirit of self-judgment. He who of old would have spared the cities of the plain had ten righteous men been found in Sodom, had looked in vain for any appreciable group in Judea who mourned before Him because of the abounding evil. He would separate any such from the apostate nation, associating them with Himself in judgment upon the rest. In a remarkable vision this was made clear to the prophet.

"Then he cried in mine ears with a loud voice, saying, Cause ye them that have charge over the city to draw near, every man with his destroying weapon in his hand. And behold, six men came from the way of the upper gate, which lieth toward the north, every man with his slaughter weapon in his hand; and one man in the midst of them clothed in linen, with a writer's inkhorn by his side. And they went in, and stood beside the brazen altar. And the glory of the God of Israel was gone up from the cherub, whereupon it was, to the threshold of the house: and he called to the man clothed in linen, who had the writer's inkhorn by his side. And Jehovah said unto him, Go through the midst of the city, through the midst of Jerusalem, and set a mark upon the foreheads of the men that sigh and that cry over all the abominations that are done in the midst thereof"—vers. 1-4.

One can see in this the inspiration of John Bunyan's graphic picture of the call to devotion to the Lord's battles as beheld by the pilgrim in the Interpreter's house. Bunyan's whole being was saturated with the Scriptures, which colored all his thinking and writing.

A voice is heard calling from the sanctuary for those who are in authority in Jerusalem to draw near with the swords of judgment in their hands.

To this call six men responded in the vision, each one armed to deal with offenders against the law of God. Among these was a secretary, or recorder, robed in linen, the symbol of righteousness, and having a writer's inkhorn by his side according to the custom of those days. All these men took their positions before the brazen altar, which speaks of the cross work of our Lord Jesus Christ, and in the light of which the whole world of the impenitent is to be judged.

The prophet sees the glory of the God of Israel which had gone up from its accustomed place between the cherubim over the mercy-seat, now hovering over the threshold of the house. The throne of God is no longer a throne of grace but of judgment, for grace has been spurned and God's holiness defied.

The voice is heard again, and is identified as that of Jehovah Himself. He commands the man clothed in linen, who had the writer's inkhorn, to go through the midst of the city of Jerusalem, and to set a mark upon the foreheads of those who manifested exercise of soul by sighing and crying because of the manifold abominations being practiced on every hand. One is reminded of the 144,000 out of all the tribes of Israel who are to be sealed in their foreheads just before the great tribulation bursts upon the world in all its terrible fury. And we think today of those who, having turned to God in repentance and trusted the Lord Jesus Christ, are sealed by the Holy Spirit and thus marked off from those who are to be Anathema Maranatha—devoted to judgment at the coming of the Lord. The nature of the mark on the foreheads of those sealed in this vision is not indicated, but it certainly was a sign that they had judged themselves before God and now sided with Him in His attitude toward the iniquities of Judah.

"And to the others he said in my hearing, Go ye through the city after him, and smite: let not your eye spare, neither have ye pity; slay utterly the old man, the young man and the virgin, and little children and women; but come not near any man upon whom is the mark: and begin at My sanctuary. Then they began at the old men that were before the house. And he said unto them, Defile the house, and fill the courts with the slain: go ye forth. And they went forth, and smote in the city"—vers. 5-7.

As we read these words we cannot fail to connect them with the solemn message of 1 Peter 4:17, 18: "For the time is come for judgment to begin at the house of God: and if it begin first at us, what shall be the end of them that obey not the gospel of God? And if the righteous scarcely be saved, where shall the ungodly and sinner appear?"

The armed executors of justice were commanded to go through Jerusalem and smite down all who did not have the seal on their foreheads, and the word was, "Begin at My sanctuary." Thus the judgment commenced with the priest of the Lord who had profaned His name. Even so, God will deal in stern retribution with all who profess His name today but who have only a form of godliness while denying its power. The Lord will not spare the professing church if its members spurn His Word and trample on His grace, turning that grace into lasciviousness.

Because the people of Judah had profaned the temple by their idolatries, God would give it up to further defilement by the dead bodies of those who had rebelled against Him.

"And it came to pass, while they were smiting, and I was left, that I fell upon my face, and cried, and said, Ah Lord Jehovah! wilt Thou destroy all the residue of Israel in Thy pouring out of Thy wrath upon Jerusalem? Then said He unto me, The iniquity of the house of Israel and Judah is exceeding great, and the land is full of blood, and the city full of wresting of judgment: for they say, Jehovah hath forsaken the land, and Jehovah seeth not. And as for Me also, Mine eye shall not spare, neither will I have pity, hut I will bring their way upon their head. And, behold, the man clothed in linen, who had the inkhorn by his side, reported the matter, saying, I have done as Thou hast commanded me"—vers. 8-11.

Stirred to the depths of his being by this vision of the slaughter of priests and people (so soon to be accomplished by the Chaldean armies), Ezekiel fell down on his face before God and pleaded that He would not destroy all the remnant of Israel when He poured out His wrath upon Jerusalem. God answered by declaring that conditions were such that judgment could no longer be delayed, and inasmuch as the whole people had departed from Him, and had refused all entreaty to repent and seek His face, judgment without mercy should be meted out to them.

But this did not mean that He had forgotten the few in the land who sighed and cried because of conditions which they could not remedy. He had commanded the destroyers already, saying, "Come not near any man upon whom is the mark." This indicated clearly His care for the faithful remnant.

As the first part of the vision came to an end the man with the inkhorn reported, saying, "I have done as Thou hast commanded me." This was to reassure the prophet concerning those who had humbled themselves before God and mourned because of the sin of Judah.

Chapter Ten The Divine Chariot Reappears

This tenth chapter gives a continuation of the vision, the first part of which is recorded in chapter 9. The man clothed with linen who had the inkhorn by his side is still before us and acts as the direct representative of God in judgment. Ezekiel's attention was turned away from the earthly sanctuary to the heavens above. He says:

"Then I looked, and behold, in the firmament that was over the head of the cherubim there appeared above them as it were a sapphire stone, as the appearance of the likeness of a throne. And he spake unto the man clothed in linen, and said, Go in between the whirling wheels, even under the cherub, and fill both thy hands with coals of fire from between the cherubim, and scatter them over the city. And he went in in my sight. Now the cherubim stood on the right side of the house, when the man went in; and the cloud filled the inner court. And the glory of Jehovah mounted up from the cherub, and stood over the threshold of the house; and the house was filled with the cloud, and the court was full of the brightness of Jehovah's glory. And the sound of the wings of the cherubim was heard even to the outer court, as the voice of God Almighty when He speaketh. And it came to pass, when he commanded the man clothed in linen, saying, Take fire from between the whirling wheels, from between the cherubim, that he went in, and stood beside a wheel. And the cherub stretched forth his hand from between the cherubim unto the fire that was between the cherubim, and took thereof, and put it into the hands of him that was clothed in linen, who took it and went out. And there appeared in the cherubim the form of a man's hand under their wings"—vers. 1-8.

So marvelous and sublime is this vision that it is almost beyond human power to fully understand and appreciate it. We see here, as in chapter 1, the divine chariot in which Jehovah rides majestically through the universe, ordering everything according to the counsel of His own will. The prophet looked up and saw in the firmament that was over the head of the cherubim, a sapphire stone, as the appearance of the likeness of a throne. It is the throne of the moral Governor of the universe. No matter how confused and confusing conditions may be on earth,

"God sits exalted on His throne,

And ruleth all things well."

At His command the man clothed with linen was seen entering in between the whirling wheels under the cherubim. There his hands were filled with coals of fire from between these glorious beings— fire which was to be scattered over the city, indicating that the hour of its judgment had come.

We have something very similar in the book of the Revelation, in the eighth chapter, where the angel-priest is seen standing at the golden altar, offering up before God the smoke of the incense with prayers of His suffering saints on the earth. In response to these prayers the angel takes the censer and fills it with the fire of the altar and casts it upon the earth, thus indicating that the judgments of God are to be poured out upon this guilty world. And so here in Ezekiel 10, God's patience having been exhausted, the people of Judah having sinned until there was no hope of repentance, the hour of their doom had struck. They could not see what was going on in the heavens; they did not realize that coals of fire from between the cherubim were being scattered over the city; but they were soon to know the meaning of all this in all its terror and its horror.

As the prophet beheld, the cherubim stood on the right side of the house when the man went in, and the cloud, we are told, filled the inner court. Then he saw the glory of Jehovah mounting up from the cherubim and standing suspended over the threshold of the house which was filled with the cloud, and the court, too, was resplendent with the brightness of Jehovah's glory.

Though the ears of the sinners of Judah were deaf to it all, the sound of the wings of the cherubim was heard even to the outer court, as the voice of God Almighty when He speaketh. He commanded the man clothed in linen, bidding him take the fire from between the whirling wheels from between the cherubim—a command that was obeyed immediately. Hands that had been hidden formerly beneath the wings of these executors of the divine government, reached out and took the fire and put it into the hands of this man who received it and went out. It was the form of a man's hand that was seen under the wings, suggesting that God was reaching down to clasp the hand of His creatures and would have poured out upon them His rich grace had they been prepared to receive it, but now He must deal in judgment.

"And I looked, and behold, four wheels beside the cherubim, one wheel beside one cherub, and another wheel beside another cherub; and the appearance of the wheels was like unto a beryl stone. And as for their appearance, they four had one likeness, as if a wheel had been within a wheel. "When they went, they went in their four directions: they turned not as they went, but to the place whither the head looked they followed it; they turned not as they went. And their whole body, and their backs, and their hands, and their wings, and the wheels, were full of eyes round about, even the wheels that they four had. As for the wheels, they were called in my hearing, the whirling wheels. And every one had four faces: the first face was the face of the cherub, and the second face was the face of a man, and the third the face of a lion, and the fourth the face of an eagle"—vers. 9-14.

The wheels of government, as we saw in chapter 1, are intimately connected with the cherubim. There are wheels within wheels, because the counsels of God are being carried out even though man cannot comprehend them. At the very time that the Lord had to visit in judgment the city where He had placed His name, He was so overruling in connection with His faithful remnant that even the haughty Gentile oppressor would find it in his heart to show them mercy.

Nothing can turn aside these wheels of government to the place whither the head looked; that is, the head of the chariot. They followed it and turned not as they went. Puny man attempts to defy God, but it will result only in his being crushed beneath these mighty wheels. None who have ever hardened themselves against Him have prospered; and yet those wheels do not represent mere arbitrary fate, but the wheels themselves were full of eyes—eyes roundabout; eyes that speak of intelligence; the eyes of the Lord, in every place beholding the evil and the good. For the judgment of God is according to truth. There is nothing capricious about His government: He will not render unto man more than his right.

We have noticed already in our comments on the first chapter the significance of the four faces of the cherubim and so need not dwell upon that here.

"And the cherubim mounted up: this is the living creature that I saw by the river Chebar. And when the cherubim went, the wheels went beside them; and when the cherubim lifted up their wings to mount up from the earth, the wheels also turned not from beside them. When they stood, these stood; and when they mounted up, these mounted up with them: for the spirit of the living creature was in them"—vers. 15-17.

Very definitely Ezekiel identifies this vision of the living creature with that which he saw previously by the River Chebar, but again he emphasizes the fact that the wheels were under the direct control of the cherubim. When they lifted up their wings to mount up from the earth the wheels also turned not from beside them; when the cherubim stood, the wheels were still; and when they soared up into the heavens the wheels were lifted up with them, for the spirit of the one was in the other.

"And the glory of Jehovah went forth from over the threshold of the house, and stood over the cherubim. And the cherubim lifted up their wings, and mounted up from the earth in my sight when they went forth, and the wheels beside them: and they stood at the door of the east gate of Jehovah's house; and the glory of the God of Israel was over them above"—vers. 18, 19.

As Ezekiel continued to gaze upon this wondrous scene he beheld the Shekinah glory issue forth from over the threshold of the house and rise up into the heavens until it stood over the cherubim; and then, as though riding majestically through the universe in the divine chariot, it crossed to the door of the east gate of Jehovah's house, and for a time seemed to be suspended above that entrance. It was as though Jehovah was loth to forsake His sanctuary. He lingered still in the place where He had set His name, but there was no evidence whatever of repentance on the part of the people, and so in a short time the glory was to ascend to heaven never to be seen again until the Lord Jesus Christ appeared on this earth.

"This is the living creatine that I saw under the God of Israel by the river Chebar; and I knew that they were cherubim. Every one had four faces, and every one four wings; and the likeness of the hands of a man was under their wings. And as for the likeness of their faces, they were the faces which I saw by the river Chebar, their appearances and themselves; they went every one straight forward"—vers. 20-22.

Again the prophet identifies the vision with the living creature which he had seen by the River Chebar. Observe that the living creature is under the God of Israel. God Himself is invisible. His attributes are manifested in the cherubim. "Justice and judgment," the Psalmist tells us, "are the habitation of Thy throne" (Psalm 89:14), and these attributes are exemplified in the angelic figures.

How solemn the repetition of the words "They went every one straight forward." Oh, the folly of supposing that it is possible for human power to thwart the will of God!

Chapter Eleven The End Of The Vision

The eleventh chapter gives us the last part of the remarkable vision which came to Ezekiel in the sixth year, as mentioned in 8:11. The prophet still speaks of what he saw when, by the Spirit, he was given to behold conditions prevailing in Jerusalem, and God's attitude toward them. The Lord made these things known to him in order that he might press home upon the consciences of those who had been taken captive the importance of heeding the Word of the Lord as given by Jeremiah, a brother-prophet, that the captives should settle down in the lands wherein they had been placed by their conquerors, and should build houses and plant vineyards and prepare for a stay in the land of the stranger for a period of at least seventy years, during which time the land was to keep sabbath.

Against this command many revolted. They supposed the Lord would intervene and open the way for them to return to Palestine. False prophets, who had risen up, encouraged them in this expectation. It was against these men that many of Ezekiel's messages were directed.

"Moreover the Spirit lifted me up, and brought me unto the east gate of Jehovah's house, which looketh eastward: and behold, at the door of the gate five and twenty men; and I saw in the midst of them Jaazaniah the son of Azzur, and Pelatiah the son of Benaiah, princes of the people. And He said unto me, Son of man, these are the men that devise iniquity, and that give wicked counsel in this city; that say, The time is not near to build houses: this city is the caldron, and we are the flesh. Therefore prophesy against them, prophesy, O son of man"—vers. 1-4.

In the spirit Ezekiel once more was carried to the east gate of the temple court. There, by the door of the gate he beheld five and twenty men, princes of Israel—men who represented the attitude of the people toward God. Among these, two are mentioned by name, Jaazaniah the son of Azzur, and Pelatiah the son of Benaiah. It is evident that these two must have had special influence among the people and are, therefore, singled out in this way.

63

The word of the Lord came, saying, "Son of man, these are the men that devise iniquity, and that give wicked counsel in this city." Jerusalem was besieged by the Chaldean armies. By the mouth of Jeremiah God had counseled capitulation to the demands of the foe, and had promised that those who willingly gave themselves up would go into captivity, but that their lives would be preserved; whereas the rest—those who refused to obey—would be utterly destroyed by these leaders opposing the word of the Lord and ridiculing the counsel given by Jeremiah.

They insisted that this was no time to build houses; that is, in the lands of their captivity, and in mockery they exclaimed, "This city is the caldron, and we are the flesh." That is, they recognized the fact that Jerusalem was as a caldron with a living fire beneath and above it, and they like to the flesh within. Nevertheless, they still preached, Peace, peace, when there was no peace, assuring the people that in a little while the Chaldean armies would turn away from Jerusalem and the holy city be preserved from judgment.

In opposition to their optimistic prophecies God again spoke through Ezekiel.

"And the Spirit of Jehovah fell upon me, and He said unto me, Speak, Thus saith Jehovah: Thus have ye said, O house of Israel; for I know the things that come into your mind. Ye have multiplied your slain in this city, and ye have filled the streets thereof with the slain. Therefore thus saith the Lord Jehovah: Your slain whom ye have laid in the midst of it, they are the flesh, and this city is the caldron; hut ye shall be brought forth out of the midst of it. Ye have feared the sword; and I will bring the sword upon you, saith the Lord Jehovah. And I will bring you forth out of the midst thereof, and deliver you into the hands of strangers, and will execute judgments among you. Ye shall fall by the sword; I will judge you in the border of Israel; and ye shall know that I am Jehovah. This city shall not be your caldron, neither shall ye be the flesh in the midst thereof; I will judge you in the border of Israel; and ye shall know that I am Jehovah: for ye have not walked in My statutes, neither have ye executed Mine ordinances, but have done after the ordinances of the nations that are round about you"—vers. 5-12.

He who knows all things not only heard the words of these leaders but also knew the thoughts that were in their hearts, and He declared, "Thus have ye said, O house of Israel; for I know the things that come into your mind." The slain had been multiplied in the city, and the streets filled with dead bodies. These were indeed the flesh, and the city truly was the caldron. And in accordance with the word of the Lord through His prophets, Jerusalem would be taken by the enemy, and those who were not slain would be brought forth out of the midst of it and delivered into the hands of strangers who would be God's instruments to execute judgments upon the inhabitants of Jerusalem. Escape would be impossible. Try as they might they could not deliver themselves from their cruel foes; throughout all the land they would be given up to judgment, and would know that Jehovah had spoken when these things were fulfilled. Not in Jerusalem alone but also throughout all the land of Israel would they know the vengeance of the Chaldeans, which would be all the fiercer because of the prolongation of the siege of the city. Israel had no title to cry for help from God, for they had not walked in His statutes nor carried out His ordinances, but they had behaved themselves in accordance with the ways of the heathen round about them.

"And it came to pass, when I prophesied, that Pelatiah the son of Benaiah died. Then fell I down upon my face, and cried with a loud voice, and said, Ah Lord Jehovah! wilt Thou make a full end of the remnant of Israel?"—ver. 13.

Even while the words were in Ezekiel's mouth he saw in the vision that Pelatiah dropped dead. Evidently this actually occurred in Jerusalem at this very time. Stirred to the depth of his heart by the beginning of the fulfilment of his words, he fell down upon his face and mourned before God, saying, "Ah Lord Jehovah! wilt Thou make a full end of the remnant of Israel?"

The Lord answered, revealing the love of His heart toward His erring people and promising to meet, in grace, any who turned to Him, even in the land of their captivity, while judgment must have its way with those who refused to hear His voice.

"And the word of Jehovah came unto me, saying, Son of man, thy brethren, even thy brethren, the men of thy kindred, and all the house of Israel, all of them, are they unto whom the inhabitants of Jerusalem have said, Get you far from Jehovah; unto us is this land given for a possession. Therefore say, Thus saith the Lord Jehovah: Whereas I have removed them far off among the nations, and whereas I have scattered them among the countries, yet will I be to them a sanctuary for a little while in the countries where they are come. Therefore say, Thus saith the Lord Jehovah: I will gather you from the peoples, and assemble you out of the countries where ye have been scattered, and I will give you the land of Israel. And they shall come thither, and they shall take away all the detestable things thereof and all the abominations thereof from thence. And I will give them one heart, and I will put a new spirit within you; and I will take the stony heart out of their flesh, and will give them a heart of flesh; that they may walk in My statutes, and keep Mine ordinances, and do them: and they shall be My people, and I will be their God. But as for them whose heart walketh after the heart of their detestable things and their abominations, I will bring their way upon their own heads, saith the Lord Jehovah"—vers. 14-21.

Jehovah's words were addressed, as before, to Ezekiel as "Son of man." His own near kinsmen were among those who had rebelled against the Lord, and they, with others, had been removed far off among the nations, but God would never forget any who, in the land of their captivity, turned to Him. He said, "Yet will I be to them a sanctuary for a little while in the countries where they are come." The temple might be destroyed. No place on earth would any longer be designated as that where Jehovah had set His name, but no soul would ever seek Him in vain. No matter what the circumstances in which His people were found, if any turned to Him with all their hearts He would reveal Himself to them and would Himself be a sanctuary unto them. Moreover, in due time He will gather a remnant of His people back to their own land.

Notice the definite promise, "I will gather you from the peoples, and assemble you out of the countries where ye have been scattered, and I will give you the land of Israel. And they shall come thither, and they shall take away all the detestable things thereof and all the abominations thereof from thence."

When that day comes the remnant will be accepted of God as the nation and will be regenerated. He says, "I will give them one heart, and I will put a new spirit within you; and I will take the stony heart out of their flesh, and will give them a heart of flesh; that they may walk in My statutes, and keep Mine ordinances, and do them: and they shall be My people, and I will be their God."

This promise has never yet been fulfilled. The present return of many Jews to Palestine, while still in unbelief, is in one sense a partial fulfilment of this prophecy; it is, doubtless, preparatory to it. But when the actual fulfilment comes the people themselves will return to the Lord; they will judge their sins, and bowing before God will confess their guilt, even the guilt, as we now know, of the rejection of their promised Messiah; and when they thus turn back in heart to God He will establish them in the land, and will give them a new nature through a second birth, even as He does to all individuals now who turn to the Lord Jesus Christ for salvation.

But when they do come there will be no blessing for those who persist in taking the path of self-will and who go on defiantly in their sins. The word of the Lord is, "I will bring their way upon their own heads."

"Then did the cherubim lift up their wings, and the wheels were beside them; and the glory of the God of Israel was over them above. And the glory of Jehovah went up from the midst of the city, and stood upon the mountain which is on the east side of the city. And the Spirit lifted me up, and brought me in the vision by the Spirit of God into Chaldea, to them of the captivity. So the vision that I had seen went up from me. Then I spake unto them of the captivity all the things that Jehovah had showed me"—vers. 22-25.

As the vision came to an end and Ezekiel beheld the cherubim lift up their wings with the wheels of government beside them, he saw the glory of the God of Israel over them above. It was evident that

God still lingered in mercy, even though that mercy was despised, for the glory of Jehovah went up from the midst, then stood upon the mountain, which is on the east side of the city. This is the Shekinah glory which had dwelt between the cherubim in the Holiest of all. It now stood over upon the Mount of Olives, the very place where the Lord Jesus Himself was to stand before He ascended to heaven. The last the prophet saw of the glory in this vision it still waited there upon the mountain top, as though God was reluctant to forsake His people, in spite of the fact that they had proven so disobedient and hardhearted.

As the vision passed Ezekiel opened his eyes to find himself in the land of Chaldea on the banks of the Chebar with a group of the captives gathered about him, to whom he revealed all that he had seen and heard.

Chapter Twelve Jerusalem's Destruction Impending

In chapters 12 to 16 we have another series of prophetic messages, all having to do with the predicted destruction of Jerusalem, and the captivity of the people of Judah. Though so long-suffering, God could no longer condone the wickedness of Judah, so there was nothing to do but to carry out His judgments against the people whom He loved so tenderly, but who had shown such utter indifference to His holy will. Zedekiah, to whom Jeremiah had witnessed so faithfully, had given no evidence whatever of repentance, and so he who sat upon the throne of Jehovah (Jeremiah 29:21) was doomed, not only to be degraded from his royal estate but also to go sightless down to Babylon as a subject-vassal of Nebuchadnezzar.

In the first part of this chapter Ezekiel was commanded to gain the attention of his fellow-captives by acting out the departure from Jerusalem.

"The word of Jehovah also came unto me, saying, Son of man, thou dwellest in the midst of the rebellious house, that have eyes to see, and see not, that have ears to hear, and hear not; for they are a rebellious house. Therefore, thou son of man, prepare thee stuff for removing, and remove by day in their sight; and thou shalt remove from thy place to another place in their sight: it may be they will consider, though they are a rebellious house. And thou shalt bring forth thy stuff by day in their sight, as stuff for removing; and thou shalt go forth thyself at even in their sight, as when men go forth into exile. Dig thou through the wall in their sight, and carry out thereby. In their sight shalt thou bear it upon thy shoulder, and carry it forth in the dark; thou shalt cover thy face, that thou see not the land: for I have set thee for a sign unto the house of Israel. And I did so as I was commanded: I brought forth my stuff by day, as stuff for removing, and in the even I digged through the wall with my hand; I brought it forth in the dark, and bare it upon my shoulder in their sight"—vers. 1-7.

Though a man of God, Ezekiel himself dwelt in the midst of a rebellious people who did not use their eyes to see nor their ears to hear, but persisted in the path of folly and self-will. Ezekiel was commanded to prepare his goods for removing; that is, he was to pack up everything as though he were getting ready to leave his present place of abode; then as night drew on he was to remove to a new location, but furtively, as we are told, as men go forth into exile. Instead of passing through the gate of the enclosure in which he dwelt, he was commanded to dig through the wall and carry out his goods through the breach that was made. His face was to be covered that he might not see the land, for he was intended to be a sign unto the house of Israel, picturing to them the condition of the thousands of Judah who would seek to flee from the Chaldeans, only to be captured by them and led away into the stranger's land.

The prophet did as he was commanded and went forth in the dark, bearing his goods upon his shoulder, in the sight of the people who doubtless looked on curiously.

"And in the morning came the word of Jehovah unto me, saying, Son of man, hath not the house of Israel, the rebellious house said unto thee, What doest thou? Say thou unto them, Thus saith the Lord Jehovah: This burden concerneth the prince in Jerusalem, and all the house of Israel among whom they are. Say, I am your sign: like as I have done, so shall it be done unto them; they shall go into exile, into captivity. And the prince that is among them shall bear upon his shoulder in the dark, and shall go forth: they shall dig through the wall to carry out thereby: he shall cover his face, because he shall not see the land with his eyes. My net also will I spread upon him, and he shall be taken in My snare; and I will bring him to Babylon to the land of the Chaldeans; yet shall he not see it, though he shall die there. And I will scatter toward every wind all that are round about him to help him, and all his bands; and I will draw out the sword after them. And they shall know that I am Jehovah, when I shall disperse them among the nations, and scatter them through the countries. But I will leave a few men of them from the sword, from the famine, and from the pestilence; that they may declare all their abominations among the nations whither they come; and they shall know that I am Jehovah"—vers. 8-16.

The day following the acted parable of the previous verses the word of Jehovah again came to Ezekiel, inquiring what impression his actions had made upon the rebellious house of Israel. Had they asked him, "What doest thou?" he was to make known unto them the burden of Jehovah concerning Zedekiah, the prince in Jerusalem, and all the house of Israel who still remained in the land. He was to explain that he himself was their sign; that as he had done, so should it be done unto them. They were all doomed to go into exile. Even the prince himself, that is, King Zedekiah, would endeavor to escape from the city, bearing a few of his possessions upon his shoulder even as one of the common people. In his effort to thwart the purpose of Nebuchadnezzar to take him captive he would flee in the dark after digging through the wall, and would seek to save his life by becoming a fugitive and hiding in some almost inaccessible place. Nevertheless he would be taken captive, and as a bird in a snare, he would be brought to Babylon, to the land of the Chaldeans. But he was destined never to see that land even though he was to dwell in it for a number of years, un- til finally death released him. This prophecy had its terrible fulfilment, as we know, when his two sons were slain before his eyes, after which those eyes were put out, so that the last memory he had of things seen would be the death of his children.

Following in the wake of the king's captivity would come the scattering of Judah throughout all the lands of earth; nor would this complete their judgment, for wherever they went God Himself would draw out the sword after them, and they would learn through experiences of deepest grief and sorrow the folly of having forsaken the Lord God. Dispersed among the nations and scattered throughout the countries they would remain a separated people, against whom the bitter enmity of their neighbors would burn.

A few of them, nevertheless, would be saved from the sword, the famine, and the pestilence, that they might declare, or acknowledge, all their abominations among the nations whither they came; thus they should know that they had to do with Jehovah.

"Moreover the word of Jehovah came to me, saying, Son of man, eat thy bread with quaking, and drink thy water with trembling and with tearfulness; and say unto the people of the land, Thus saith the Lord Jehovah concerning the inhabitants of Jerusalem, and the land of Israel: They shall eat their bread with fearfulness, and drink their water in dismay, that her land may be desolate, and despoiled of all that is therein, because of the violence of all them that dwell therein. And the cities that are inhabited shall be laid waste, and the land shall be a desolation; and ye shall know that I am Jehovah"—vers. 17-20.

Thus Ezekiel would continue to be a sign unto the people. In accordance with the word of the Lord, he ate his bread with quaking, and drank his water with trembling and with fearfulness. In this way he was to picture the unhappy conditions under which the people of Judah would live when carried away from their own land after their cities had been laid waste and the land itself become a desolation.

In imminent fear of their lives, never knowing from one day to another what new calamity might come upon them, the unhappy captives would be in constant dread because of the violence of their enemies. Not only during the time of Nebuchadnezzar's sway, but also down through all the centuries since has this been the unhappy portion of the nation of Israel. Never fully at home anywhere, they have lived in continual fear and uncertainty, and all because they knew not the time of their visitation.

For many years God's prophets had been warning the people of the dire calamities that would come upon them if they persisted in refusing to obey the word of Jehovah, but they had spurned these testimonies and mistreated the messengers. Because sentence against their evil ways was not immediately executed they put off from them the day of reckoning, hoping that it might never come in their time. Of this we next read:

"And the word of Jehovah came unto me, saying, Son of man, what is this proverb that ye have in the land of Israel, saying, The days are prolonged, and every vision faileth? Tell them therefore, Thus saith the Lord Jehovah: I will make this proverb to cease, and they shall no more use it as a proverb in Israel; but say unto them, The days are at hand, and the fulfilment of every vision. For there shall be no more any false vision nor flattering divination within the house of Israel. For I am Jehovah; I will speak, and the word that I shall speak shall be performed; it shall be no more deferred: for in your days, O rebellious house, will I speak the word, and will perform it, saith the Lord Jehovah"—vers. 21-25.

The majority of the people of Israel and Judah were of the same spirit as those of our own time, who, when they hear the truth that the Lord Jesus is to return again, cry out in derision, "Where is the promise of His coming? for since the fathers fell asleep, all things continue as they were from the beginning of the creation" (2 Peter 3:4). So those of old said, "The days" (that is, the days in which God was waiting in mercy ere visiting judgment upon His people) "are prolonged, and every vision faileth." They did not look for the prophet's visions to materialize, but God's word came, saying, "I will make this proverb to cease, and they shall no more use it as a proverb in Israel"; for contrary to what they had said, the days were at hand, and every vision of judgment was about to be fulfilled. Moreover, the false prophets were to be cut off in Jehovah's anger; there should be no more any false vision nor flattering divination. God's word alone should stand. He had spoken, and His word should be performed, nor should the predicted doom be longer deferred. In their days, He declared, He would give the final commandment that would bring down the judgment upon that rebellious house.

"Again the word of Jehovah came to me, saying, Son of man, behold, they of the house of Israel say, The vision that he seeth is for many days to come, and he prophesieth of times that are afar off. Therefore say unto them, Thus saith the Lord Jehovah: There shall none of My words be deferred any more, but the word which I shall speak shall be performed, saith the Lord Jehovah"—vers. 26-28.

A second time Jehovah gave the same message through His servant. Even though He had spoken so definitely, in their folly and unbelief the house of Israel continued to say, "The vision that he seeth is for many days to come, and he prophesieth of times

73

that are far off." With a foolhardy optimism they put away the evil day, and went on carelessly in their sin and ungodliness, thinking they would escape the predicted judgments, and that if they came at all they would fall upon a future generation. But God declared that none of His words should be deferred any more; that which He had spoken was now to be performed immediately, and thus the people would know that they had to do with a God who never calls back His words.

We may also see in all this a picture of that which prevails in Christendom at the present time. While the Scriptures clearly indicate the fact that we are living in the closing days of this dispensation, the professing Church, with very few exceptions, has settled down complacently in the world, and its leaders endeavor to make the people believe that those who talk of judgment beginning at the house of God are misguided fanatics, and that conditions were never better than those that now prevail. Yet the Word of God declares that, "As the days of Noah were, so shall also the coming of the Son of Man be" (Matthew 24:37); for as corruption and violence filled the antediluvian world, so we see corruption and violence on every hand today, and in the Church itself the characteristics of the last days, as depicted in 2 Timothy 3, are everywhere prevalent.

Oh, that we might have eyes to see and ears to hear, to understand the signs of the times and take heed to the Word of the Lord.

Chapter Thirteen Lying Prophets Rebuked

At the time when these providential judgments were being meted out to Israel, already there were not wanting false prophets who dared to declare that Ezekiel's predictions were the ravings of an ill-natured pessimist, and that the hour of Jerusalem's deliverance and Judah's triumph was near, when the Chaldean armies would be driven from the land of Palestine, defeated and utterly humiliated. To these vain optimists Ezekiel was commanded to speak in the name of Jehovah, declaring that they themselves were doomed to perish with the rest of the apostate nation when the full wrath of the Lord should fall upon them.

"And the word of Jehovah came unto me, saying, Son of man, prophesy against the prophets of Israel that prophesy, and say thou unto them that prophesy out of their own heart, Hear ye the word of Jehovah: thus saith the Lord Jehovah, Woe unto the foolish prophets, that follow their own spirit, and have seen nothing! O Israel, thy prophets have been like foxes in the waste places. Ye have not gone up into the gaps, neither built up the wall for the house of Israel, to stand in the battle in the day of Jehovah. They have seen falsehood and lying divination, that say, Jehovah saith; but Jehovah hath not sent them: and they have made men to hope that the word would be confirmed. Have ye not seen a false vision, and have ye not spoken a lying divination, in that ye say, Jehovah saith; albeit I have not spoken?"—vers. 1-7.

Professing to speak by the Spirit of the Lord, these false prophets had but given utterance to the promptings of their own spirits. They expressed only what they vainly hoped might be the outcome of the conflict then going on. Their whole attitude was the result of wishful thinking. Failing to recognize the cause of the suffering of Judah, and thus not understanding the attitude of Jehovah toward the people called by His name, they predicted only that which they fondly hoped would come to pass.

Thus they were hindrances rather than helpers, making the people comfortable in their sins. Like foxes in the deserts, or rather, as jackals in the wilderness feeding on carrion, they were worthless messengers because they had no word from Jehovah.

They had not attempted to get at the root of the trouble by calling on Israel to judge the idolatry and all its attendant evils, which had led them so far astray and hidden Jehovah's face from them.

Declaring the Lord had sent them to give assurance of coming deliverance, they made the people trust in a lie which would never be confirmed. Theirs was a vain or empty vision and a false divination, for in spite of their pretension to represent Jehovah, He had not spoken through them.

In every age when God has been dealing with His professed people because of their sins and apostasy there have been such false prophets who have sought to lull the offenders to sleep in a false confidence, assuring them that all is well and there need be no fear of judgment falling upon them. How these prophets abound in Christendom today! With the Judge standing at the door, they continue to cry, "Peace, peace, when there is no peace!"

"Therefore thus saith the Lord Jehovah: because ye have spoken falsehood, and seen lies, therefore, behold, I am against you, saith the Lord Jehovah. And My hand shall be against the prophets that see false visions, and that divine lies: they shall not he in the council of My people, neither shall they be written in the writing of the house of Israel, neither shall they enter into the land of Israel; and ye shall know that I am the Lord Jehovah. Because, even because they have seduced My people, saying, Peace; and there is no peace; and when one buildeth up a wall, behold, they daub it with untempered mortar: say unto them that daub it with untempered mortar, that it shall fall: there shall be an overflowing shower; and ye, O great hailstones, shall fall; and a stormy wind shall rend it"—vers. 8-11.

Like a careless or unfaithful workman who would build up a wall by attempting to cement the stones together with untempered mortar, so these lying prophets endeavored to build up the morale of their brethren who looked to them for guidance, by leading them to trust in a lie. Because of this God had set His face against them. They were doomed to die in their captivity, never again to see the land to which they declared the scattered nation would soon return in triumph.

The very names of these so-called seers were to be blotted out of the records of Israel because they had endeavored to discredit the testimony of the Lord, as given through His inspired representatives. The time would soon come when their falsity should be made manifest. Then the very people who had been deceived by them would ridicule their unfounded pretensions to be mouthpieces of Jehovah.

"Lo, when the wall is fallen, shall it not be said unto you, Where is the daubing wherewith ye have daubed it? Therefore thus saith the Lord Jehovah: I will even rend it with a stormy wind in My wrath; and there shall be an overflowing shower in Mine anger, and great hailstones in wrath to consume it. So will I break down the wall that ye have daubed with untempered mortar, and bring it down to the ground, so that the foundation thereof shall be uncovered; and it shall fall, and ye shall be consumed in the midst thereof: and ye shall know that I am Jehovah. Thus will I accomplish My wrath upon the wall, and upon them that have daubed it with untempered mortar; and I will say unto you, The wall is no more, neither they that daubed it; to wit, the prophets of Israel that prophesy concerning Jerusalem, and that see visions of peace for her, and there is no peace, saith the Lord Jehovah"—vers. 12-16.

A wall speaks of protection and separation. The wall built with untempered mortar was destined to collapse, exposing the people to the power of the Chaldeans. In that day these self-styled optimists would become the objects of the scorn and contempt of those who had been misled by their lying predictions.

Back of Nebuchadnezzar's armies was God Himself. It was He who would use these cruel foes to destroy the wall and to consume the people from off the land. In His wrath He was about to visit His indignation upon them because of their manifold iniquities of which they refused to repent. Their prophets cried, "Peace"; but the Lord declared, "There is no peace." How could there be when the law of God was flouted, and His Word despised?

"And thou, son of man, set thy face against the daughters of thy people, that prophesy out of their own heart; and prophesy thou against them, and say, Thus saith the Lord Jehovah: Woe to the women that sew pillows upon all elbows, and make kerchiefs for the head of persons of every stature to hunt souls! Will ye hunt the souls of My people, and save souls alive for yourselves? And ye have profaned Me among My people for handfuls of barley and for pieces of bread, to slay the souls that should not die, and to save the souls alive that should not live, by your lying to My people that hearken unto lies. Wherefore thus saith the Lord Jehovah: Behold, I am against your pillows, wherewith ye there hunt the souls to make them fly, and I will tear them from your arms; and I will let the souls go, even the souls that ye hunt to make them fly. Your kerchiefs also will I tear, and deliver My people out of your hand, and they shall be no more in your hand to be hunted; and ye shall know that I am Jehovah"—vers. 17-21.

There were not only false prophets, but also false prophetesses at this time. Often when men have failed it has pleased God to speak through faithful women. But in those days the women were as false and faithless as the men. They too prophesied smooth things and tried to make the people comfortable in their sins. So God pronounced a woe against them.

The expression, "The women that sew pillows (or cushions) to all armholes (or wristbands)," is admittedly a difficult passage to explain. Some think the reference is to binding charms and amulets upon their clothing; others think that it was simply a suggestive adornment that implied there was no danger to avoid, and so they were prepared to rest comfortably without fear of evil. The other expression, "That make kerchiefs for the head of persons of every stature," is also somewhat perplexing. But may it not also suggest careless adornment in order to banish the fear of calamity and incite to increased mirth and vanity?

The verse that follows seems to coincide with this thought. Like harlots adorning themselves in order to attract unwary victims, these false prophetesses made everything as pleasing as they could in order to ensnare the souls of those who might be inclined to heed the word of the Lord as given by Ezekiel and others, who were divinely inspired and who warned of judgment to come.

"Because with lies ye have grieved the heart of the righteous, whom I have not made sad, and strengthened the hands of the wicked, that he should not return from his wicked way, and be saved alive; therefore ye shall no more see false visions, nor divine divinations: and I will deliver My people out of your hand; and ye shall know that I am Jehovah"—vers. 22, 23.

Where conscience was at all active the heart was saddened by all this wicked perversion of the truth of God. The righteous were grieved as they saw the wicked lulled into a state of carnal security, from which only judgment would awaken them, when it would be too late for repentance. False teaching always tends to strengthen people, who accept it, in their wickedness and to make them believe that no matter how they live they will be secure from divine wrath.

God may seem tolerant of that which is untrue and unreal for a time, but He will deal eventually with those who propagate error, and will deliver His people from their hand.

Chapter Fourteen Too Late For Intercession

We are told in the book of Proverbs that if men refuse to heed the voice of God when He speaks in grace, calling to repentance, the day will come when they shall call on Him for mercy and He will refuse to heed their cry. This is what we have emphasized in the present chapter.

It was very evident that the Jews' case had become extremely critical. Those who had counted on the withdrawal of the Chaldean armies and the fulfilment of the predictions of peace made by their false prophets, were beginning to feel that, after all, they were in a far worse case than they had supposed; and so a deputation of the leaders called on Ezekiel to confer with him as to whether there might be any hope of Jehovah's intervention on their behalf.

"Then came certain of the elders of Israel unto me, and sat before me. And the word of Jehovah came unto me, saying, Son of man, these men have taken their idols into their heart, and put the stumblingblock of their iniquity before their face: should I be inquired of at all by them? Therefore speak unto them, and say unto them, Thus saith the Lord Jehovah: Every man of the house of Israel that taketh his idols into his heart, and putteth the stumblingblock of his iniquity before his face, and cometh to the prophet; I Jehovah will answer him therein according to the multitude of his idols; that I may take the house of Israel in their own heart, because they are all estranged from Me through their idols"—vers. 1-5.

Before any of these elders uttered a word, God Himself spoke to Ezekiel, declaring that He who seeth not as man seeth but discerns the thoughts and intents of the heart, had already judged these men as those who had set up their idols in their own hearts and put the stumblingblock of their iniquities before their faces. Why, then, should they come to a prophet of God to inquire of him? They had no desire to do the will of God; therefore they had no title to seek relief from Him. As long as conditions continued as they were, there could be no answer of peace. Jehovah declared that all those of the house of Israel who had set up idols in their hearts and who persisted in their iniquities, which had thus become a national stumbling-block, deserved no answer, save an answer in judgment in accordance with the idolatry that they had pursued. God would deal with them as He saw them to be inwardly, not in accordance with their lip profession as they pretended to reverence Him.

He commanded that Ezekiel simply confirm the prophecies of judgment that had already gone forth.

"Therefore say unto the house of Israel, Thus saith the Lord Jehovah: Return ye, and turn yourselves from your idols; and turn away your faces from all your abominations. For every one of the house of Israel, or of the strangers that sojourn in Israel, that separateth himself from Me, and taketh his idols into his heart, and putteth the stumblingblock of his iniquity before his face, and cometh to the prophet to inquire for himself of Me; I Jehovah will answer him by Myself: and I will set My face against that man, and will make him an astonishment, for a sign and a proverb, and I will cut him off from the midst of My people; and ye shall know that I am Jehovah. And if the prophet be deceived and speak a word, I, Jehovah, have deceived that prophet, and I will stretch out My hand upon him, and will destroy him from the midst of My people Israel. And they shall bear their iniquity:, the iniquity of the prophet shall be even as the iniquity of him that seeketh unto him; that the house of Israel may go no more astray from Me, neither defile themselves any more with all their transgressions; but that they may be My people, and I may be their God, saith the Lord Jehovah"—vers. 6-11.

In his mercy He called upon the people to turn again to Him, to put away their idols, to judge all these abominations after which they had gone for so long. If they were prepared to do this, He would still heed their cry. In fact, wherever there was an individual of the house of Israel or of the strangers who were dwelling among the people of Israel, God would hear in mercy if they turned to Him in truth, but where they persisted in their idolatry He could only set His face against them and pour out His wrath upon them.

He declared that those who went on in their sins would become an astonishment, a sign, and a proverb to the nations, and would be cut off from *She* midst of Israel. Thus by His judgments they should know it was Jehovah with whom they had to do.

As for the false prophets who were misleading them, the Lord Himself took the responsibility for having permitted this; for it is a principle in Scripture that when men refuse the truth, God Himself often gives them up to falsehood. Even as in the last days of the great tribulation, those who receive not the love of the truth that they might be saved, will be given up to strong delusion that they might believe the lie of the Antichrist, and so all be judged which obey not the truth but have pleasure in unrighteousness.

We may think it is just a matter of chance when one man receives the testimony of the Lord and turns to Him in repentance and faith and seeks to walk in His truth, while others are carried away by false systems, many of which have become most popular in our own days. In the first instance it is the Spirit of God Himself who reveals to man his need, and then shows how Christ has met that need; whereas, in the other case, when people have refused the truth of God and resisted the Holy Spirit, He allows their minds to be blinded and permits them to be deluded by false teachings which, if followed to the end, result in their everlasting doom.

Our Lord Jesus warned against blind leaders of the blind, both of whom fall into the ditch at last. To Ezekiel God declared that the people who followed after that which was false should bear their iniquities, and the punishment of the pretended prophet should be even as that of those who trusted in his messages.

In order that the house of Israel might realize the folly of turning away from Jehovah, and might learn from His judgments the importance of walking in His truth, and so might not go farther astray nor be defiled any more with the things that had rendered them so unclean in His sight, there is more than a suggestion in verse 11, that there was still hope if they would turn to God. In that case He would again acknowledge them as His people, and He would manifest Himself as their God. But alas, there was no response! They persisted in their evil way; therefore God declared that they must be given up to judgment.

"And the word of Jehovah came unto me, saying, Son of man, when a land sinneth against Me by committing a trespass, and I stretch out My hand upon it, and break the staff of the bread thereof, and send famine upon it, and cut off from it man and beast; though these three men, Noah, Daniel, and Job, were in it, they should deliver but their own souls by their righteousness, saith the Lord Jehovah. If I cause evil beasts to pass through the land, and they ravage it, and it be made desolate, so that no man may pass through because of the beasts; though these three men were in it, as I live, saith the Lord Jehovah, they should deliver neither sons nor daughters; they only should be delivered, but the land should be desolate. Or if I bring a sword upon that land, and say, Sword, go through the land; so that I cut off from it man and beast; though these three men were in it, as I live, saith the Lord Jehovah, they should deliver neither sons nor daughters, but they only should be delivered themselves. Or if I send a pestilence into that land, and pour out My wrath upon it in blood, to cut off from it man and beast; though Noah, Daniel, and Job, were in it, as I live, saith the Lord Jehovah, they should deliver neither son nor daughter; they should but deliver their own souls by their righteousness"—vers. 12-20.

While the hypocritical elders waited, hoping for an answer that might promise deliverance from their present awful plight, God commanded Ezekiel to tell them that they had gone beyond the place where He would listen to intercession on their behalf. The people of the land had so thoroughly committed themselves to iniquity and had been so unfaithful to the covenant which God had made with them that He was now stretching out His hand against them and would give them over to famine in addition to the other troubles that had come upon them. Even though such godly and devoted men as Noah, the outstanding witness for God before the flood; Daniel, who at this very time was in Babylon being prepared of God for a remarkable ministry in future days; or Job the patriarch who had been so severely tested and come through so triumphantly, should all be together in the land and should make intercession on its behalf, still they would deliver but their own souls by their righteousness. Their pleadings could not avail for the apostate nation.

If conditions in the land became so evil that wild and savage beasts increased to such an extent as to endanger the lives of the few who were left in it so that no one dared appear on the highway because of these beasts, even then, though these three men should be among the remnant and should plead on their behalf, still God declared they should deliver neither sons nor daughters but only themselves, and the land should be left to desolation. Or if the sword of the enemy were allowed to prevail, as it would very soon, when God Himself should command the sword to go through the land to cut off man and beast from it, if these three men should be in it and should stand before Jehovah and plead for the people, still He would not answer. He would recognize their own righteousness, but their prayer would avail for no one else. Or if pestilence, which so often follows bloody warfare, should take its terrible toll of those who remained, cutting off man and beast, Noah, Daniel, and Job would be unable to avert the judgment, let them plead as they might.

"For thus saith the Lord Jehovah: How much more when I send My four sore judgments upon Jerusalem, the sword, and the famine, and the evil beasts, and the pestilence, to cut off from it man and beast! Yet, behold, therein shall be left a remnant that shall be carried forth, both sons and daughters: behold, they shall come forth unto you, and ye shall see their way and their doings; and ye shall be comforted concerning the evil that I have brought upon Jerusalem, even concerning all that I have brought upon it. And they shall comfort you, when ye see their way and their doings; and ye shall know that I have not done without cause all that I have done in it, saith the Lord Jehovah"—vers. 21-23.

We may notice a very close connection between the threatened evils mentioned here and the four horsemen of the Apocalypse. In Ezekiel we read of warfare, famine, evil beasts, and pestilence. These are called Jehovah's "four sore judgments." In the Apocalypse we have, first, the white horse of peace, then the red horse of war, followed by the black horse of famine, and the corpse-colored horse of pestilence. These are all providential judgments which God sends upon the nations when they turn away from Him.

But there is a rainbow of hope seen even in the dark clouds of judgment, as we notice in verses 22 and 23, wherein God speaks of a remnant that shall be carried forth and shall learn from what has come upon them and the rest, and as a result, will turn to the Lord and be comforted concerning the evil that He was bringing upon Jerusalem. These were to be the witnesses of God's loving care over all who, in their hearts, turned back to Him, and so made it possible for Him in righteousness to act for their blessing. Realizing the sinfulness of the nation to which they belonged they would recognize the fact that God had not acted arbitrarily, but had good reasons for dealing with them in the manner in which He did.

Chapter Fifteen Israel An Unfruitful Vine

As every Bible student knows, there are different plants or trees used in the Scriptures as types or symbols of the nation of Israel, God's earthly people. Four of these are brought together in the parable of Jotham, as found in Judges 9:8-21. These are the olive, the fig-tree, the vine, and the bramble-bush. As we learn in Jeremiah 11:16, 17, and in Romans 11, the olive-tree represents Israel in covenant relationship with God. For the present the covenant is in abeyance, and Israel is scattered among the nations. The Gentiles now enjoy the privileges that might have been Israel's had they been faithful to the Lord. In a future day, however, because of the unfaithfulness of the Gentiles, they will be set to one side and Israel grafted again into their own olive-tree. The fig-tree speaks of Israel nationally; perhaps more particularly of the Jews as such—that is, the descendants of Judah and Benjamin who were in the land when the Lord Himself came. This fig-tree failed to bear fruit for God, and so is under a curse. There will be no fruit until, through infinite grace, the nation will be restored to God and to their land.

The vine tells us of Israel looked at as a people in spiritual relationship with God, who should have brought forth the peaceable fruit of righteousness to His glory. He planted them a noble vine and cared for them in every possible way, as we read in Isaiah 5, but there was no fruit for Himself. In the book of Hosea (10:1) we read, "Israel is an empty vine, he bringeth forth fruit unto himself." So when the Lord Jesus was about to be crucified He declared that Israel's house was left unto them desolate, and announced that He Himself was the true Vine, and all who professed faith in Him are the branches.

The bramble-bush pictures in a very graphic way what Israel has become as under divine judgment, instead of being a blessing to the world. The name of God is blasphemed among the Gentiles through them, as we read in Romans 2:24.

In our present chapter Ezekiel is called upon to consider the vine-tree from God's standpoint.

"And the word of Jehovah came unto me, saying, Son of man, what is the vine-tree more than any tree, the vine-branch which is among the trees of the forest? Shall wood he taken thereof to make any work? or will men take a pin of it to hang any vessel thereon? Behold, it is cast into the fire for fuel; the fire hath devoured both the ends of it, and the midst of it is burned: is it profitable for any work? Behold, when it was whole, it was meet for no work: how much less, when the fire hath devoured it, and it is burned, shall it yet be meet for any work!"—vers. 1-5.

The vine was created by God for but one special purpose, and that is to bear fruit. Compared with other trees it is a crooked, twisted dwarf, whose wood is of very little use. It could not be made into boards for building purposes; it is so soft in texture that one could not even make tent-pins of it to place upon the center pole in order to hang vessels thereon, as is customary among nomadic peoples. It is almost worthless even as fuel, for in a few moments it is utterly consumed, and it would take an enormous amount of fagots of the vine to keep up a fire for any length of time. It is utterly unprofitable for any work. But if it bears rich, luscious grapes it fulfils the purpose of its creation. So when God used the vine as a figure of Israel it was in view of their spiritual relationship to Him. If this relationship were maintained in purity and holiness there would be precious fruit borne by the nation for His honor and glory. Some day this shall be, when regenerated Israel shall blossom and bud and fill the face of the whole earth with fruit; but in the meantime we see this people scattered among the nations and a testimony wherever they go to the divine displeasure.

"Therefore thus saith the Lord Jehovah: As the vine-tree among the trees of the forest, which I have given to the fire for fuel, so will I give the inhabitants of Jerusalem. And I will set My face against them; they shall go forth from the fire, but the fire shall devour them; and ye shall know that I am Jehovah, when I set My face against them. And I will make the land desolate, because they have committed a trespass, saith the Lord Jehovah"—vers. 6-8.

Just as the vine-dresser roots out of his vineyard worthless vines and consumes them in the fire, so God was giving the inhabitants of Jerusalem into the hands of the Chaldeans that they might be destroyed. Because of their unfaithfulness and corruption He had set His face against them, declaring that the fire of judgment should devour them, and thus they should know that He, Jehovah, was dealing with them because of their sins. Their land was to become desolate because of the great trespass which they had committed against His holy name. In the book of the Revelation we have God's final dealings with the apostate part of Israel just before the return of Messiah, when a remnant will be recognized by Him and planted again in the land of Palestine, to become a fruitful vine through the millennial age. John saw in vision a mighty angel come forth from the temple which is in heaven, having a sharp sickle in his hand, and he heard another angel commanding the first one to send forth "the sharp sickle, and gather the clusters of the vine of the earth; for her grapes are fully ripe" (Rev. 14:18). God had said through Isaiah, "He looked that it should bring forth grapes, and it brought forth wild grapes" (Isa. 5:2). These tell out the condition of the people in their complete repudiation of God's Word and of His Son, their own Messiah, whom they still failed to recognize.

We are told that the angel cast his sickle into the earth and gathered the vintage of the earth and cast it into the wine-press—the great wine-press of the wrath of God—and the wine-press was trodden without the city, and there came out blood from the winepress, even to the bridles of the horses, as far as six hundred furlongs. This is the actual length of the land of Palestine, and the vision clearly intimates that the entire land will be drenched with blood—the blood of those who have apostatized from Jehovah in the awful days of the great tribulation. Then will God's judgment be poured out upon the vine of the earth. Following this, when the Son of Man descends to take the kingdom, He will recognize a spared remnant as His own vine, and will place them again in the very land where judgment will have been executed upon the wicked.

In the interval, between the rejection of Israel—the Lord said, "Behold, your house is left unto you desolate" (Matt. 23:38)—and the time of Jacob's trouble, the Lord Jesus Himself, as the True

Vine, brings forth fruit unto the Father through those who in infinite grace have been linked up with Him not in profession but in reality. It is well to remember that there are no natural branches in the living Vine; all must be grafted in. Where the graft does not strike—that is, where there is only profession and not life, there will be no fruit; but where there is actual union in life there will be fruit unto God—fruit which is precious in His sight. In order that more fruit may be produced He cleanses the branches, prunes them as He sees fit, and rejoices when they bring forth much fruit.

Chapter Sixteen Israel Favored Of God But Faithless

This lengthy chapter, in the very nature of things, could not very well have been divided inasmuch as it gives a complete outline of God's ways with Israel from the very beginning, and their ungrateful response to His loving-kindness. There is much here against which the mind revolts—much that is so indelicate according to our way of speaking, much that is loathsome and even grossly sordid. But we need to remember that sin is the vilest thing in all the universe. And Israel's sin in turning away from the true and living God to the worship of the idols of the nations roundabout her, was of a most revolting character, for that idolatry was linked with very corrupt and immoral practices. Therefore God used the method employed here, indelicate as it may seem to people of refined tastes and clean minds, to portray the filthiness of such sin and iniquity as that of which this nation had been guilty. No carefully chosen words or guarded expressions can make wickedness any less repulsive than it really is in the sight of a holy God.

"Again the word of Jehovah came unto me, saying, Son of man, cause Jerusalem to know her abominations; and say, Thus saith the Lord Jehovah unto Jerusalem: Thy birth and thy nativity is of the land of the Canaanite; the Amorite was thy father, and thy mother was a Hittite. And as for thy nativity, in the day thou wast born thy navel was not cut, neither wast thou washed in water to cleanse thee; thou wast not salted at all, nor swaddled at all. No eye pitied thee, to do any of these things unto thee, to have compassion upon thee; but thou wast cast out in the open field, for that thy person was abhorred, in the day that thou wast born"—vers. 1-5.

Israel here is likened to an unwanted female babe exposed for death, thrown out by its parents immediately after birth and left to perish in its uncleanness.

Canaan was the home of the Amorite and the Hittite. Israel's parentage as a nation was traced back to these idolatrous tribes. The ordinary care given to a newborn child had not been hers. The inhabitants of the land repudiated her and endeavored to rid themselves of her from the beginning.

Nevertheless God in mercy and loving-kindness looked upon Israel and intervened in her behalf, as the next verses remind us.

"And when I passed by thee, and saw thee weltering in thy blood, I said unto thee, Though thou art in thy blood, live; yea, I said unto thee, Though thou art in thy blood, live. I caused thee to multiply as that which groweth in the field, and thou didst increase and wax great, and thou attainedst to excellent ornament; thy breasts were fashioned, and thy hair was grown; yet thou wast naked and bare. Now when I passed by thee, and looked upon thee, behold, thy time was the time of love; and I spread my skirt over thee, and covered thy nakedness: yea, I sware unto thee, and entered into a covenant with thee, saith the Lord Jehovah, and thou becamest Mine. Then washed I thee with water; yea, I thoroughly washed away thy blood from thee, and 1 anointed thee with oil. I clothed thee also with broidered work, and shod thee with sealskin, and I girded thee about with fine linen, and covered thee with silk. And I decked thee with ornaments, and I put bracelets upon thy hands, and a chain on thy neck. And I put a ring upon thy nose, and earrings in thine ears, and a beautiful crown upon thy head. Thus wast thou decked with gold and silver; and thy raiment was of fine linen, and silk, and broidered work; thou didst eat fine flour, and honey, and oil; and thou wast exceeding beautiful, and thou didst prosper unto royal estate. And thy renown went forth among the nations for thy beauty; for it was perfect, through My majesty which I had put upon thee, saith the Lord Jehovah"—vers. 6-14.

Jehovah looked upon the infant nation in pity and tender consideration. Instead of permitting her enemies to destroy her, He threw the mantle of His protection over her, took her up in grace, nourished and cherished her, saw her develop as from a neglected infant into a fair and beautiful maiden.

In His tender love He cleansed, clothed and adorned her, making her to become the most favored of nations, a witness to His great compassion and His omnipotent power. Thus she became renowned throughout the world, and even the nations that knew not her God, could not fail to realize that she was specially favored by Him who had become her Deliverer and Protector. All was of Him. He acted according to the love of His heart not according to any merit He saw in her.

Instead of responding to such goodness by loyalty to her Redeemer-God, she proved utterly faithless, as the next section reveals.

"But thou didst trust in thy beauty, and playedst the harlot because of thy renown, and pouredst out thy whoredoms on every one that passed by; his it was. And thou didst take of thy garments, and madest for thee high places decked with divers colors, and playedst the harlot upon them: the like things shall not come, neither shall it be so. Thou didst also take thy fair jewels of My gold and of My silver, which I had given thee, and madest for thee images of men, and didst play the harlot with them; and thou tookest thy broidered garments, and coveredst them, and didst set Mine oil and Mine incense before them. My bread also which I gave thee, fine flour, and oil, and honey, wherewith I fed thee, thou didst even set it before them for a sweet savor; and thus it was, saith the Lord Jehovah. Moreover thou hast taken thy sons and thy daughters, whom thou hast borne unto Me, and these hast thou sacrificed unto them to be devoured. Were thy whoredoms a small matter, that thou hast slain My children, and delivered them up, in causing them to pass through the fire unto them? And in all thine abominations and thy whoredoms thou hast not remembered the days of thy youth, when thou wast naked and bare, and wast weltering in thy blood"—vers. 15-22.

Pride is latent in the human heart. We who have nothing of which to be proud, are prone to take credit to ourselves for any success or special favor God bestows upon us, forgetting that we have nothing which we have not received.

So Israel became vainglorious and trusted in her own beauty— that beauty which the Lord her God had put upon her, which should have led her to devote herself to Him alone. She used it to draw to herself the admiration and lascivious affection of the idolatrous nations from which she had been called to separation. Like an unfaithful wife preferring others to her own husband she became filthy and defiled. Spiritual fornication and adultery is the unholy union of the people of God with the world, even as James says, "Ye adulterers and adulteresses, know ye not that the friendship of the world is enmity with God? Whosoever therefore will be a friend of the world is the enemy of God" (James 4:4). This immoral relationship is also used as a symbol of idolatry, turning from the one true God to the worship of idols. Of all this Israel had been guilty, and although God had sent His prophets to plead with her to forsake her evil way, she refused to hearken, and persisted in her wicked harlotry, so that God was now about to cast her off as one with whom it was useless to plead any longer. But ere declaring this He gave further proof of her perfidy.

"And it is come to pass after all thy wickedness (woe, woe unto thee! saith the Lord Jehovah), that thou hast built unto thee a vaulted place, and hast made thee a lofty place in every street. Thou hast built thy lofty place at the head of every way, and hast made thy beauty an abomination, and hast opened thy feet to every one that passed by, and multiplied thy whoredom. Thou hast also committed fornication with the Egyptians, thy neighbors, great of flesh; and hast multiplied thy whoredom, to provoke Me to anger. Behold therefore, I have stretched out My hand over thee, and have diminished thine ordinary food, and delivered thee unto the will of them that hate thee, the daughters of the Philistines, that are ashamed of thy lewd way. Thou hast played the harlot also with the Assyrians, because thou wast insatiable; yea, thou hast played the harlot with them, and yet thou wast not satisfied. Thou hast moreover multiplied thy whoredom unto the land of traffic, unto Chaldea; and yet thou wast not satisfied herewith"—vers. 23-29.

Instead of either turning from her corrupt ways, or even manifesting a measure of restraint, the very-pleadings of the Lord through His prophets had the opposite effect, apparently; for Israel increased in her wickedness, becoming guilty of more and greater abominations as the years went on, so that even "the daughters of the Philistines" were astonished and ashamed of her lewdness. Her zest for new forms of idolatry seemed insatiable. She followed the vile nature worship of the Assyrians with which the most detestable sexual impurity was connected, and still she was not satisfied, for satisfaction can never be found apart from conformity to and delight in the will of God.

The charge against her is continued in verses 30 to 34.

"How weak is thy heart, saith the Lord Jehovah, seeing thou doest all these things, the work of an impudent harlot; in that thou buildest thy vaulted place at the head of every way, and makest thy lofty place in every street, and hast not been as a harlot, in that thou scornest hire. A wife that committeth adultery! that taketh strangers instead of her husband! They give gifts to all harlots; but thou givest thy gifts to all thy lovers, and bribest them, that they may come unto thee on every side for thy whoredoms. And thou art different from other women in thy whoredoms, in that none followeth thee to play the harlot; and whereas thou givest hire, and no hire is given unto thee, therefore thou art different"—vers. 30-34.

The slave of her own lusts, Israel fancied herself free while attempting to enjoy the licentiousness into which she had plunged and which she imagined was liberty—freedom from all restraint; whereas it was actually bondage of the worst kind. Too weak to resist solicitation to sin she plunged madly on in her downward course like "a wife that committeth adultery! that taketh strangers instead of her husband!"

Ordinarily those going in to harlots expect to pay for the gratification of their voluptuous desires. But so low had Israel fallen that she was as one who was so insatiable in her unholy appetite that she was paying a terrible price for such gratification. It is a sordid picture indeed, but it shows how low a people may fall who turn their backs upon revealed truth and learn to love darkness rather than light, because their deeds are evil.

Therefore judgment could no longer be deferred. The very holiness of God demanded that He deal with such unspeakable corruption.

"Wherefore, O harlot, hear the word of Jehovah: Thus saith the Lord Jehovah, Because thy filthiness was poured out, and thy nakedness uncovered through thy whoredoms with thy lovers; and because of all the idols of thy abominations, and for the blood of thy children, that thou didst give unto them; therefore behold, I will gather all thy lovers, with whom thou hast taken pleasure, and all them that thou hast loved, with all them that thou hast hated; I will even gather them against thee on every side, and will uncover thy nakedness unto them, that they may see all thy nakedness. And I will judge thee, as women that break wedlock and shed blood are judged; and I will bring upon thee the blood of wrath and jealousy. I will also give thee into their hand, and they shall throw down thy vaulted place, and break down thy lofty places; and they shall strip thee of thy clothes, and take thy fair jewels; and they shall leave thee naked and bare. They shall also bring up a company against thee, and they shall stone thee with stones, and thrust thee through with their swords. And they shall burn thy houses with fire, and execute judgments upon thee In the sight of many women; and I will cause thee to cease from playing the harlot, and thou Shalt also give no hire any more. So will I cause My wrath toward thee to rest, and My jealousy shall depart from thee, and I will be quiet, and will be no more angry. Because thou hast not remembered the days of thy youth, but hast raged against Me in all these things; therefore, behold, I also will bring thy way upon thy head, saith the Lord Jehovah: and thou shalt not commit this lewdness with all thine abominations"—vers. 35-43.

Judgment is God's strange work. He delights in mercy and "doth not afflict willingly nor grieve the children of men" (Lamentations 3:33). But when every effort to recover people from their wilfulness and wickedness proves abortive His wrath must have its way.

In this section the Lord specifies very definitely the reasons why He could no longer tolerate the behavior of His covenant people. Not only were they guilty of all the vileness charged against them, but also they were destroying their own children by their evil example. As they had behaved so shamelessly God would put them to shame before the "lovers" on whom they had doted. He would deal with them as women who break wedlock should be dealt with, and He would bring down upon their guilty heads the punishment that they deserved. They should be stripped of all that He had given them—their land would be overrun by those with whom they had committed spiritual fornication. As they had proven utterly recreant to the promises they had made to the Lord, so He would be bound no longer by His promises to them. He was about to visit upon them the fruit of their own evil ways and reward them according to the perfidy of their hearts.

In their disobedience to His word they had sunk to the level of the cities of the plain which God had destroyed with fire from heaven because of their unnatural vices.

"Behold, every one that useth proverbs shall use this proverb against thee, saying, As is the mother, so is her daughter. Thou art the daughter of thy mother, that loatheth her husband and her children; and thou art the sister of thy sisters, who loathed their husbands and their children: your mother was a Hittite, and your father an Amorite. And thine elder sister is Samaria, that dwelleth at thy left hand, she and her daughters; and thy younger sister, that dwelleth at thy right hand, is Sodom and her daughters. Yet hast thou not walked in their ways, nor done after their abominations; but, as if that were a very little thing, thou wast more corrupt than they in all thy ways. As I live, saith the Lord Jehovah, Sodom thy sister hath not done, she nor her daughters, as thou hast done, thou and thy daughters. Behold, this was the iniquity of thy sister Sodom: pride, fulness of bread, and prosperous ease was in her and in her daughters; neither did she strengthen the hand of the poor and needy. And they were haughty, and committed abomination before Me: therefore I took them away as I saw good. Neither hath Samaria committed half of thy sins; but thou hast multiplied thine abominations more than they, and hast justified thy sisters by all thine abominations which thou hast done. Thou also, bear thou thine own shame, in that thou hast given judgment for thy sisters; through thy sins that thou hast committed more abominable than they, they are more righteous than thou: yea, be thou also confounded, and bear thy shame, in that thou hast justified thy sisters"—vers. 44-52.

The cities of Sodom and Gomorrah were thriving communities when Abraham first entered the land. They were destroyed in judgment when the cup of their iniquity became full. Now Judah had shown herself to be of the same character as they. She was morally their daughter, and, "As is the mother so is her daughter." Samaria, her elder sister, had been judged already. The Assyrians had carried the ten tribes into captivity because of their iniquity. But instead of learning from this and humbling themselves before God and turning from their filthiness, Judah had perpetrated even greater wickedness until now "there was no remedy."

"And I will turn again their captivity, the captivity of Sodom and her daughters, and the captivity of Samaria and her daughters, and the captivity of thy captives in the midst of them; that thou mayest bear thine own shame, and mayest be ashamed because of all that thou hast done, in that thou art a comfort unto them. And thy sisters, Sodom and her daughters, shall return to their former estate; and Samaria and her daughters shall return to their former estate; and thou and thy daughters shall return to your former estate. For thy sister Sodom was not mentioned by thy mouth in the day of thy pride, before thy wickedness was uncovered, as at the time of the reproach of the daughters of Syria, and of all that are round about her, the daughters of the Philistines, that do despise unto thee round about. Thou hast borne thy lewdness and thine abominations, saith Jehovah. For thus saith the Lord Jehovah: I will also deal with thee as thou hast done, who hast despised the oath in breaking the covenant"—vers. 53-59.

In the times of restitution of all things spoken of by God's holy prophets (Acts 3:21) even Sodom and her daughters, the sister cities of the plain will be restored, when the desert shall be made to blossom as a rose. This refers not to the eventual salvation of the sinners of those cities, who are, as Jude tells us, suffering the vengeance of eternal fire (Jude 7), but to rebuilding of the cities themselves in millennial days, when they will be inhabited by a regenerated people dwelling in peace under Messiah's benevolent yet righteous sway. In that day Israel and Judah shall "return to their former estate of blessing" under the fostering care of the God they had so dishonored in the past.

Judah had despised the people of Sodom as sinners above all others; yet her own behavior was even more shameful than theirs. So the Lord declared He would deal with them according to their doings as those who had "despised the oath in breaking the covenant."

This however should not be forever. In a future day He would take them up again, after they had humbled themselves in His sight and forsaken the sins that had provoked Him to anger.

"Nevertheless I will remember My covenant with thee in the days of thy youth, and I will establish unto thee an everlasting covenant. Then shalt thou remember thy ways, and be ashamed, when thou shalt receive thy sisters, thine elder sisters and thy younger; and I will give them unto thee for daughters, but not by thy covenant. And I will establish My covenant with thee; and thou shalt know that I am Jehovah; that thou mayest remember, and be confounded, and never open thy mouth any more, because of thy shame, when I have forgiven thee all that thou hast done, saith the Lord Jehovah"—vers. 60-63.

How precious these closing verses of this long chapter which has been such a sad and gruesome recital of the lewdness and unfaithfulness of Israel!

Though they had forgotten Him and broken the covenant, so far as their responsibility was concerned—that is, the legal covenant into which they had entered at Sinai—God still remembered the unconditional covenant He had made with Abraham, Isaac, and Jacob, and He would fulfil those promises in spite of the failure of the nation as such, His is an everlasting covenant, and as David said, is "ordered in all things, and sure" (2 Sam. 23:5).

In the day when He shall turn their hearts back to Himself they will become ashamed, both Israel and Judah, of all the evil they have done; and they will become a means of blessing to others when God takes them up in grace again. His covenant shall be established, and they who had behaved so badly will loathe themselves because of their iniquities, and rejoice in His favor when He shall forgive all their iniquities, or as the Authorized Version puts it, "When He is pacified toward them for all that they have done."

Only through the work of Christ on the cross is this blessedness to be theirs. That work is not mentioned here, but it is unfolded elsewhere in the prophetical writings as the only basis upon which God can meet and bless those who had become so polluted by sin.

Part I, Prophecies Relating To Israel (chapters 17-24)

Chapter Seventeen
The Eagles, The Cedar, And The Vine

Again we find God speaking to the people, through His servant, in parable form. The first part of the parable refers to Nebuchadnezzar's former onslaught upon Palestine and the captivity of the king of Judah.

"And the word of Jehovah came unto me, saying, Son of man, put forth a riddle, and speak a parable unto the house of Israel; and say, Thus saith the Lord Jehovah: A great eagle with great wings and long pinions, full of feathers, which had divers colors, came unto Lebanon, and took the top of the cedar: he cropped off the topmost of the young twigs thereof, and carried it unto a land of traffic; he set it in a city of merchants. He took also of the seed of the land, and planted it in a fruitful soil; he placed it beside many waters; he set it as a willow-tree. And it grew, and became a spreading vine of low stature, whose branches turned toward him, and the roots thereof were under him: so it became a vine, and brought forth branches, and shot forth sprigs"—vers. 1-6.

In the great eagle we have a picture of the Chaldean monarch, who had flown, as it were, on mighty wings from Babylon to the land of Israel where he "took the highest branch of the cedar"; that is, he carried Judah's king into captivity. Babylon itself is the city of merchants mentioned here, for at this time it was the great commercial center of all Asia.

After deposing Jehoiakim, and a little later his son Jehoiachin, Nebuchadnezzar took Jehoiakim's brother Mattaniah, changed his name to Zedekiah, and set him over the kingdom of Judah, doubtless hoping that he would rule in subservience to himself. The brief reign of Jehoiachin is passed over almost unnoticed here. Zedekiah is pictured as the spreading vine of low stature. He did not possess any of the qualities that make for a successful administrator. He was loyal neither to the God of Israel nor to his heathen overlord, but began plotting almost immediately with the ruler of Egypt to free himself from Babylon's thralldom. There is no contradiction in speaking of him as a willow, and a spreading vine. The figure refers of course to what is now called the weeping willow, which is of vine-like appearance.

"There was also another great eagle with great wings and many feathers: and, behold, this vine did bend its roots toward him, and shot forth its branches toward him, from the beds of its plantation, that he might water it. It was planted in a good soil by many waters, that it might bring forth branches, and that it might bear fruit, that it might be a goodly vine. Say thou, Thus saith the Lord Jehovah: Shall it prosper? shall He not pull up the roots thereof, and cut off the fruit thereof, that it may wither; that all its fresh springing leaves may wither? and not by a strong arm or much people can it be raised from the roots thereof. Yea, behold, being planted, shall it prosper? shall it not utterly wither, when the east wind toucheth it? it shall wither in the beds where it grew"—vers. 7-10.

This second great eagle was the king of Egypt, Pharaoh-Hophra, with whom Zedekiah sought to make a league in order to secure his assistance in throwing off the Chaldean yoke. But God had decreed that no such cabal should prosper. Egypt was as a bruised reed, and reliance upon it was in vain and doomed to end only in worse conditions for Judah than if Zedekiah had kept the oath of allegiance to Nebuchadnezzar. What Zedekiah failed to see was that God had given Judah into the hands of the Chaldeans as a punishment for their many sins and abominable idolatries. It behooved them, therefore, to bow the head in submission to the yoke and not to attempt a revolt against it.

The divine interpretation of the parable is given in the verses that follow:

"Moreover the word of Jehovah came unto me, saying, Say now to the rebellious house, Know ye not what these things mean! Tell them, Behold, the king of Babylon came to Jerusalem, and took the king thereof, and the princes thereof, and brought them to him to Babylon. And he took of the seed royal, and made a covenant with him; he also brought him under an oath, and took away the mighty of the land; that the kingdom might be base, that it might not lift itself up, but that by keeping his covenant it might stand. But he rebelled against him in sending his ambassadors into Egypt, that they might give him horses and much people. Shall he prosper? shall he escape that doeth such things? shall he break the covenant, and yet escape? As I live, saith the Lord Jehovah, surely in the place where the king dwelleth that made him king, whose oath he despised, and whose covenant he brake, even with him in the midst of Babylon he shall die. Neither shall Pharaoh with his mighty army and great company help him in the war, when they cast up mounds and build forts, to cut off many persons. For he hath despised the oath by breaking the covenant; and behold, he had given his hand, and yet hath done all these things; he shall not escape. Therefore, thus saith the Lord Jehovah: As I live, surely Mine oath that he hath despised, and My covenant that he hath broken, I will even bring it upon his own head. And I will spread My net upon him, and he shall be taken in My snare, and I will bring him to Babylon, and will enter into judgment with him there for his trespass that he hath trespassed against Me. And all his fugitives in all his bands shall fall by the sword, and they that remain shall be scattered toward every wind: and ye shall know that I, Jehovah, have spoken it"—vers. 11-21.

That which was difficult for Israel to realize was that their own God was now arrayed against them, and He it was who had exalted Nebuchadnezzar and given him authority over the nations; so that it was in his power to remove or set up kings at his own will.

While, doubtless, Nebuchadnezzar himself was unaware of the divine counsels, nevertheless, he acted under the guidance of that Jehovah whom he knew not, when he took Jehoiachin into captivity and set up the puppet king Zedekiah with whom he had made a covenant, and who had sworn by a solemn oath that he would rule as his representative in Jerusalem. By his vacillation and crafty plotting, Zedekiah aroused the ire of his overlord and exposed himself to the indignation of God, the Judge of all the earth, who loves truth and hates deceit and falsehoods Therefore Ezekiel predicted that the wretched king of Judah, who had despised the oath he had taken and violated the covenant to which he had agreed, should be taken captive by Nebuchadnezzar and carried to Babylon, there to learn in bitterness and sorrow the folly of trifling with God and scheming to thwart His counsels. But although all was so dark for Judah at that time, God had not forgotten His promise to David that he should never want a man to sit upon his throne; and so in due time Israel's restoration should take place and a Son of David rule in Jerusalem and on Mount Zion, over all the earth.

"Thus saith the Lord Jehovah: I will also take of the lofty top of the cedar, and will set it; I will crop off from the topmost of its young twigs a tender one, and I will plant it upon a high and lofty mountain: in the mountain of the height of Israel will I plant it; and it shall bring forth boughs, and bear fruit, and be a goodly cedar: and under it shall dwell all birds of every wing; in the shade of the branches thereof shall they dwell. And all the trees of the field shall know that I, Jehovah, have brought down the high tree, have exalted the low tree, have dried up the green tree, and have made the dry tree to flourish: I, Jehovah, have spoken and have done it"—vers. 22-24.

This "tender shoot" is the Man whose name is the "Branch" of Zechariah 6:12, who shall grow up in His place and build the temple of the Lord. He is "Great David's Greater Son," the "Root and Offspring of David" (Rev. 22:16), whom God designates in Zechariah 3:8 as "My Servant the Branch." Of Him, Isaiah prophesied that He should be as "A Rod out of the stem of Jesse, and a Branch shall grow out of his roots" (11:1).

When He came in God's appointed time He was rejected by His own people, but when He returns in power and might He will take the kingdom and administer the affairs of this universe for the glory of God and the blessing of all mankind. Then the high tree of Gentile supremacy will be cut down, and the low tree of Judah shall be made to flourish when the kingdoms of this world become the kingdom of our God and His Christ. This is decreed by Him who cannot lie, and will be brought to pass in the day of Jehovah's power.

Chapter Eighteen Principles Of The Divine Government

There are certain great principles that run throughout Scripture. Of these, two are outstanding: namely, grace and government. In every dispensation all who have ever been saved were saved by God's free grace. Grace is not only unmerited favor, but also it is favor to those who have merited the very opposite. God has dealt with repentant sinners in grace because of the redemptive work of our Lord Jesus Christ. That work had a backward and a forward aspect as we are told in Romans 3:24-26: "Being justified freely by His grace through the redemption that is in Christ Jesus: whom God hath set forth to be a propitiation through faith in His blood, to declare His righteousness for the remission of sins that are past, through the forbearance of God; to declare, I say, at this time His righteousness: that He might be just, and the Justifier of him which believeth in Jesus." The expression "for the remission of sins that are past" might better be rendered "for the pretermission of sins." That is, the meaning is not simply that God now forgives our past sins when we believe in the Lord Jesus, but also He forgave or remitted the sins of those who lived in past ages, before Christ died, in view of the work He was pledged to perform. And now, because of that finished work, God can be just, and the Justifier of all who have faith in Him who was delivered for our offences and raised again for our justification.

But grace does not set aside government. All believers today are under the government of God the Father who, without respect of persons, judgeth according to every man's work (1 Peter 1:17). It is true today, as in past ages, that whatsoever a man soweth, that shall he also reap (Galatians 6:7). This is true of all men whether saints or sinners. There are temporal consequences that follow sin, which may go on all through life, even though God has forgiven the sin itself; as in David's case. Nathan said by divine authority, "The Lord also hath put away thy sin." But he added, "The sword shall never depart from thine house" (2 Samuel 12:7-15).

It is important to understand this in order that one may not misconstrue the teaching of this chapter, as also of chapter 33, in this same book. Both have to do with the divine government in this world and not with the question of how a guilty sinner may be cleansed from his sin and saved for eternity.

Let us look, then, at the opening section.

"The word of Jehovah came unto me again, saying, What mean ye, that ye use this proverb concerning the land of Israel, saying, The fathers have eaten sour grapes, and the children's teeth are set on edge? As I live, saith the Lord Jehovah, ye shall not have occasion any more to use this proverb in Israel. Behold, all souls are Mine; as the soul of the father, so also the soul of the son is Mine: the soul that sinneth, it shall die"—vers. 1-4.

The people of Israel, notably Judah, at this time sought to impugn the righteousness of God in visiting temporal judgments upon them, on the ground that He was punishing them for the sins of their fathers; whereas they themselves were guiltless of any offences that deserved such drastic measures as God was taking with them, "The fathers," they said, "have eaten sour grapes, and the children's teeth are set on edge."

But God justified His governmental dealings with them from the very opposite standpoint. He was the moral Governor of the world. All men (souls) should be subject to Him because He created them all. He deals with each one individually according to his record or behavior. Therefore, "the soul that sinneth, it shall die." This was what the law declared. God had said, "He that doeth these things shall live in them" (Leviticus 18:5). This was not a promise of eternal life in heaven, but of long life on the earth to him who was obedient to the divine law. The violation of that law exposed one to the penalty of death.

But God who is long-suffering and merciful did not visit this penalty upon the offender immediately. He left room for repentance and reformation of life, as so often illustrated in His dealings with men. So He shows how ready He is to pardon and set aside the immediate judgment of physical death if there be evidence of a changed attitude on the part of the offender. Wherever men are found who endeavor to do what is just and right toward God and their fellows, they are promised life even though none can claim to have kept the law in every point.

"But if a man be just, and do that which is lawful and right, and hath not eaten upon the mountains, neither hath lifted up his eyes to the idols of the house of Israel, neither hath denied his neighbor's wife, neither hath come near to a woman in her impurity, and hath not wronged any, but hath restored to the debtor his pledge, hath taken nought by robbery, hath given his bread to the hungry, and hath covered the naked with a garment; he that hath not given forth upon interest, neither hath taken any increase, that hath withdrawn his hand from iniquity, hath executed true justice between man and man, hath walked In My statutes, and hath kept Mine ordinances, to deal truly; he is just, he shall surely live, saith the Lord Jehovah"—vers. 5-9.

"If a man be just"; that is, if one behaves himself righteously—if he walks uprightly and his life is one of integrity and moral rectitude, God takes note of this, and He deals with man accordingly.

If one shuns idolatry, keeps himself from immorality of every kind, deals honorably with all men so that his business affairs are above reproach, is charitable toward and considerate of the poor and needy, and has endeavored to deal truly with all men, honoring the law of God by obedience to its precepts, then he may know that "he shall surely live, saith the Lord Jehovah." Do not confuse this with the gospel. This has to do with blessing on earth, not with things eternal.

But what if a man has been characterized by the virtues described in verses 5 to 9, and has a son who, presuming on God's favor to his father, becomes lax as to morals and careless as to his manner of living? Will the righteousness of his father avail to shield him from the judgment of God? The answer is given in the next paragraph.

"If he beget a son that is a robber, a shedder of blood, and that doeth any one of these things, and that doeth not any of those duties, but even hath eaten upon the mountains, and denied his neighbor's wife, hath wronged the poor and needy, hath taken by robbery, hath not restored the pledge, and hath lifted up his eyes to the idols, hath committed abomination, hath given forth upon interest, and hath taken increase; shall he then live? He shall not live: he hath done all these abominations; he shall surely die; his blood shall be upon him"—vers. 10-13.

Hezekiah was such an one as the father, mentioned above. Manasseh, his ungodly son, is well depicted in the description given here. Alas, that the children of upright parents do not always walk in the ways of their fathers! Where such is not the case the son must answer to God individually for his own wickedness. So, no matter how good a father may have been, if his son turns away from the teaching and example of his sire and plunges into licentiousness, idolatry, extortion and other vices, he will be punished accordingly; "he shall surely die; his blood shall be upon him." He cannot blame anyone else for his suffering. He brings it down upon his own head.

Just as a righteous father's good behavior will not shield a stubborn and rebellious son from the divine government, so a wicked father's offences will not hinder God from dealing kindly with a son who repents and turns to Him.

"Now, lo, if he beget a son, that seeth all his father's sins, which he hath done, and feareth, and doeth not such like; that hath not eaten upon the mountains, neither hath lifted up his eyes to the idols of the house of Israel, hath not defiled his neighbor's wife, neither hath wronged any, hath not taken aught to pledge, neither hath taken by robbery, but hath given his bread to the hungry, and hath covered the naked with a garment; that hath withdrawn his hand from the poor, that hath not received interest nor increase, hath executed Mine ordinances, hath walked in My statutes; he shall not die for the iniquity of his father, he shall surely live. As for his father, because he cruelly oppressed, robbed his brother, and did that which is not good among his people, behold, he shall die in his iniquity"—vers. 14-18.

God the righteous Ruler over men takes note of the piety and obedience of a son, even though his father may have been very wicked and ungodly. Where the son seeks to obey the divine precepts and to shun iniquitous behavior, God will reward him accordingly. If he learns by the folly of his father that it is indeed an evil and a bitter thing to plunge headlong into lascivi- ousness and corruption, that God is displeased with one who oppresses the poor or is indifferent to their needs and turns a deaf ear to their pitiful plea for assistance, and so looks compassionately upon the poverty-stricken and shares his wealth with them, while endeavoring to keep himself morally clean, "he shall surely live." The wicked father will be judged, but the upright son will be honored of God: therefore the proverb they used to excuse themselves and to blame God for their troubles was not true.

"Yet say ye, Wherefore doth not the son bear the iniquity of the father? When the son hath done that which is lawful and right, and hath kept all My statutes, and hath done them, he shall live. The soul that sinneth, it shall die: the son shall not bear the iniquity of the father, neither shall the father bear the iniquity of the son; the righteousness of the righteous shall be upon him, and the wickedness of the wicked shall be upon him"—vrs. 19, 20.

In this sense the son did not bear the iniquity of the father. His teeth were not set on edge because the father had eaten sour grapes. But each one had to give his own individual account unto God who dealt with him according to the righteous or unrighteous way in which he conducted himself.

Nor does this principle contradict the revelation given by God to Moses in which He spoke of Himself as "visiting the iniquity of the fathers upon the children unto the third and fourth generation of them that hate Me; and showing mercy unto thousands of them that love Me, and keep My commandments" (Exodus 20:5, 6). There is a fearful entail of physical weakness and often of spiritual blindness in which the children of ungodly, immoral parents participate. But even these children will find God ready to bless if they themselves turn from their iniquity. But let none presume upon God being better than His Word. Remember that if one chooses to turn from the path of rectitude to that of lawlessness he must suffer accordingly, "the wickedness of the wicked shall be upon him."

"But if the wicked turn from all his sins that he hath committed, and keep all My statutes, and do that which is lawful and right, he shall surely live, he shall not die. None of his transgressions that he hath committed shall be remembered against him: in his righteousness that he hath done he shall live. Have I any pleasure in the death of the wicked? saith the Lord Jehovah; and not rather that he should return from his way, and live? But when the righteous turneth away from his righteousness, and committeth iniquity, and doeth according to all the abominations that the wicked man doeth, shall he live? None of his righteous deeds that he hath done shall be remembered: in his trespass that he hath trespassed, and in his sin that he hath sinned, in them shall he die"—vers. 21-24.

In order that none may misunderstand, God, as it were, repeats Himself in a most clear and definite manner. Painstakingly He reiterates what has been set forth already, that none may despair, no matter how far from Him they have wandered. He has no pleasure in the death of the wicked, but rather desires that everyone should return from his evil way and so find the path of life.

The two roads—that of wickedness and that of right-living—are portrayed clearly. Each man can choose for himself which one he will take. But let him be assured of this, that if he turns away from righteousness none of his past good behavior shall avail to save him from death. He will die in his trespass that he has trespassed, and in his sin that he has sinned.

"Yet ye say, The way of the Lord is not equal. Hear now, O house of Israel: Is not My way equal? are not your ways unequal? When the righteous man turneth away from his righteousness, and committeth iniquity, and dieth therein; in his iniquity that he hath done shall he die. Again, when the wicked man turneth away from Ms wickedness that lie hath committed, and doeth that which is lawful and right, he shall save his soul alive. Because he considered, and turneth away from all his transgressions that he hath committed, he shall surely live, he shall not die. Yet saith the house of Israel, The way of the Lord is not equal. O house of Israel, are not My ways equal? are not your ways unequal? Therefore I will judge you, O house of Israel, every one according to his ways, saith the Lord Jehovah. Return ye, and turn yourselves from all your transgressions; so iniquity shall not he your ruin. Cast away from you all your transgressions, wherein ye have transgressed; and make you a new heart and a new spirit: for why will ye die, O house of Israel? For I have no pleasure in the death of him that dieth, saith the Lord Jehovah: wherefore turn yourselves, and live"—vers. 25-32.

All is summed up in this stirring paragraph. Israel's complaint against God is answered fully, and the integrity of His government is defended. They had said, "The way of the Lord is not equal"; whereas it was their ways that were unequal. They were blaming God for their afflictions when they should have blamed themselves.

Although suffering under His hand because of their past departure from Him, it was not yet too late to turn back to Him, the source of all blessing. If they would do this, although captives among their enemies, iniquity should not be their ruin, but they would find God waiting to be gracious to them. An entirely new attitude on their part would enable Him to undertake for them in righteousness and yet in mercy and loving-kindness. He yearned over them and reminded them once more that He had no pleasure in the death of him that dieth. Therefore He pleaded, crying, "Why will ye die, O house of Israel?...Wherefore turn yourselves, and live." Where there was response to this plea and true repentance and turning to God in faith, they would indeed be born again. But the great theme of the chapter is government, rather than saving grace.

Chapter Nineteen The Fallen Prince Of Judah

This chapter brings the present series to an end. In it God shows why the promises made to Judah of old seemed to fail of fulfilment. These had been predicated on the obedience of the people. But both they and their rulers had forfeited all title to blessing by their corrupt behavior. The Lord makes this plain, although He speaks in parabolic form as He so frequently does in this book.

"Moreover, take thou up a lamentation for the princes of Israel, and say, What was thy mother? A lioness: she couched among lions, in the midst of the young lions she nourished her whelps. And she brought up one of her whelps: he became a young lion, and he learned to catch the prey; he devoured men. The nations also heard of him; he was taken in their pit; and they brought him with hooks unto the land of Egypt"—vers. 1-4.

In the previous chapters we have seen exposed the guilt of the people. Now the Lord makes manifest the wickedness of their kings. While only two are brought definitely before us, suggesting that this lamentation was intended to exercise the conscience of Zedekiah; yet the same evil ways had characterized all the last four kings of Judah. We may think of both Judah and Jerusalem, the capital city, as represented by the mother lioness. God had said of old through Jacob, "Judah is a lion's whelp" (Genesis 49:9); and Balaam had depicted the nation that he could not curse, in the same way: "Behold the people shall rise up as a great lion, and lift up himself as a young lion" (Numbers 23:24). It is true the same figure is used of other tribes than Judah, as Gad (Deut. 33:20), and Dan (Deut. 33:22). But here in Ezekiel it is evident that Judah is in view, as the royal tribe with her place in Jerusalem. From this tribe He was to come, through David's line, who should be the Lion of the tribe of Judah, who shall fulfil at last all the promises of God (Rev. 5:5).

Upon the death of the godly king Josiah, his son Jehoahaz, or Shallum, as he is otherwise called, was crowned king in his father's stead. He is the young lion spoken of here. But he proved to be an unprincipled weakling, and was taken captive by Pharaoh-Necho and carried down to Egypt, never to return to the land of Palestine.

"Now when she saw that she had waited, and her hope was lost, then she took another of her whelps, and made him a young lion. And he went up and down among the lions; he became a young lion, and he learned to catch the prey; he devoured men. And he knew their palaces, and laid waste their cities; and the land was desolate, and the fulness thereof, because of the noise of his roaring. Then the nations set against him on every side from the provinces; and they spread their net over him; he was taken in their pit. And they put him in a cage with hooks, and brought him to the king of Babylon; they brought him into strongholds, that his voice should no more be heard upon the mountains of Israel"— vers. 6-9.

When it became apparent that it was hopeless to look for the return of Jehoahaz, Jehoiakim, whom the king of Egypt had set up in place of his brother, was recognized as king; but after eleven years he was carried to Babylon. Then in their desperation the people of Judah turned to the son of Jehoiakim, a youth of eighteen years of age, whose name closely resem- bled that of his father, Jehoiachin, or Jeconiah. He seems to be the young lion referred to here, as it was he and not his father whom Judah herself chose as king. But his reign was for less than four months, for Nebuchadnezzar came again into the land and carried him away in chains to Babylon, setting up Mattaniah, older brother of the deposed king, in his stead, and changing his name to Zedekiah. It was he who sat on the throne at this time; and it was his heart and conscience that this lamentation over the departed glory of the throne of David, was designed to reach; but alas, he was too far gone in the path of self-will to heed the message addressed to him. Therefore the fate of all the three kings before him might well serve as a warning to him. Actually because of his perversity he was to suffer worse things than any of them, for his sons were to be slain before his eyes, and then those eyes were to be put out and he himself carried as a blind and brokenhearted man to Babylon.

"Thy mother was like a vine, in thy blood, planted by the waters: it was fruitful and full of branches by reason of many waters. And it had strong rods for the sceptres of them that bare rule, and their stature was exalted among the thick boughs, and they were seen in their height with the multitude of their branches. But it was plucked up in fury, it was cast down to the ground, and the east wind dried up its fruit: its strong rods were broken off and withered; the fire consumed them. And now it is planted in the wilderness, in a dry and thirsty land. And fire is gone out of the rods of its branches, it hath devoured its fruit, so that there is in it no strong rod to be a sceptre to rule. This is a lamentation, and shall be for a lamentation"—vers. 10-14.

In this part of the lamentation God reverts to a figure formerly used. Judah was like a vine, which at one time had been fruitful and had spread abroad because of the blessing of the Lord when she walked in obedience to His Word. So rich was her fruitage that she is represented as a great vine with many spreading branches, supported by strong rods that the clusters of grapes might be properly harvested. But a change had come about because of her revolt from the law of God. She had chosen the path of self-will, and so the surrounding nations were permitted to destroy her branches, and the east wind of adversity wrought havoc with her fruit. Now she was as a broken, withered vine planted in the desert where all was waste and dry. Moreover, the fire of judgment had devoured the rods and the branches until at last "there was no sceptre to rule." The last of her kings was about to go into captivity, and she should never know again a king of David's line until He shall come, whose right it is to reign, our Lord Jesus Christ, who shall yet sit upon the throne of His father David and build again the tabernacle of David that is fallen down.

The departed sceptre may seem to be in contradiction of Genesis 49:10, "The sceptre shall not depart from Judah, nor a lawgiver" (or the ruler's staff) "from between his feet, until Shiloh come; and unto Him shall the gathering of the people be." But here it is evidently the tribal sceptre, not the royal sceptre, that is in view. Judah remained a distinct and separate tribe until Shiloh—the Prince of Peace—came the first time, only to be rejected. Jacob's prophecy shall have its complete fulfilment when He comes again and the people shall gather together unto Him, owning Him as their rightful King.

Chapter Twenty Jehovah's Faithfulness And Israel's Unfaithfulness

Beginning with the first verse of this twentieth chapter and continuing through chapter 23, we have a series of prophecies which bear the general date of the seventh year of the captivity. The first one was delivered on the tenth day of the fifth month. In this series God continues His expostulations with Israel because of their unfaithfulness to the covenant into which they had entered; while on the other hand, He stresses His own unfailing adherence to the promises He Himself had made to their fathers.

"And it came to pass in the seventh year, in the fifth month, the tenth day of the month, that certain of the elders of Israel came to inquire of Jehovah, and sat before me. And the word of Jehovah came unto me, saying, Son of man, speak unto the elders of Israel, and say unto them, Thus saith the Lord Jehovah: Is it to inquire of me that ye are come? As I live, saith the Lord Jehovah, I will not be inquired of by you. Wilt thou judge them, son of man, wilt thou judge them? Cause them to know the abominations of their fathers; and say unto them, Thus saith the Lord Jehovah: In the day when I chose Israel, and sware unto the seed of the house of Jacob, and made Myself known unto them in the land of Egypt, when I sware unto them, saying, I am Jehovah your God; in that day I sware unto them, to bring them forth out of the land of Egypt into a land that I had searched out for them, flowing with milk and honey, which is the glory of all lands. And I said unto them, Cast ye away every man the abominations of his eyes, and defile not yourselves with the idols of Egypt; I am Jehovah your God. But they rebelled against Me, and would not hearken unto Me; they did not every man cast away the abominations of their eyes, neither did they forsake the idols of Egypt. Then I said I would pour out My wrath upon them, to accomplish My anger against them in the midst of the land of Egypt. But I wrought for My name's sake, that it should not be profaned in the sight of the nations, among which they were, in whose sight I made Myself known unto them, in bringing them forth out of the land of Egypt"—vers. 1-9.

Upon the date mentioned above, an unspecified number of the elders of Israel came to Ezekiel and sat down before him that he might inquire of Jehovah on their behalf. Outwardly they seemed to be subject to His word and ready to submit to His will, but it was very evident that there had been no real repentance or facing of their sins in the presence of God. Therefore, He said through His servant, "Is it to inquire of Me that ye are come?" He declared that He would not be inquired of by them: they were not on praying ground because of their wilful disobedience to His word, and their determined opposition to His truth. Therefore, as speaking for God, Ezekiel was to take the place of a judge among them, and to set before them in unmistakable terms the abominations of their fathers in which they themselves were also walking. God retraced their history from the day He brought them out of Egypt, when He revealed Himself to them as Jehovah their God, the Eternal One with whom they had entered into covenant. He had promised and sworn by Himself that He would deliver them from the land of bondage and bring them into a land which He Himself had selected for them—a land flowing with milk and honey, which He described as "the glory of all lands."

One who visits Palestine today may find it difficult to see just how language such as this could apply to it, but when God brought His people into Canaan He strengthened them against their enemies and multi- plied them there, and enabled them to build great and beautiful cities. As they cultivated the hills and the valleys, His blessing rested upon their efforts to such an extent that they had abundance of all things. That which made Palestine the glory of all lands, however, was the fact that it was there that Jehovah manifested Himself, and there at Jerusalem He had set His name. From Jerusalem word had gone out into all the world that God the Creator of all things was there known and honored; and so those who desired to learn of Him came from distant places, like the Queen of Sheba, to be instructed concerning the name of the Lord. Though for centuries that land has lain desolate, the temple has been utterly destroyed, and an infidel shrine erected in its place, yet in a future day it will once more become the glory of all lands when the people of Israel shall be restored to the Lord, and He Himself will be manifested among them. Then the law shall go forth from Mount Zion, and all nations will flow unto it to worship the King who will reign in righteousness over a regenerated world.

The sins of Israel defiled the land to such an extent that the indignation of Jehovah had to be visited upon a disobedient and gainsaying people, even when they dwelt in Egypt and were specifically warned against the idolatry of that land. They had soon turned away from the truth revealed to them, and actually worshiped the idols of Egypt so that God's wrath and anger had been poured out upon them before they left that place of bondage; in fact, one would gather from these verses that it was in judgment that God had stirred up Pharaoh to enslave them and make their lives so hard and bitter. Nevertheless, He had wrought for His own name's sake, in order that that name should not be profaned in the sight of the nations; and so, in due time, He had intervened in mercy and brought the people forth out of the land of Egypt. We might think that from the days of Joseph until Moses they had lived as a separate people in the land of the stranger, but this passage throws a lurid light upon their behavior in those years and after, when a new king arose who knew not Joseph.

It is evident, therefore, that they had forgotten to a great extent the revelation God had made to Abraham, Isaac, and Jacob, so that the message brought by Moses came to many as a new revelation of Jehovah, as the God of their fathers, who loved them still in spite of their waywardness, and had heard their cry and come down to deliver them.

One might have supposed that the remarkable signs given to them and the many wonderful evidences of God's loving care would have turned them forever from idolatry and given them to honor Him alone, who had redeemed them to Himself; but, even after they left Egypt, they were ready at the slightest occasion to lapse into disobedience and idolatry.

"So I caused them to go forth out of the land of Egypt, and brought them into the wilderness. And I gave them My statutes, and showed them Mine ordinances, which if a man do, he shall live in them. Moreover also I gave them My sabbaths, to be a sign between Me and them, that they might know that I am Jehovah that sanctifieth them. But the house of Israel rebelled against Me in the wilderness: they walked not in My statutes, and they rejected Mine ordinances, which if a man keep, he shall live in them; and My sabbaths they greatly profaned. Then I said, I would pour out My wrath upon them in the wilderness, to consume them. But I wrought for My name's sake, that it should not be profaned in the sight of the nations, in whose sight I brought them out. Moreover also I sware unto them in the wilderness, that I would not bring them into the land which I had given them, flowing with milk and honey, which is the glory of all lands; because they rejected Mine ordinances, and walked not in My statutes, and profaned My sabbaths: for their heart went after their idols. Nevertheless Mine eye spared them, and I destroyed them not, neither did I make a full end of them in the wilderness"—vers. 10-17.

It was the Lord Himself who brought them into the wilderness, and there at Sinai, gave them His statutes and showed them His ordinances, concerning which He said, "Which if a man do, he shall live in them." There, too, He made known unto them His sabbaths to be a sign between Him and them, the weekly memorial that He was Jehovah, their Sanctifier. But even in the wilderness they rebelled against Him and refused to walk in His statutes. They rejected His ordinances and profaned His sabbaths; thus they had forfeited all title to blessing, and God, in righteousness, might have given them up to utter destruction had it not been that He was concerned for the glory of His own name.

Speaking anthropomorphically, He declared He would pour out His wrath upon them in the wilderness to consume them, even as we know He threatened to do when He proposed to Moses that the people should be destroyed, and a new nation should come from him who had brought them thus far on their way. But when Moses interceded for them God wrought for His name's sake. He would not have the heathen around say that He was unable to bring His people into the land He had promised; and therefore, although He swore in His wrath that all those of adult age should perish in the wilderness, nevertheless He brought their children to that land flowing with milk and honey, as He had promised.

The real reason for Israel's failure is given in verse 16, "Their heart went after their idols." How manifestly this was seen when they came to Aaron crying, "Up, make us gods, which shall go before us; for as for this Moses, this man that brought us up out of the land of Egypt, we know not what is become of him" (Exod. 32:1). They preferred an image which they could see to the living God who could not be seen by mortal eye. So they turned to idolatry, rejecting God's ordinances and refusing to walk in His statutes and profaning His sabbaths. But though He visited them from time to time with judgments because of their sins, nevertheless, as a nation He spared them, and did not utterly destroy them nor make a full end of them in the wilderness.

After pronouncing judgment on the older generation He called upon their children to walk in obedience that thereby they might enter into blessing.

"And I said unto their children in the wilderness, Walk ye not in the statutes of your fathers, neither observe their ordinances, nor defile yourselves with their idols. I am Jehovah your God: walk in My statutes, and keep Mine ordinances, and do them; and hallow My sabbaths; and they shall be a sign between Me and you, that ye may know that I am Jehovah your God. But the children rebelled against Me; they walked not in My statutes, neither kept Mine ordinances to do them, which if a man do, he shall live in them; they profaned My sabbaths. Then I said I would pour out My wrath upon them, to accomplish My anger against them in the wilderness. Nevertheless I withdrew My hand, and wrought for My name's sake, that it should not be profaned in the sight of the nations, in whose sight I brought them forth. Moreover I sware unto them in the wilderness, that I would scatter them among the nations, and disperse them through the countries; because they had not executed Mine ordinances, but had rejected My statutes, and had profaned My sabbaths, and their eyes were after their fathers' idols. Moreover also I gave them statutes that were not good, and ordinances wherein they should not live; and I polluted them in their own gifts, in that they caused to pass through the fire all that openeth the womb, that I might make them desolate, to the end that they might know that I am Jehovah"—vers. 18-26.

One might have thought that the children would have learned from the folly of their parents that it is indeed an evil thing and bitter to turn away from the word of the Lord, but these soon manifested the traits of their fathers and denied themselves with idolatry. Again and again God pleaded with them to obey His word, to keep His ordinances and to do them, to hallow His sabbaths; but they rebelled against Him and spurned His testimonies. We have a sad example of this in their terrible failure at Baal-peor, when they mingled with the idolatrous people about them, and so sinned against God that in His wrath He smote them and would have destroyed them had it not been for the intercession of Moses and Aaron. He withdrew His hand and again wrought for His own name's sake that it should not be profaned in the sight of the heathen.

But He warned His people that if they continued in their disobedience the day would come when they would be scattered among the nations and dispersed throughout all countries—a warning which has had a terrible fulfilment throughout the centuries.

Because they turned away from those statutes and ordinances which were meant for their blessing, He chose their delusions and gave them up to statutes that were not good, and ordinances wherein they should not live; so He permitted them to sink to the degradation of Moloch worship and all its kindred abominations, thus going down to the level of the vilest of the heathen whom He cast out before them. Their behavior in the land was even worse than that which characterized them in the wilderness.

"Therefore, son of man, speak unto the house of Israel, and say unto them, Thus saith the Lord Jehovah: In this moreover have your fathers blasphemed Me, in that they have committed a trespass against Me. For when I had brought them into the land, which I sware to give unto them, then they saw every high hill, and every thick tree, and they offered there their sacrifices, and there they presented the provocation of their offering; there also they made their sweet savor, and they poured out there their drink-offerings. Then I said unto them, What meaneth the high place whereunto ye go? So the name thereof is called Bamah unto this day. Wherefore say unto the house of Israel, Thus saith the Lord Jehovah: Do ye pollute yourselves after the manner of your fathers? and play ye the harlot after their abominations? and when ye offer your gifts, when ye make your sons to pass through the fire, do ye pollute yourselves with all your idols unto this day? and shall I be inquired of by you, O house of Israel? As I live, saith the Lord Jehovah, I will not be inquired of by you; and that which cometh into your mind shall not be at all, in that ye say, We will be as the nations, as the families of the countries, to serve wood and stone"—vers. 27-32.

After Jehovah had fulfilled His word and brought them through the wilderness and led them into Canaan under the leadership of Joshua, it was not long until they followed in the ways of the nations which they were commanded to destroy. They erected shrines to false gods and goddesses upon every high hill and under every great tree, and there they sacrificed to demons and not to God. By such conduct they polluted themselves after the manner of their fathers and were guilty of spiritual harlotry. They did for their false gods what they never would have been asked to do for Jehovah: they sacrificed their own children, causing them to pass through the fire unto Moloch, and so polluted themselves that God could no longer tolerate them. He would not be inquired of by them. They had sought to be as the nations around; and as the nations, He would deal with them in judgment.

Nevertheless He had not forgotten His promise to Abraham—a promise reiterated again and again to his descendants. And so in verses 33 to 44 Ezekiel was given to foretell Israel's future restoration, when all their past failure shall be blotted out, and they shall be restored to the Lord.

"As I live, saith the Lord Jehovah, surely with a mighty hand, and with an outstretched arm, and with wrath poured out, will I be King over you. And I will bring you out from the peoples, and will gather you out of the countries wherein ye are scattered, with a mighty hand, and with an outstretched arm, and with wrath poured out; and I will bring you into the wilderness of the peoples, and there will I enter into judgment with you face to face. Like as I entered into judgment with your fathers in the wilderness of the land of Egypt, so will I enter into judgment with you, saith the Lord Jehovah. And I will cause you to pass under the rod, and I will bring you into the bond of the covenant; and I will purge out from among you the rebels, and them that transgress against Me; I will bring them forth out of the land where they sojourn, but they shall not enter into the land of Israel: and ye shall know that I am Jehovah. As for you, O house of Israel, thus saith the Lord Jehovah: Go ye, serve every one his idols, and hereafter also, if ye will not hearken unto Me; but My holy name shall ye no more profane with your gifts, and with your idols"—vers. 33-89.

Despite all their wilfulness Jehovah was still their King, and in due time His authority shall be openly manifested. In that day He will bring them out from all the nations and countries wherein they have been scattered. With a mighty hand and outstretched arm, and with wrath poured out upon those who continue in their apostasy, He will bring the remnant into what He calls "the wilderness of the peoples," and there will enter into judgment with them face to face. As of old He had dealt with their fathers in the wilderness adjoining the land of Egypt, so will He in this coming day deal with the nation that is as a scattered people among the Gentiles, because He will own them still as His. He will deal with them in chastisement, causing them to pass under the rod like sheep being marked off by their shepherd. In that day they will be brought again into the bond of the covenant, and He will purge out from among them the rebels, and all that transgress against Him. From every land where they have sojourned He will bring them into the land of Israel, and they shall know in that day that He is indeed Jehovah, the Eternal One with whom they have to do. That the time had not come for this, however, was evident; and so Ezekiel was commanded to say to the elders who came inquiring, "Go ye, serve every one his idols, and hereafter also, if ye will not hearken unto Me; but My holy name shall ye no more profane with your gifts, and with your idols." Until the day of their redemption as a people they would be given up to hardness of heart and left to their own devices.

"For in My holy mountain, in the mountain of the height of Israel, saith the Lord Jehovah, there shall all the house of Israel, all of them, serve Me in the land: there will I accept them, and there will I require your offerings, and the first-fruits of your oblations, with all your holy things. As a sweet savor will I accept you, when I bring you out from the peoples, and gather you out of the countries wherein ye have been scattered; and I will be sanctified in you in the sight of the nations. And ye shall know that I am Jehovah, when I shall bring you into the land of Israel, into the country which I sware to give unto your fathers. And there shall ye remember your ways, and all your doings, wherein ye have polluted yourselves; and ye shall loathe yourselves in your own sight for all your evils that ye have committed. And ye shall know that I am Jehovah, when I have dealt with you for My name's sake, not according to your evil ways, nor according to your corrupt doings, O ye house of Israel, saith the Lord Jehovah"—vers. 40-44.

What a delightful picture the prophet here portrays! He speaks of a day when Jerusalem will again be recognized as the holy mount of God, "the mountain of the height of Israel," when the restored people will be back in their land, there to serve the One from whom they had wandered so long. Once more they will bring to Him their offerings and the first-fruits of their oblations with all their holy things. He will accept their worship and their thanksgiving when He has gathered them out from the people and brought them back from the countries wherein they have been scattered; for then He will be sanctified in them in the sight of all nations. How near that day may be we cannot say. The present return of many of the Jewish people to Palestine in their unbelief may be indeed a preparation for the complete fulfilment of the prophecy. But when these words actually come to pass, the Jewish people will return not only to the land but also to Jehovah Himself. Then they will look back with shame upon their former evil ways, and will loathe themselves in their own sight for all the wickedness of which they have been guilty, as they realize that Jehovah has dealt with them, not according to their evil ways nor according to their corrupt doing, but according to the loving-kindness of His own heart.

123

The concluding verses of the chapter remind us of the Lord's words to the daughters of Jerusalem as He was going out to die: "If they do these things in a green tree, what shall be done in the dry?" The green tree is that in which life is found; the dry tree is dead and fit only for the fire. So we read:

"And the word of Jehovah came unto me, saying, Son of man, set thy face toward the south, and drop thy word toward the south, and prophesy against the forest of the field in the south; and say to the forest of the south, Hear the word of Jehovah: Thus saith the Lord Jehovah, Behold, I will kindle a fire in thee, and it shall devour every green tree in thee, and every dry tree: the flaming flame shall not be quenched, and all faces from the south to the north shall be burnt thereby. And all flesh shall see that I, Jehovah, have kindled it; it shall not be quenched. Then said I, Ah Lord Jehovah! They say of me, Is he not a speaker of parables?"—vers. 45-49.

Ezekiel was to set his face toward the south—that is, toward the land of Israel, having especially in mind the forests of Lebanon; and he was to declare, in the name of Jehovah, "Thus saith the Lord Jehovah, Behold, I will kindle a fire in thee, and it shall devour «very green tree in thee, and every dry tree: the flaming flame shall not be quenched, and all faces from the south to the north shall be burnt thereby." In His indignation against the people who had so dishonored Him, He would pour out His judgments upon them as a whole, so that all flesh would recognize that it was He indeed who was thus visiting His people in His wrath and pouring out upon them the fires of judgment which could not be quenched until all those who persisted in their iniquities had been destroyed. But even after Ezekiel proclaimed this solemn message he recognized that the people were not taking in the seriousness of his words. To them he was but a speaker of parables—parables which they could not seem to understand.

Chapter Twenty-one The Parting Of The Ways

In God's dealings, both with individuals and with nations, He first instructs, then admonishes if they turn away from His word. Where repentance is manifested He delights to pour out blessing, but where instructions and pleadings are met with determined and wilful rejection, He deals finally in judgment. This comes out very clearly in the present chapter, where we see that all His pleadings with Judah had availed nothing so far as bringing them to repentance was concerned. Consequently, the destroyer of the Gentiles was permitted to come down upon the land, taking vengeance on those who had so utterly disregarded the covenant made between Jehovah and Israel at Sinai.

"And the word of Jehovah came unto me, saying, Son of man, set thy face toward Jerusalem, and drop thy word toward the sanctuaries, and prophesy against the land of Israel; and say to the land of Israel, Thus saith Jehovah: Behold, I am against thee, and will draw forth My sword out of its sheath, and will cut off from thee the righteous and the wicked. Seeing then that I will cut off from thee the righteous and the wicked, therefore shall My sword go forth out of its sheath against all flesh from the south to the north: and all flesh shall know that I, Jehovah, have drawn forth My sword out of its sheath; it shall not return any more. Sigh therefore, thou son of man; with the breaking of thy loins and with bitterness shalt thou sigh before their eyes. And it shall be, when they say unto thee, Wherefore sighest thou? that thou shalt say, Because of the tidings, for it cometh; and every heart shall melt, and all hands shall be feeble, and every spirit shall faint, and all knees shall be weak as water: behold, it cometh, and it shall be done, saith the Lord Jehovah"—vers. 1-7.

The term "son of man" used here in ver. 2, and elsewhere in this book, seems to designate Ezekiel as the representative man standing for God among His people in a day of apostasy. He who had pleaded on their behalf was now called upon to set his face against Jerusalem and to declare the judgments that were destined to fall upon the land of Israel which was covered with

125

heathen sanctuaries, all of which were an offense to Jehovah who had declared Himself to be the one true and living God. Because of their many sins He arrayed Himself against them and was about to draw His sword out of its sheath and cut them off as a people. This would involve the destruction of the righteous with the wicked; it could not be otherwise when an invading army swept over the land. But though the righteous may have to suffer in a temporal way, their souls will be gathered with all those in whom God had found faith throughout the centuries.

The sword of the Lord in this instance was really the sword wielded by Nebuchadnezzar. In other words, God had put that sword into his hands and instructed him to use it against all flesh from the south to the north, that all in those nations might know that it was a divine judgment which was falling upon them.

Though it was given to Ezekiel to declare this, there was not to be on his part any hardness of spirit or inward satisfaction when he saw his prophecies being fulfilled; rather he was to deliver the word of Jehovah in bitterness of soul as he realized what his people were to suffer because of their many offenses. He could not but sigh even as he proclaimed the word. When his hearers should look on and ask the reason for this perturbation of spirit, he was to reply that it was on account *of* the invading armies, before which every heart should melt, and their own hands should be feeble, and the spirit of every man in Israel should faint, and all knees should be weak as water. Nothing could now restrain the judgment so long deserved, but which God held in check ever since the days of the godly king Josiah.

The prophet has more to tell us about the sword of the Lord in verses 8 to 17.

"And the word of Jehovah came unto me, saying, Son of man, prophesy, and say, Thus saith Jehovah: Say, A sword, a sword, it is sharpened, and also furbished; it is sharpened that it may make a slaughter; it is furbished that it may be as lightning: shall we then make mirth? the rod of My son, it contemneth every tree. And it is given to be furbished, that it may be handled: the sword, it is sharpened, yea, it is furbished, to give it into the hand of the slayer. Cry and wail, son of man; for it is upon My people, it is upon all the princes of Israel: they are delivered over to the sword with My people; smite therefore upon thy thigh. For there is a trial; and what if even the rod that contemneth shall be no more? saith the Lord Jehovah. Thou therefore, son of man, prophesy, and smite thy hands together; and let the sword be doubled the third time, the sword of the deadly wounded: it is the sword of the great one that is deadly wounded, which entereth into their chambers. I have set the threatening sword against all their gates, that their heart may melt, and their stumblings be multiplied: ah! it is made as lightning, it is pointed for slaughter. Gather thee together, go to the right, set thyself in array, go to the left, whithersoever thy face is set. I will also smite My hands together, and I will cause My wrath to rest: I, Jehovah, have spoken it"—vers. 8-17.

Jehovah commanded Ezekiel to cry, "A sword, a sword, it is sharpened, and also furbished"; that is, scoured in order that it might gleam brightly as it flashed in the hands of the warrior, like lightning striking down all who came in its way.

In view of the terrible conditions which this implied, the question is asked, Shall we then make mirth? The human heart is ever ready to minimize and make light of the judgments of God, and men, instead of being sobered by divine visitations and brought to repentance, often try to forget unpleasant conditions, and in order to keep their morale, join in all kinds of folly and sin—like those of whom we read in the book of Revelation, who will be making merry in the day of wrath, sending presents one to another. Times such as those that Israel was called to pass through and which many nations have endured in the last half' century, call for sobriety and seriousness of purpose rather than for careless joviality and merriment.

"No room for mirth or trifling here

For worldly hope or worldly fear,

If life so soon is gone,

If now the Judge is at the door,

And all mankind must stand before

The inexorable throne."

It is far better, in such solemn times, to go to the house of mourning than to the house of feasting, as the preacher tells us in the book of Ecclesiastes; but men in their folly try to forget reality by frivolous behavior and incitement to joviality. If ever there was a time when people ought to be serious, it is when the judgments of God are abroad in the land and when the rod of chastisement is falling upon His people.

This furbished sword of the Lord is sharpened that it might deal out death to everyone who dared to stand against it. It was to be given into the hand of the slayer; namely, the King of Babylon and his armies. To stand against these would be useless, for God had forsaken His people because of their sins. Therefore. Ezekiel was to cry and wail because of the judgments that were to fall on his people and upon all the princes of Israel, who were to be delivered over to the sword and smitten upon the thigh—that is, in the place of strength—they were to be cut down in weakness. Nothing could turn back the invader now: the day for repentance is past. The sword which had already been unsheathed in the hand of Pharaoh, and earlier by Nebuchadnezzar, was now to be used the third time, and is designated as the sword of the deadly wounded. Against all the gates of the cities of Judah this glittering sword was to be seen until the hearts of the people should melt and they would stumble in their blindness and wickedness as the Chaldean armies, like lightning, came down upon the land. It made no difference where the people should turn, whether they went to the right or to the left, God's wrath would find them out and they would fall before the invader, for Jehovah had spoken it.

In verses 18 to 23 we see the King of Babylon standing at the parting of the ways, where the slightest thing might have turned him northward rather than southward to invade the land of Palestine, but inasmuch as God Himself had decreed the latter, the king's own diviners advised him to take that course.

"The word of Jehovah, came unto me again, saying, Also, thou son of man, appoint thee two ways, that the sword of the King of Babylon may come; they twain shall come forth out of one land: and mark out a place, mark it out at the head of the way to the city. Thou shalt appoint a way for the sword to come to Kabbah of the children of Amnion, and to Judah in Jerusalem the fortified. For the King of Babylon stood at the parting of the way, at the head of the two ways, to use divination: he shook the arrows to and fro, he consulted the teraphim, he looked in the liver. In his right hand was the divination for Jerusalem, to set battering rams, to open the mouth in the slaughter, to lift up the voice with shouting, to set battering rams against the gates, to cast up mounds, to build forts. And it shall be unto them as a false divination in their sight, who have sworn oaths unto them; but He bringeth iniquity to remembrance, that they may be taken"—vers. 18-23.

Two ways were marked out for the Chaldean armies: a road leading toward the north, up into Ammon; another toward the land of Judah. Nebuchadnezzar is represented as pausing at the intersection of the roads, not fully decided whether to besiege Rabbah, the capital of the Ammonites, or to go on to Jerusalem, the capital of Judah. He called his soothsayers to advise him as to which city he should first seek to subdue. Using various means of divination, such as shaking of arrows, consulting with teraphim, or luck-pieces as we say, and slaughtering of victims and looking into the liver in order to assist in these prognostications, they pointed out that everything indicated that he should go to Jerusalem. Little did they know, and little did he understand that, after all, it was the very God of Israel who Himself was overruling in all this and leading the haughty king from the land of Shinar, to move upon the Holy City which had become so defiled by Israel's sin. It was God Himself who had brought the iniquity to remembrance that they might be destroyed and taken captive by this heathen prince.

The king of Judah is addressed directly in the verses that follow:

"Therefore thus saith the Lord Jehovah: Because ye have made your iniquity to be remembered, in that your transgressions are uncovered, so that in all your doings your sins do appear; because that ye are come to remembrance, ye shall be taken with the hand. And thou, O deadly wounded wicked one, the prince of Israel, whose day is come, in the time of the iniquity of the end, thus saith the Lord Jehovah: Remove the mitre, and take off the crown; this shall be no more the same; exalt that which is low, and abase that which is high. I will overturn, overturn, overturn it: this also shall l)e no more, until He come whose right it is; and I will give it Him"—vers. 24-27.

This is one of the most striking prophecies in the Old Testament. It tells of the complete setting aside of the royal house of David because of the wickedness of its princes until the day in which Messiah should come and set up the kingdom so long predicted. In spite of all the warnings they had received, the kings who sat upon David's throne had gone farther and farther from God until their iniquity and transgressions had become so flagrant that He could no longer condone them and consent to dwell among His people; therefore, He declared, "O deadly-wounded wicked one, the prince of Israel, whose day is come in the time of the iniquity of the end." There was to be no further respite. The warnings that had fallen from the lips of all the prophets must now culminate in condign judgment, and so the decree went forth, "Remove the mitre, and take off the crown; this shall be no more the same." That is, there shall be no more a man of David's line sitting on the throne of David until great David's greater Son should appear in power and glory.

God says, "I will overturn, overturn, overturn it: this also shall be no more, until He come whose right it is; and I will give it Him." Since the carrying away of the people to Babylon, following the destruction of Jerusalem, there has never been a king recognized by God as sitting upon the throne of Israel. Hosea's prophecy, found in the third chapter of his remarkable book, has had its fulfilment. Israel still abides without a king, without a prince, without a priest, and so shall it abide until Messiah Himself appears the second, time to take His great power and reign.

"And thou, son of man, prophesy, and say, Thus saith the Lord Jehovah concerning the children of Amnion, and concerning their reproach; and say thou, A sword, a sword is drawn, for the slaughter it is furbished, to cause it to devour, that it may be as lightning; while they see for thee false visions, while they divine lies unto thee, to lay thee upon the necks of the wicked that are deadly wounded, whose day is come in the time of the iniquity of the end. Cause it to return into its sheath. In the place where thou wast created, in the land of thy birth, will I judge thee. And I will pour out Mine indignation upon thee; I will blow upon thee with the fire of My wrath; and I will deliver thee into the hand of brutish men, skilful to destroy. Thou shalt be for fuel to the fire; thy blood shall be in the midst of the land; thou shalt be no more remembered: for I, Jehovah, have spoken it"—vers. 28-32.

In these last verses of the chapter we learn that even though Ammon had escaped the sword of judgment for the moment because of Nebuchadnezzar's turning toward Jerusalem, nevertheless they, too, were to feel the sharpness of that sword when a little later Nebuchadnezzar would turn against them also. While they had not been in covenant relation with God as Israel was, nevertheless their wickedness and corruption had so offended the Holy One of Israel that He was about to judge them and pour out His indignation upon them, blowing upon them in the fire of His wrath, even as upon His own people whom the Ammonites had often persecuted in the past.

Chapter Twenty-two The Bloody And Defiled City

When God set His name at Jerusalem and appointed it to be the capital of Immanuel's land, He called it "the Holy City." Such it had been in former days when His people gathered there to worship in His sanctuary, and the voice of praise and thanksgiving ascended with the smoke of the incense to heaven. But alas, all this had been changed. By the wickedness of its people Jerusalem had become so utterly denied that God was now about to forsake it completely. Instead of being a city of truth and righteousness it was filled with falsehood and wickedness; instead of being a citadel of holiness it had become unclean with the blood of thousands of little children who had been offered in sacrifice to Moloch. Idolatry with its false priests reared its horrid head in the very place where once the priests of the Lord honored His name. Time after time God had sent His prophets to protest against the evils that were manifest among His people, but things had grown worse and worse until now the city was so wholly polluted that He was about to give it over to the cruel enemies who were besieging it.

Surely, there are lessons in all this for the professing Church today. In the beginning, as recorded in the book of Acts, and as we may gather from a careful reading of the Epistles and the messages to the seven churches of Asia in the book of The Revelation, the people of God of this age of grace delighted in His Word and loved His truth, clinging to the name of the Lord Jesus and seeking to honor Him; but little by little declension came in; the Church took up with the ways of the heathen, out of which she had been called; and finally, we find the Lord Himself declaring that He is about to spue her out of His mouth. Nevertheless, so long as the Saviour tarries, a remnant will abide to whom the things of God shall be precious; but when these are taken away at the coming of our Lord Jesus Christ and our gathering together unto Him, all that is left of Christendom will be rejected by God, and finally fall under His judgment when the Lord Jesus appears in flaming fire, taking vengeance on those that know not God.

"Moreover the word of Jehovah came unto me, saying, And thou, son of man, wilt thou judge, wilt thou judge the bloody city? then cause her to know all her abominations. And thou shalt say, Thus saith the Lord Jehovah: A city that sheddeth blood in the midst of her, that her time may come, and that maketh idols against herself to defile her! Thou art become guilty in thy blood that thou hast shed, and art defiled in thine idols which thou hast made; and thou hast caused thy days to draw near, and art come even unto thy years: therefore have I made thee a reproach unto the nations, and a mocking to all the countries. Those that are near, and those that are far from thee, shall mock thee, thou infamous one, and full of tumult"—vers. 1-5.

Ezekiel was called upon to act as a judge in the name of the Lord, bringing to the inhabitants of Jerusalem the divine indictment of their manifold crimes and offenses against the law of the Lord which they had spurned. The city had become completely defiled by the blood shed in the midst of her; that is, primarily the blood of the poor innocents, which, in their fanaticism, the people had devoted in sacrifice to their vile demon gods. Then too, we may think of blood shed because of the miscarriage of justice, when those who protested against the sins of the people were hated and slain by their fellows. Because of all this Jerusalem had become a reproach and a mocking in the countries roundabout, even as we are told in the New Testament that through apostate Judaism the name of God was blasphemed among the Gentiles. They who should have ever witnessed to Jehovah's faithfulness and by holy lives have manifested their subjection to and appreciation of His Word, had sunk to so low a depth that their heathen neighbors looked on with amazement and ridiculed their pretensions of being the chosen people of the Lord.

Item after item follows, indicating the low level morally to which the leaders of Israel had sunk.

"Behold, the princes of Israel, every one according to his power, have been in thee to shed blood. In thee have they set light by father and mother; in the midst of thee have they dealt by oppression with the sojourner; in thee have they wronged the fatherless and the widow. Thou hast despised My holy things, and

133

hast profaned My sabbaths. Slanderous men have been in thee to shed blood; and in thee they have eaten upon the mountains: in the midst of thee they have committed lewdness. In thee have they uncovered their fathers' nakedness; in thee have they humbled her that was unclean in her impurity. And one hath committed abominations with his neighbor's wife; and another hath lewdly defiled his daughter-in-law; and another in thee hath humbled his sister, his father's daughter. In thee have they taken bribes to shed blood; thou hast taken interest and increase, and thou hast greedily gained of thy neighbors by oppression, and hast forgotten Me, saith the Lord Jehovah"—vers. 6-12.

The princes of Israel who should have led the people in devotion to the Lord, were the chief trespassers. In the guilty city the children spurned the guidance of their parents, setting light by father and mother; they oppressed the strangers who sojourned among them: they wronged the fatherless and the widow. Instead of reverently regarding the holy things of the Lord, they despised His sacrifices and profaned His sabbaths. By false accusation they caused the innocent to be put to death; and worshiped the gods of the heathen upon the high places. Abominable excesses of the vilest character were linked with all this heathen worship so that they behaved more like beasts than rational human beings.

We shrink from meditating upon or even reading the awful charges brought out in verses 10 and 11, but God draws aside the veil by which they attempted to cover their filthiness, and shows up their moral defilement in all its dreadfulness. All things are naked and open to His holy eyes, and He cannot but deal in judgment with those guilty of such sins as are here described. Bribery, and that of the worst type, was also common among them. Even the magistrates accepted gifts in order to bias their attitude toward those unjustly accused before them, so that they condemned to death the innocent that they themselves might be enriched. Extortion and covetousness were prevalent among all classes—all these evils were the result of their having forgotten God, the One who had delivered them from Egypt and had watched over them through all the years of their sojourn in Canaan.

"Behold, therefore, I have smitten My hand at thy dishonest gain which thou hast made, and at thy blood which hath been in the midst of thee. Can thy heart endure, or can thy hands be strong, in the days that I shall deal with thee? I, Jehovah, have spoken it, and will do it. And I will scatter thee among the nations, and disperse thee through the countries; and I will consume thy filthiness out of thee. And thou shalt be profaned in thyself, in the sight of the nations; and thou shalt know that I am Jehovah"— vers. 13-16.

How could the Holy One of Israel do other than express His disapproval of those who were so guilty and who gave no evidence whatever of a desire to repent and get right with Him whom they had so dishonored.

The challenge of ver. 14 might well speak to any today who are bent upon taking their own way and have refused to heed the voice of God calling to repentance and to subjection to His Word: "Can thy heart endure or can thy hands be strong, in the days that I shall deal with thee?" Men may flaunt the will of God while in health and strength, and because sentence against their evil works is not immediately carried out they may think that God has forgotten, but the day is surely coming when He will arise in His wrath to visit upon the wilful and disobedient His indignation against sin and iniquity. What human heart can then bear up in that awful day, or whose hands will be strong enough to hold back or to resist the omnipotent power of the God they have defied? That which Jehovah has declared must come to pass; though judgment is His strange work, and He has no pleasure in the death of the wicked, yet His very holiness demands that sin be punished.

How literally have verses 15 and 16 been fulfilled! For centuries, yes, for two millenniums, Israel has been scattered among the nations and dispersed throughout the countries. Eventually, as a result of the suffering they are called upon to endure, a remnant at least will face their sins, confess their iniquities, and look upon Him whom they have pierced: then their filthiness shall be consumed out of them, and they shall know that Jehovah is indeed their God. Until that day they remain among the nations

135

as dross rather than the precious treasure they once were in the eyes of the Lord.

"And the word of Jehovah came unto me, saying, Son of man, the house of Israel is become dross unto Me: all of them are brass and tin and iron and lead, in the midst of the furnace; they are the dross of silver. Therefore thus saith the Lord Jehovah: Because ye are all become dross, therefore, behold, I will gather you into the midst of Jerusalem. As they gather silver and brass and iron and lead and tin into the midst of the furnace, to blow the fire upon it, to melt it; so will I gather you in Mine anger and in My wrath, and I will lay you there, and melt you. Yea, I will gather you, and blow upon you with the fire of My wrath, and ye shall be melted in the midst thereof. As silver is melted in the midst of the furnace, so shall ye be melted in the midst thereof; and ye shall know that I, Jehovah, have poured out My wrath upon you"—vers. 17-22.

The figure used in this paragraph is that of the casting of various metals into the crucible and exposing them to furnace heat in order that they may be melted together, and then the different metals be separated, one from the other. Of silver, which reflects the face of the refiner, there was very little, for few indeed heeded the voice of the Lord. The great majority were like brass and iron and lead, base metals which God could only cast away in His wrath and indignation.

We know that when Messiah comes He shall sit as a Refiner of silver, and then there will be manifested a people to the praise of the Lord who shall reflect His image and glorify Him in the earth.

The last section is a somewhat lengthy one, including verses 23 to 31.

"And the word of Jehovah came unto me, saying, Son of man, say unto her, Thou art a land that is not cleansed, nor rained upon in the day of indignation. There is a conspiracy of her prophets in the midst thereof, like a roaring lion ravening the prey: they have devoured souls; they take treasure and precious things; they have made her widows many in the midst thereof. Her priests have done violence to My law, and have profaned My holy things: they have made no distinction between the holy and the common, neither have they caused men to discern between the unclean and the clean, and have hid their eyes from My sabbaths, and I am profaned among them. Her princes in the midst thereof are like wolves ravening the prey, to shed blood, and to destroy souls, that they may get dishonest gain. And her prophets have daubed for them with untempered mortar, seeing false visions, and divining lies unto them, saying, Thus saith the Lord Jehovah, when Jehovah hath not spoken. The people of the land have used oppression, and exercised robbery; yea, they have vexed the poor and needy, and have oppressed the sojourner wrongfully. And I sought for a man among them, that should build up the wall, and stand in the gap before Me for the land, that I should not destroy it; but I found none. Therefore have I poured out Mine indignation upon them; I have consumed them with the fire of My wrath: their own way have I brought upon their heads, saith the Lord Jehovah"—vers. 23-31.

Here the Lord again emphasizes the defiled condition of the land of Israel and its barrenness because He had withdrawn the rains on account of His displeasure with His people. Moreover, there was, as it were, a conspiracy of her prophets—that is, those who professed to speak in the name of the Lord, who themselves being deceived sought to deceive the people by promising peace when there was no peace. Their soft words and false predictions proved the ruin of many souls and led to the loss of Israel's treasure and precious things. Widows were multiplied because husbands went forth at the bidding of these prophets to defend the land when God Himself had declared He would not protect them against their enemies. The priests in the temple profaned the holy things of Jehovah as they carried on their hypocritical service. There was no longer a distinction made between the things that were of God and those that had to do with the common life of the people; neither did they discern between that which was clean and that which was unclean. The sabbaths of the Lord, which were given for their blessing, were no longer valued but rather profaned.

Again an indictment is brought against the princes because, instead of shepherding the flock, they were like fierce ravening wolves let loose upon the people, shedding the blood of the innocent and destroying souls in order that they might thereby enrich themselves. The prophets, like man-pleasing preachers today, sought to make the people comfortable in their sins, thus daubing with untempered mortar, seeing false visions and divining lies in the name of the Lord of truth. The people followed after their unreliable spiritual guides, giving themselves over to oppression and robbery and affliction, rather than aiding the poor and needy.

Under such conditions Jehovah looked for even one man among them who should act for Him, standing against the iniquities and building up the wall of the city and closing its gaps, but He found none. Ezekiel himself, we must remember, was no longer in Palestine but on the banks of the River Chebar in Chaldea. In the land itself and in the defiled city there was not one to plead for the people, save Jeremiah, whose message was spurned, and he himself cast into prison. Therefore, there was none to stand between the people and the judgment that their sins deserved; so God declared He was pouring out His indignation upon them and consuming them with the fire of His wrath—and all this because of their own wilfulness; they had taken their own way, and so brought down these calamities upon their guilty heads.

Chapter Twenty-three The Apostasy Of Israel And Judah

In this lengthy chapter God once more goes over the ground of His controversy with Israel and Judah, picturing them as two sisters whom He brought up out of the land of Egypt and charged to be faithful to Him, but who both turned away from Him, following idolatry in its vilest forms.

"The word of Jehovah came again unto me, saying, Son of man, there were two women, the daughters of one mother: and they played the harlot in Egypt; they played the harlot in their youth; there were their breasts pressed, and there was handled the bosom of their virginity. And the names of them were Oholah the elder, and Oholibah her sister: and they became Mine, and they bare sons and daughters. And as for their names, Samaria is Oholah, and Jerusalem Oholibah"—vers. 1-4.

The word "Oholah" means "her tent"; whereas "Oholibah" means "My tent is in her." "Tent" and "tabernacle" are of course the same thing, so that the meaning is clear. Jehovah never identified Himself with the worship which Jeroboam set up for the ten tribes. The sanctuary to which the people there went was simply their own tabernacle, but it was otherwise with Judah: God Himself had set up His tabernacle in the midst of her; He dwelt in Judah and linked His name with Jerusalem in a way He never did with the ten tribes after they revolted from subjection to the house of David. At last they went wholly over to the same type of idolatry as that which characterized Israel up to the time that they were carried away into Assyria.

As we have already seen, spiritual adultery is idolatry, turning away from the one true and living God to idols; and God uses the figure of an unchaste woman to represent both Israel and Judah in their grave sin of infidelity toward Him. People of fastidious taste and delicacy of sentiment naturally shrink from reading such verses as these, but we need to remember the words that describe sin are in themselves not unclean or unholy; it is the evils that are back of the words that are so vile in the sight of God and should be detested by every right-minded person.

139

"And Oholah played the harlot when she was Mine; and she doted on her lovers, on the Assyrians her neighbors, who were clothed with blue, governors and rulers, all of them desirable young men, horsemen riding upon horses. And she bestowed her whoredoms upon them, the choicest men of Assyria all of them; and on whomsoever she doted, with all their idols she defiled herself. Neither hath she left her whoredoms since the days of Egypt; for in her youth they lay with her, and they handled the bosom of her virginity; and they poured out their whoredom upon her. Wherefore I delivered her into the hand of her lovers, into the hand of the Assyrians, upon whom she doted. These uncovered her nakedness; they took her sons and her daughters; and her they slew with the sword: and she became a byword among women; for they executed judgments upon her"—vers. 5-10.

Under the figure of harlotry God here sets forth the sin to which Israel in the north had given herself. She had followed after all the evil ways of her unclean idolatrous neighbors, and so eventually God Himself had forsaken her. One might have supposed that all this would have had a salutary effect upon the people of Judah and would have led them to abhor the sins that had brought ruin upon their neighbors to the north; but alas, alas, so prone is the heart of man to evil, and so true is it that "evil communications corrupt good manners," that Judah soon went just as far into the same type of wickedness and spiritual lewdness as did her sister in the north. All this comes out clearly in verses 11 to 21.

"And her sister Oholibah saw this, yet was she more corrupt in her doting than she, and in her whoredoms which were more than the whoredoms of her sister. She doted upon the Assyrians, governors and rulers, her neighbors, clothed most gorgeously, horsemen riding upon horses, all of them desirable young men. And I saw that she was defiled; they both took one way. And she increased her whoredoms; for she saw men portrayed upon the wall, the images of the Chaldeans portrayed with vermilion, girded with girdles upon their loins, with flowing turbans upon their heads, all of them princes to look upon, after the likeness of the Babylonians in Chaldea, the land of their nativity. And as soon as she saw them she doted upon them, and sent messengers unto them into Chaldea. And the Babylonians came to her into the bed of love, and they defiled her with their whoredom, and she was polluted with them, and her soul was alienated from them. So she uncovered her whoredoms, and uncovered her nakedness: then My soul was alienated from her, like as My soul was alienated from her sister. Yet she multiplied her whoredoms, remembering the days of her youth, wherein she had played the harlot in the land of Egypt. And she doted upon their paramours, whose flesh is as the flesh of asses, and whose issue is like the issue of horses. Thus thou calledst to remembrance the lewdness of thy youth, in the handling of thy bosom by the Egyptians for the breasts of thy youth"—vers. 11-21.

Because of her vileness God, the Holy One, could no longer condone her offenses, and must deal with her as her sins deserved in accordance with His warnings.

"Therefore, O Oholibah, thus saith the Lord Jehovah: Behold, I will raise up thy lovers against thee, from whom thy soul is alienated, and I will bring them against thee on every side: the Babylonians and all the Chaldeans, Pekod and Shoa and Koa, and all the Assyrians with them; desirable young men, governors and rulers all of them, princes and men of renown, all of them riding upon horses. And they shall come against thee with weapons, chariots, and wagons, and with a company of peoples; they shall set themselves against thee with buckler and shield and helmet round about: and I will commit the judgment unto them, and they shall judge thee according to their judgments. And I will set My jealousy against thee, and they shall deal with thee in fury; they shall take away thy nose and thine ears; and thy residue shall fall by the sword: they shall take thy sons and thy daughters; and thy residue shall be devoured by the fire. They shall also strip thee of thy clothes, and take away thy fair jewels. Thus will I make thy lewdness to cease from thee, and thy whoredom brought from the land of Egypt; so that thou shalt not lift up thine eyes unto them, nor remember Egypt any more. For thus saith the Lord Jehovah: Behold, I will deliver thee into the hand of them whom thou hatest, into the hand of them from whom thy soul is alienated; and they shall deal with thee in hatred, and shall take away all thy labor, and shall leave thee naked and bare; and the nakedness of thy whoredoms shall be uncovered, both thy lewdness and thy whoredoms"—vers. 22-29.

Such words as these require very little comment. They are too plain to need exposition. The language used is so clear that any reader will understand readily why God was thus dealing with His people. In spite of all His expostulations they had persisted in their unclean behavior and had laughed to scorn the admonitions of the prophets He sent to them.

"These things shall be done unto thee, for that thou hast played the harlot after the nations, and because thou art polluted with their idols. Thou hast walked in the way of thy sister; therefore will I give her cup into thy hand. Thus saith the Lord Jehovah: Thou shalt drink of thy sister's cup, which is deep and large; thou shalt be laughed to scorn and had in derision; it containeth much. Thou shalt be filled with drunkenness and sorrow, with the cup of astonishment and desolation, with the cup of thy sister Samaria. Thou shalt even drink it and drain it out, and thou shalt gnaw the sherds thereof, and shalt tear thy breasts; for I have spoken it, saith the Lord Jehovah. Therefore thus saith the Lord Jehovah: Because thou hast forgotten Me, and cast Me behind thy back, therefore bear thou also thy lewdness and thy whoredoms"—vers. 30-35.

God was about to give them up to the same kind of punishment that had been meted out already to Sa- maria, and they should learn in bitterness of soul what it meant to depart from the living God—from Him who would so gladly have cast all their sins behind His back if they had but turned to Him in contrition of heart.

He chides them because, having forgotten Him, they had cast His Word behind their backs and given themselves up to every type of idolatry.

"Jehovah said moreover unto me: Son of man, wilt thou judge Oholah and Oholibah? Then declare unto them their abominations. For they have committed adultery, and blood is in their hands; and with their idols have they committed adultery; and they have also caused their sons, whom they bare unto Me, to pass through the fire unto them to be devoured. Moreover this they have done unto Me: they have denied My sanctuary in the same day, and have profaned My sabbaths. For when they had slain their children to their idols, then they came the same day into My sanctuary to profane it; and, lo, thus have they done in the midst of My house. And furthermore ye have sent for men that come from afar, unto whom a messenger was sent, and, lo, they came; for whom thou didst wash thyself, paint thine eyes, and deck thyself with ornaments, and sit upon a stately bed, with a table prepared before it, whereupon thou didst set Mine incense and Mine oil. And the voice of a multitude being at ease was with her: and with men of the common sort were brought drunkards from the wilderness; and they put bracelets upon the hands of them twain, and beautiful crowns upon their heads"—vers. 36-42.

Israel and Judah both had been warned of the peril involved in apostasy; yet both had deliberately turned away from the truth they had once known and given themselves over to following after the ways of the surrounding nations. They had defiled the sanctuary of Jehovah and profaned His sabbaths, doing for their idols what God never would have asked them to do for Him—sacrificing their own children at the behest of the demon-inspired priests of their high places. Like an unchaste woman who sought in every way to at- tract men to her, they had made every effort to incorporate into their own economy the ways of the heathen, both religious and political; and thus had so dishonored God that He could do no other than repudiate them and visit judgment upon their heads.

"Then said I of her that was old in adulteries, Now will they play the harlot with her, and she with them. And they went in unto her, as they go in unto a harlot: so went they in unto Oholah and unto Oholibah, the lewd women. And righteous men, they shall judge them with the judgment of adulteresses, and with the judgment of women that shed blood; because they are adulteresses, and blood is in their hands. For thus saith the Lord

Jehovah: I will bring up a company against them, and will give them to be tossed to and fro and robbed. And the company shall stone them with stones, and despatch them with their swords; they shall slay their sons and their daughters, and burn up their houses with fire. Thus will I cause lewdness to cease out of the land, that all women may be taught not to do after your lewdness. And they shall recompense your lewdness upon you, and ye shall bear the sins of your idols; and ye shall know that I am the Lord Jehovah"—vers. 43-49.

Solemn indeed are the words with which this section closes. How unspeakably sad the state into which Judah had fallen! She who had once been a bright gem in the diadem of Jehovah now had fallen to the very lowest depth, and God was about to cast her out of His sight, to send her down to Babylon—there to learn in bitterness of soul what a mistake she had made in rejecting Him and refusing to heed His Word and following after the strange gods of the nations, which, in reality, are no gods but simply demons seeking the destruction of those who sacrifice to them.

Chapter Twenty-four The Death Of The Prophet's Wife A Sign To Israel

The prophecies recorded in the last four chapters seem all to have been delivered in the seventh year of King Jehoiachin's captivity (20:1). The message of chapter 24 is dated on the tenth day of the tenth month of the ninth year. Despite all the optimistic promises made by false prophets who declared that the scattered families of Judah would soon return in peace to their land, conditions continued to grow worse.

"Again, in the ninth year, in the tenth month, in the tenth day of the month, the word of Jehovah came unto me, saying, Son of man, write thee the name of the day, even of this selfsame day: the king of Babylon drew close unto Jerusalem this selfsame day. And utter a parable unto the rebellious house, and say unto them, Thus saith the Lord Jehovah, Set on the caldron, set it on, and also pour water into it: gather the pieces thereof into it, even every good piece, the thigh, and the shoulder; fill it with the choice bones. Take the choice of the flock, and also a pile of wood for the bones under the caldron; make it boil well; yea, let the bones thereof be boiled in the midst of it"—vers. 1-5.

Nebuchadnezzar, who was now the reigning monarch, had gone up against Jerusalem a second time, and God was about to use him to execute His judgment upon the guilty city whose inhabitants still seemed insensible of the real danger to which they were exposed. Ezekiel again likens Jerusalem to a great cooking vessel, and its inhabitants as the flesh to be boiled in it. The army of the Chaldeans surrounding the city were like the fire which should cause the pot to boil furiously until those within the city were utterly destroyed.

In the verses that follow he enlarges upon this illustration, applying it with terrible force to the people of the stricken city where once Jehovah had set His name, but which He now disowned because of its manifold iniquities.

"Wherefore thus saith the Lord Jehovah: Woe to the bloody city, to the caldron whose rust is therein, and whose rust is not gone out of it! take out of it piece after piece; no lot is fallen upon it. For her blood is in the midst of her; she set it upon the bare rock; she poured it not upon the ground, to cover it with dust. That it may cause wrath to come up to take vengeance, I have set her blood upon the bare rock, that it should not be covered. Therefore thus saith the Lord Jehovah: Woe to the bloody city! I also will make the pile great. Heap on the wood, make the fire hot, boil well the flesh, and make thick the broth, and let the bones be burned. Then set it empty upon the coals thereof, that it may be hot and the brass thereof may burn, and that the filthiness of it may be molten in it, that the rust of it may be consumed. She hath wearied herself with toil; yet her great rust goeth not forth out of her; her rust goeth not forth by fire. In thy filthiness is lewdness: because I have cleansed thee and thou wast not cleansed, thou shalt not be cleansed from thy filthiness any more, till I have caused My wrath toward thee to rest. I, Jehovah, have spoken it: it shall come to pass, and I will do it; I will not go back, neither will I spare, neither will I repent; according to thy ways, and according to thy doings, shall they judge thee, saith the Lord Jehovah"—vers. 6-14.

Instead of "the holy city," Jerusalem is called "the bloody city," for it had become utterly filthy and defiled by the idolatrous wickedness of its people. Like a disgusting mess simmering in its own filth, the doomed inhabitants were exposed to the vengeance of the God whose law they had spurned and whose grace they had despised. As they had poured out their sacrifices upon the high places to their false gods who were powerless to save, so should they be emptied out upon the top of the rock and cast into the dust as unclean and unfit for God's acceptance. He Himself would make the pile for fire great against them, and instead of baring His arm to deliver them He would give them up to that destruction which their sins deserved. Jerusalem is again likened to a false and unchaste woman who has broken wedlock. She had wearied herself with lies in her effort to cover her infamy and hide her shame, but all was of no avail. So manifest was her corruption that her filthiness and lewdness could not be purged or cleansed away until she had endured the fury of the Lord which her guilt deserved.

What God had spoken He would surely bring to pass. There would be no changing His mind or giving further opportunity to repent. They had sinned beyond remedy, and so judgment must take its course.

"Also the word of Jehovah came unto me, saying, Son of man, behold, I take away from thee the desire of thine eyes with a stroke: yet thou shalt neither mourn nor weep, neither shall thy tears run down. Sigh, but not aloud, make no mourning for the dead; bind thy headtire upon thee, and put thy shoes upon thy feet, and cover not thy lips, and eat not the bread of men. So I spake unto the people in the morning; and at even my wife died; and I did in the morning as I was commanded"—vers. 15-18.

In this section we have a personal experience of the prophet. His wife, whom he loved tenderly, was to be taken away suddenly by death; yet he was not to show any outward sign of mourning, for as he suffered so should the people as a whole suffer. He was commanded to refrain from weeping for the dead, but was to endure in stolid silence the grief which he was called to face.

That day he prophesied as usual, though with this heavy cloud hanging over his head; and at evening his wife died. His heart must indeed have been heavy, but in the morning he gave no evidence of the grief that was stirring within his soul except that he remained dumb, much to the astonishment of the people who undoubtedly knew of his sincere affection for his wife. They wondered at his apparent indifference.

"And the people said unto me, Wilt thou not tell us what these things are to us, that thou doest so? Then I said unto them, The word of Jehovah came unto me, saying, Speak unto the house of Israel, Thus saith the Lord Jehovah: Behold, I will profane My sanctuary, the pride of your power, the desire of your eyes, and that which your soul pitieth; and your sons and your daughters whom ye have left behind shall fall by the sword. And ye shall do as I have done: ye shall not cover your lips, nor eat the bread of men. And your tires shall be upon your heads, and your shoes upon your feet: ye shall not mourn nor weep; but ye shall pine away in your iniquities, and moan one toward another. Thus shall

Ezekiel be unto you a sign; according to all that he hath done shall ye do: when this cometh, then shall ye know that I am the Lord Jehovah"—vers. 19-24.

When his neighbors questioned Ezekiel as to his strange behavior he explained that his loss was but a small one as compared with the sorrows and bereavements that were to come to the inhabitants of Jerusalem and all the people of Israel.

The Lord God had decreed that because of their behavior His sanctuary would be given over to profanation and destruction. Israel, the desire of His eyes, was to be given up to death. Her sons and daughters were to perish by the sword of a cruel and vindictive enemy. So terrible would be the carnage that the survivors would be literally paralyzed with horror and would be dumb in the greatness of their grief. Thus, they should do as he, the prophet, had done in the hour of his soul's distress—they should not put on the gar- ments of mourning nor show signs of their anguish because of the dead. Rather were they destined to pine away in their own sins, grieving because of what they themselves were called upon to endure.

In this way Ezekiel was their sign; for they should do as he had done when the word of the Lord had been fulfilled, and they should know that He was the Lord God who executed judgment against the unconfessed sin of His people.

"And thou, son of man, shall it not be in the day when I take from them their strength, the joy of their glory, the desire of their eyes, and that whereupon they set their heart, their sons and their daughters, that in that day he that escapeth shall come unto thee, to cause thee to hear it with thine ears? In that day shall thy mouth be opened to him that is escaped, and thou shalt speak, and be no more dumb: so shalt thou be a sign unto them; and they shall know that I am Jehovah"—vers. 25-27.

When the city was taken and multitudes slain and those who had escaped should come to Ezekiel for help and comfort, then he was to be dumb no longer but to speak unto them the Word of the Lord as He should give it in that day. Judgment must follow disobedience, but God delights to show mercy to all who confess and forsake their sins.

Surely there is a message in all this for us today. We who call ourselves Christians have drifted far from the truth as set forth in the Word of God. How can we hope to escape when He arises to deal in judgment with those who have turned after the things of the world, thus dishonoring His name? Oh, that there might yet be a great returning to God and His Word, that there might come revival and blessing ere the close of this dispensation of grace!

Part II, Prophecies Relating To Seven Nations With Whom Israel Had Close Relationship Or Providential Dealings (chapters 25-32)

Chapter Twenty-five
Judgments On The Surrounding Nations

In 1 Peter 4:17 we read, "For the time is come for judgment to begin at the house of God: and if it first begin at us, what shall the end be of them that obey not the gospel of God?" This suggests a principle in God's ways of dealing with His people and with the world. We see this exemplified in the present chapter. Judgment had its inception in the sanctuary of the Lord. His rod of chastisement was stretched over the city and the people called by His name. Against these, the Chaldean conqueror was to execute His vengeance because of the grave departure of Israel and Judah from the path of obedience to Jehovah. But if thus His judgment was being executed upon His own house and His own people, then the nations surrounding, whose wickedness in some respects even surpassed that of the professed people of God, need not hope to escape. Therefore the prophet was commanded to declare that the Lord's wrath was about to fall upon these contiguous peoples.

In verses 1 to 7 we have the judgment of Ammon.

"And the word of Jehovah came unto me, saying, Son of man, set thy face toward the children of Ammon, and prophesy against them: and say unto the children of Ammon, Hear the word of the Lord Jehovah: Thus saith the Lord Jehovah, Because thou saidst, Aha, against My sanctuary, when it was profaned; and against the land of Israel, when it was made desolate; and against the house of Judah, when they went into captivity: therefore, behold, I will deliver thee to the children of the east for a possession, and they shall set their encampments in thee, and make their dwellings in thee; they shall eat thy fruit, and they shall drink thy milk. And I will make Kabbah a stable for camels, and the children of Amnion a couching-place for flocks: and ye shall know that I am Jehovah. For thus saith the Lord Jehovah: Because thou hast clapped thy hands, and stamped with the feet, and rejoiced with all the despite of thy soul against the land of Israel; therefore, behold, I have stretched out My hand upon thee, and will deliver thee for a spoil to the nations; and I will cut thee off from the peoples, and I will cause thee to perish out of the countries: I will destroy thee; and thou shalt know that I am Jehovah"—vers. 1-7.

It will be remembered that the Ammonites were descended from Ammon, who was one of the illegitimate sons of Lot, the result of his incestuous relation with his own daughter, who had plied him with liquor until he fell into a drunken stupor and knew not what he was doing. The Ammonites, therefore, were in a certain sense related to the people of Israel; though that relationship was a most disgraceful one. They evidently realized that they were looked upon by Israel with a measure of contempt, because we find them from early days numbered among the enemies of God's people.

Ezekiel was commanded to set his face against these children of Ammon and prophesy against them. They had, in their supercilious pride, sneered at the sanctuary of Jehovah, and delighted in its profanation; they rejoiced when it was made desolate, and gloried in seeing the people of God go into captivity. God is never an unconcerned witness of such conduct as this on the part of the enemies of His people. He may see fit to deal with them in chastisement because of their failures, but He will not tolerate ridicule on the part of their enemies. And so in this instance He was about to deliver the Ammonites also to the children of the East for a possession: that is, they, too, were to be overrun by the Chaldeans and their armies completely defeated. Many of their people would be carried into captivity, and their great cities would become desolate; even Rabbah, which from ancient times had been recognized as their capital, would be but a stable for camels, a couching-place for flocks. Thus by bitter experience the Ammonites would be made to realize God's indignation. Because of the way they had rejoiced when they saw His judgments falling on the land of Israel, they, too, would be delivered for a spoil to the nations and would be cut off from the peoples: that is, they would cease to be recognized as an independent dominion. Ammon was to be utterly destroyed because of the indignation of the Lord.

"Thus saith the Lord Jehovah: Because that Moab and Seir do say, Behold, the house of Judah is like unto all the nations; therefore, behold, I will open the side of Moab from the cities, from his cities which are on his frontiers, the glory of the country, Beth-jeshimoth, Baal-meon, and Kiriathaim, unto the children of the east, to go against the children of Ammon; and I will give them for a possession, that the children of Ammon may not be remembered among the nations: and I will execute judgments upon Moab; and they shall know that I am Jehovah"—vers. 8-11.

In this section the prophet's attention is directed to Moab and Seir. The Moabites bore the same relationship to the people of Israel that the Ammonites did, Moab himself being the child of Lot's other daughter by her own father. The pride of Moab is referred to in other scriptures: they gloried in their fortress habitations on the heights across the Jordan, and east of the Dead Sea; they fancied that their dwellings were impregnable, but they were soon to learn by bitter experience that they were powerless to stand against the armies of Nebuchadnezzar. Idolatry of the most cruel character nourished in Moab, and led the way in the sacrificing of sons and daughters to the vile gods, such as Moloch and others that were supposed to demand such offerings in order that they might turn away their wrath from the people and give rain and blessing to the land.

Now in the hour of their extremity they would find that these false gods were powerless to defend them, and would learn that He whom they had despised was indeed Jehovah the Everlasting One.

"Thus saith the Lord Jehovah: Because that Edom hath dealt against the house of Judah by taking vengeance, and hath greatly offended, and revenged himself upon them; therefore thus saith the Lord Jehovah, I will stretch out My hand upon Edom, and - will cut off man and beast from it; and I will make it desolate from Teman; even unto Dedan shall they fall by the sword. And I will lay My vengeance upon Edom by the hand of My people Israel;

and they shall do in Edom according to Mine anger and according to My wrath; and they shall know My vengeance, saith the Lord Jehovah"—vers. 12-14.

Edom, too, was related to Israel but in a far different way to the two nations we have just been considering. We read in Genesis 36:43, "He is Esau, the father of the Edomites." That is, Edom was descended from Jacob's twin brother, and his name is practically the same as that of the first man, Adam. He represents in a very definite way the man of the flesh. He was a man of considerable nobility of character and, in some respects, more to be admired than his scheming brother, Jacob, who nevertheless valued the covenant of the Lord in a way that Esau did not. God had given to Esau the land adjoining Moab and south of the Dead Sea. Here were built great fortress cities, some of which are in existence today, and are the wonder and admiration of travelers who go to visit them. The rock city of Petra, marvelous in its architecture cut out of the mountains, is a perpetual memorial to the truth of the Word of God which declared that Edom would be utterly destroyed even though its cities would remain. Edom hated Israel, and she arrayed herself against those whom she should have befriended. Therefore, God's judgment was to fall upon Edom also, and He would do in her cities according to His anger and His wrath; thus they should know His vengeance and learn the folly of defying His omnipotent power.

"Thus saith the Lord Jehovah: Because the Philistines have dealt by revenge, and have taken vengeance with despite of soul to destroy with perpetual enmity; therefore thus saith the Lord Jehovah, Behold, I will stretch out My hand upon the Philistines, and I will cut off the Cherethites, and destroy the remnant of the sea coast. And I will execute great vengeance upon them with wrathful rebukes; and they shall know that I am Jehovah, when I shall lay My vengeance upon them"—vers. 15-17.

The Philistines were Israel's enemies from of old. They had an Egyptian origin and were descended from Caphtor. They entered Palestine from the south and, typically, would speak of men of the world intruding into the inheritance of the people of God: that is, they represented natural men with no spiritual discernment, yet taking authority over those to whom God had revealed Himself. Such Philistines abound today: unsaved men professing to be ministers of God and exercising authority over His people while actually they have never been born into His kingdom.

The Philistines had dwelt in the land for many centuries, and even in Israel's most palmy days they were never able to destroy these crafty foes; though they did at times subdue them. Now the hour had struck when God was about to deal with them because they had taken vengeance with despite of soul, endeavoring to destroy His people with perpetual enmity. Because of this they themselves were to be destroyed. They must know the awfulness of Jehovah's vengeance falling upon them; thus they, too, should know that they had to do with Jehovah the God of Israel whom they had defied.

Chapter Twenty-six God's Judgment On Tyre

The city of Tyre at the time of Jerusalem's siege was still a great and prominent commercial metropolis. Its ships visited every port of the then known world, carrying goods of all kinds from western Asia, and returning with raw materials such as could be used in Phoenicia. It was renowned as a city of pleasure-lovers who lived in independence of God and vaunted themselves in their security against their foes because of their insular position, but judgment must fall on Tyre as well as on the other peoples surrounding Israel, because of their wickedness and corruption.

"And it came to pass in the eleventh year, in the first day of the month, that the word of Jehovah came unto me, saying, Son of man, because that Tyre hath said against Jerusalem, Aha, she is broken that was the gate of the people; she is turned unto me; I shall be replenished, now that she is laid waste: therefore thus saith the Lord Jehovah, Behold, I am against thee, O Tyre, and will cause many nations to come up against thee, as the sea causeth its waves to come up. And they shall destroy the walls of Tyre, and break down her towers: I will also scrape her dust from her, and make her a bare rock. She shall be a place for the spreading of nets in the midst of the sea; for I have spoken it, saith the Lord Jehovah; and she shall become a spoil to the nations. And her daughters that are in the field shall be slain with the sword: and they shall know that I am Jehovah"—vers. 1-6.

This prophecy was given about two years after the one we have just been considering, as recorded in the previous chapter. Ezekiel was commanded to prophesy against Tyre because she had rejoiced in the grief and sorrow that had come upon Jerusalem. He pictures her as exulting in the misfortunes of her neighbor, and counting that the troubles that had befallen Jerusalem would work out for the further upbuilding of Tyre herself. Because of her heartless attitude, Jehovah declared Himself to be against her, and announced that He would cause many nations to come up and besiege her, so that it would seem that the sea itself were hurling its waves upon the doomed city. The walls of Tyre should be destroyed; her towers broken down; the very dust of her foundations scraped away so that it would appear as but a bare rock in the midst of the water. So literally has this prophecy been fulfilled that even at this very day the rocky island on which Tyre once stood is now in exactly the same condition as foretold here. It is still a place for the spreading of the nets of fishermen, and has been the astonishment of many who have beheld it throughout the centuries. The outlying villages were to be destroyed with the mother city, and this, too, came to pass in due time.

The means whereby this destruction was wrought is predicted in the next section.

"For thus saith the Lord Jehovah: Behold, I will bring upon Tyre Nebuchadnezzar king of Babylon, king of kings, from the north, "with horses, and with chariots, and with horsemen, and a company, and much people. He shall slay with the sword thy daughters in the field; and he shall make forts against thee, and cast up a mound against thee, and raise up the buckler against thee. And he shall set his battering engines against thy walls, and with his axes he shall break down thy towers. By reason of the abundance of his horses their dust shall cover thee: thy walls shall shake at the noise of the horsemen, and of the wagons, and of the chariots, when he shall enter into thy gates, as men enter into a city wherein is made a breach. With the hoofs of his horses shall he tread down all thy streets; he shall slay thy people with the sword; and the pillars of thy strength shall go down to the ground. And they shall make a spoil of thy riches, and make a prey of thy merchandise; and they shall break down thy walls, and destroy thy pleasant houses; and they shall lay thy stones and thy timber and thy dust in the midst of the waters. And I will cause the noise of thy songs to cease; and the sound of thy harps shall be no more heard. And I will make thee a bare rock; thou shalt be a place for the spreading of nets; thou shalt be built no more: for I Jehovah have spoken it, saith the Lord Jehovah"—vers. 7-14.

Nebuchadrezzar—note the spelling here, for the "R" in place of the "N," in the second to the last syllable, is found upon the bricks that composed a part of the wall of the city of Babylon;

evidently *Nebuchadrezzar* was the Chaldean form of this monarch's name; whereas the Jews called him *Nebuchadnezzar*. He little realized, when fired with ambition to be monarch of all the world, leading his armies against nation after nation, that he was really the instrument in God's hand for punishing the peoples who had turned away from the truth of God and followed after their idols. It was because of this that no power was strong enough to stand against the Chaldeans. Every engine of war then known was put into action by them and used for the breaking down of the walls and towers of the cities that they besieged; their vast cohorts of cavalry, their wagons filled with instruments to use in the siege and chariots whereby to attack their foes, made them a fearful power to be reckoned with. As we read these verses we have little difficulty visualizing the triumphant dash of the vanguard of Nebuchadnezzar's hosts as they trod down the people in the streets of the cities that they sought to destroy: none were able to resist them, nor to save their wealth from being carried away. The riches of all the subdued nations were taken as a spoil by the Babylonians and carried into the land of Shinar. All joy and gladness disappeared from the conquered city so that not even the sound of a harp was heard again among them—and all this because of the pride and folly that led Tyre to exalt itself above the people of Jehovah's choice. Again He says He will make them a bare rock and a place for the spreading of nets; furthermore, the declaration was given that Tyre would never be built again. Millenniums have gone by since these words were uttered and the fulfilment began to take place, but Tyre of the ancients is still as though it had never been. It is true that on the mainland another city bearing the same name has risen up, but it is poor and squalid indeed, as compared with the great seafaring city that was built upon the island at some distance from the shore.

"Thus saith the Lord Jehovah to Tyre: Shall not the isles shake at the sound of thy fall, when the wounded groan, when the slaughter is made in the midst of thee? Then all the princes of the sea shall come down from their thrones, and lay aside their robes, and strip off their broidered garments: they shall clothe themselves with trembling; they shall sit upon the ground, and shall tremble every moment, and be astonished at thee. And they shall take up a lamentation over thee, and say to thee, How art thou destroyed, that wast inhabited by seafaring men, the renowned city, that was strong in the sea, she and her inhabitants, that caused their terror to be on all that dwelt there! Now shall the isles tremble in the day of thy fall; yea, the isles that are in the sea shall be dismayed at thy departure"—vers. 15-18.

The many cities and nations in distant parts of the world with which the merchants of Tyre had done business would be filled with fear and dread when they heard of the fall of this great commercial center. The description here given is very much like that which we have in the book of the Revelation concerning the downfall of Babylon the Great. All hope of rehabilitation would be at an end, and with this would go all possibility of restoring the traffic in goods of every kind which had worked to the advantage of the merchantmen in distant places, who would lament with great grief and crying, exclaiming, "How art thou destroyed, that wast inhabited by seafaring men, the renowned city, that was strong in the sea!" The people of the isles—a term, by the way, that includes not only actual islands surrounded by water but also cities built upon the seashore—would tremble in the day of the fall of Tyre, not knowing what the future might have for them.

Further description of the desolation that was to come upon Tyre is given in verses 19 to 21.

"For thus saith the Lord Jehovah: When I shall make thee a desolate city, like the cities that are not inhabited; when I shall bring up the deep upon thee, and the great waters shall cover thee; then will I bring thee down with them that descend into the pit, to the people of old time, and will make thee to dwell in the nether parts of the earth, in the places that are desolate of old, with them that go down to the pit, that thou be not inhabited; and I will set glory in the land of the living. I will make thee a terror, and thou shalt no more have any being; though thou be sought for, yet shalt thou never be found again, saith the Lord Jehovah"—vers. 19-21.

She was to be so utterly destroyed that the great water would cover her foundation, and her people would be brought down into the pit: that is, into Sheol to dwell with the people of old-time who were found there in the nether parts of the earth; that is, in the lower or infernal regions. In other words, the eternal doom of the inhabitants of Tyre is linked with the temporal destruction that would come upon the city when God, in His indignation, would manifest His glory in the land of the living by the defeat of these people who had ridiculed and despised Israel—the na- tion He had chosen for Himself. They should become a terror and be rooted out of the earth, so that, although they were sought for, they would never be found again. This is in accord with the verse in the Psalms that declares, "The wicked shall be turned into hell" (that is, into Sheol), "and all the nations that forget God" (Ps. 9:17). Tyre had forgotten God, therefore the desolation that was to come upon her with the eternal doom of her people by casting them into the outer darkness in the depths of Sheol.

Chapter Twenty-seven The Doom Of Tyre, Continued

With great detail the prophet continues to describe the doom which was to come upon Tyre because of the people's attitude of self-satisfaction and independence of God, which led them into all kinds of iniquity.

"The word of Jehovah came again unto me, saying, And thou, son of man, take up a lamentation over Tyre; and say unto Tyre, O thou that dwellest at the entry of the sea, that art the merchant of the peoples unto many isles, thus saith the Lord Jehovah: Thou, O Tyre, hast said, I am perfect in beauty. Thy borders are in the heart of the seas; thy builders have perfected thy beauty. They have made all thy planks of fir-trees from Senir; they have taken a cedar from Lebanon to make a mast for thee. Of the oaks of Bashan have they made thine oars; they have made thy benches of ivory inlaid in boxwood, from the isles of Kittim. Of fine linen with broidered work from Egypt was thy sail, that it might be to thee for an ensign; blue and purple from the isles of Elishah was thine awning. The inhabitants of Sidon and Arvad were thy rowers: thy wise men, O Tyre, were in thee, they were thy pilots. The old men of Gebal and the wise men thereof were in thee thy calkers: all the ships of the sea with their mariners were in thee to deal in thy merchandise. Persia and Lud and Put were in thine army, thy men of war: they hanged the shield and helmet in thee; they set forth thy comeliness. The men of Arvad with thine army were upon thy walls round about, and valorous men were in thy towers; they hanged their shields upon thy walls round about; they have perfected thy beauty"—vers. 1-11.

This is described as a lamentation over Tyre, for judgment is never God's delight. He has no pleasure in the death of the wicked, but His heart is grieved when it becomes necessary to deal in wrath with those who have spurned His gracious expostulations, and refused to turn from their sins.

Tyre dwelt at the entry of the sea. As already mentioned, the ancient city was built upon an island which was connected with the mainland by a causeway. To her ports came ships from all nations, and from thence her own fleet went out to all the then known world. Her people gloried in their wealth, and lived luxuriously. Nothing was too good for them. From nearby lands they brought lumber of cedar and oak with which they built magnificent mansions and palaces; they reclined upon couches inlaid with ivory. Importations of fine linen from Egypt, and blue and purple cloth from distant isles decorated their homes and were made into sails for their ships. Their sailors were conscripted from the surrounding cities and districts; and the pilots of Tyre were looked upon as experts in their calling. From the city of Gebal to the north of them came workmen to assist in shipbuilding. Gebal, which was for centuries buried beneath the sands of the desert, has only recently been uncovered by archaeologists. It is possible today to walk through the streets of this ancient city and note the arrangement of the houses: it bespeaks a remarkable civilization which, however, was long since overthrown by invading armies from other countries. Upon its ruins a Roman city was erected, which, in turn, gave place to a third city, built by the Crusaders. All these are now visible to the traveler as mute evidences of the passing glory of this world. Portions of each city have been left and stand out clearly just as the different rock strata can be seen on a hillside.

From Persia, Lud, and Put, mariners were obtained to serve for the defense of Tyre, and the men of Arvad also were engaged to protect the city against its enemies.

In verses 12 to 25 we have a list of names of cities and districts with which the merchants of Tyre traded.

"Tarshish was thy merchant by reason of the multitude of all kinds of riches; with silver, iron, tin, and lead, they traded for thy wares. Javan, Tubal, and Meshech, they were thy traffickers; they traded the persons of men and vessels of brass for thy merchandise. They of the house of Togarmah traded for thy wares with horses and warhorses and mules. The men of Dedan were thy traffickers; many isles were the mart of thy hand: they brought thee in exchange horns of ivory and ebony. Syria was thy merchant by reason of the multitude of thy handiworks: they traded for thy wares with emeralds, purple, and broidered work,

161

and fine linen, and coral, and rubies. Judah, and the land of Israel, they were thy traffickers: they traded for thy merchandise wheat of Minnith, and Pannag, and honey, and oil, and balm. Damascus was thy merchant for the multitude of thy handiworks, by reason of the multitude of all kinds of riches, with the wine of Helbon, and white wool. Vedan and Javan traded with yarn for thy wares: bright iron, cassia, and calamus, were among thy merchandise. Dedan was thy trafficker in precious cloths for riding. Arabia, and all the princes of Kedar, they were the merchants of thy hand; in lambs, and rams, and goats, in these were they thy merchants. The traffickers of Sheba and Raamah, they were thy traffickers; they traded for thy wares with the chief of all spices, and with all precious stones, and gold. Haran and Canneh and Eden, the traffickers of Sheba, Asshur and Chilmad, were thy traffickers. These were thy traffickers in choice wares, in wrappings of blue and broidered work, and in chests of rich apparel, bound with cords and made of cedar, among thy merchandise. The ships of Tarshish were thy caravans for thy merchandise: and thou wast replenished, and made very glorious in the heart of the seas"—vers. 12-25.

Tarshish seems to have been a name used not simply, as some have thought, for Spain, but even including the British Isles. Observe that from Tarshish came tin and lead as well as silver and iron. The very word *Britannia* means "land of tin"; and it is believed that some of the Tyrian ships sailed beyond Gibraltar and reached Britain at a very early period.

Javan is generally supposed to refer to Greece; Tubal, and Meshech were settled by Scythian tribes, north of the Black Sea: the one in Asia, and the other in Europe. From them apparently came the Muscovites, the founders of the great Russian empire.

Togarmah is generally considered to be identical with Armenia; Dedan is somewhat uncertain, but was also located, in all likelihood, in the region of the Black Sea. Syria and Judah were respectively north and south of Tyre, Damascus being the chief city of Syria. It is not possible to identify with certainty every one of the places mentioned, some of which would have passed away forever had it not been that the names have been preserved in Ezekiel's prophecy.

Arabia, settled by the descendants of Ishmael, was already a land in which nomadic tribes raised great numbers of large and small cattle. The Sheba of ver. 22 is undoubtedly the city whose queen, centuries before, went to visit King Solomon.

It is evident from ver. 23 that the name "Eden" was applied to a part of Mesopotamia, and may indeed have been the very district in which the ancient Eden was located.

All these various places poured their riches into the markets of Tyre and obtained, in return from them, other goods which they needed in their respective localities.

It must have seemed to the haughty, independent merchant princes of this great city, that there was little likelihood of their great commercial system ever being destroyed, but just as in a future day Babylon the Great is to go down in a moment, so Tyre's judgment was to fall with terrible and sudden force upon the godless city which had dared to defy the Eternal One.

"Thy rowers have brought thee into great waters: the east wind hath broken thee in the heart of the seas. Thy riches, and thy wares, thy merchandise, thy mariners, and thy pilots, thy calkers, and the dealers in thy merchandise, and all thy men of war, that are in thee, with all thy company which is in the midst of thee, shall fall into the heart of the seas in the day of thy ruin. At the sound of the cry of thy pilots the suburbs shall shake. And all that handle the oar, the mariners, and all the pilots of the sea, shall come down from their ships; they shall stand upon the land, and shall cause their voice to be heard over thee, and shall cry bitterly, and shall cast up dust upon their heads; they shall wallow themselves in the ashes: and they shall make themselves bald for thee, and gird them with sackcloth, and they shall weep for thee in bitterness of soul with bitter mourning. And in their wailing they shall take up a lamentation for thee, and lament over thee, saying, Who is there like Tyre, like her that is brought to silence in the midst of the sea? When thy wares went forth out of the seas, thou filledst many peoples; thou didst enrich the kings of the earth with the multitude of thy riches and of thy merchandise. In the time that thou wast broken by the seas in the depths of the waters, thy merchandise and all thy company did fall in the midst of thee. All the inhabitants of the isles are astonished at thee, and their kings are horribly afraid; they are troubled in their countenance. The merchandise among the peoples hiss at thee; thou art become a terror, and thou Shalt nevermore have any being"—vera. 26-36.

Her rowers: that is, her statesmen, had brought her into great waters, and the east wind of adversity was to break her in the heart of the seas. All her wealth would then avail her nothing: her palaces, her warehouses, her great mansions, would all go down together and fall into the heart of the sea in the day of her ruin. The ships' officers, pilots, and mariners, beholding from afar the burning of the city, would bewail its utter destruction, exclaiming, "Who is there like Tyre, like her that is brought to silence in the midst of the sea?" Realizing that their opportunities for enrichment were now gone forever, they would lament with a bitter cry the overthrow of the great Phoenician metropolis which God Himself declared should never more have any being. The island city of Tyre, when once destroyed, was never to rise again.

Chapter Twenty-eight The Supernatural Ruler Of Tyre

As we read this chapter carefully it is very evident that two personalities come into view: first the literal prince of Tyre, the one who actually sat on the throne when Nebuchadnezzar's armies besieged and eventually sacked the city. But back of this earthly ruler was a sinister supernatural king who controlled the heart of the Tyrian prince, filling him with pride and self-confidence and leading him to defy the armies that God, as the Creator and Governor of the universe, had sent against him. The same thing comes out in Isa. 14, where we see Lucifer, a fallen angel, dominating the mind and controlling the spirit of the king of Babylon. These chapters throw a great deal of light on the words of the Apostle Paul in Ephesians 6. He tells us that our conflict as Christians is not with flesh and blood but is a spiritual warfare. We are called upon to put on the whole armour of God in order that we may be able to stand against the wiles of the devil, who works through "wicked spirits in the heavenlies, the world rulers of this darkness," as a more literal translation would read.

The real world rulers of the great earthly powers are not the men who seem to hold the reins of government and dominate the nations. These men are often but puppets under the control of Satan's minions, angelic personalities and powers who are doing all that they can to thwart the carrying out of God's counsels. That their efforts will avail nothing in the end is perfectly clear from Scripture; nevertheless, they are able to cause the saints of God and the peoples of the world a great deal of trouble and distress, while the conflict between righteousness and unrighteousness goes on.

The tenth chapter of the book of Daniel gives us added light as to this spiritual warfare. There we find a man of God in prayer for three full weeks; and then an amazing declaration is made by the angel Gabriel who comes at last to answer his petition. He tells the prophet that the request was granted from the first day that he began to intercede for his people; but for one-and-twenty days the prince of the kingdom of Persia withstood this angel of the

Lord. Now this prince was certainly not the man who sat on the throne of Persia but an evil angel seeking to keep that man from carrying out God's purpose regarding the restoration of His people.

Another evil prince is mentioned in the closing verses, where Gabriel tells Daniel that he must now go again to fight with the prince of Persia, and later the prince of Grecia would come into the picture; for it was under the great power of Greece that Israel was to come next; and Satan was seeking to control the rulers of that land in order that he might work evil against the people of God.

With all this in view, history becomes a most interesting study indeed. As we look back over the centuries and note the rise and fall of nations and their attitude toward the things of God, we can almost visualize the conflict going on in the heavenlies. Sometimes it looks as though Satan is about to be victor, then his hosts are driven back in ignominious defeat. Thank God, the day will soon come when Satan's last hold upon the heavenlies will come to an end, and Michael the Archangel, with his attendant angels, will participate in the final battle with Satan and his minions, as a result of which the devil and his angels will be cast out of the created heavens into the earth, where he will have great wrath, knowing that his time is short. This will be the event that will precipitate the great tribulation which immediately precedes the revelation of the Lord Jesus Christ from heaven with His holy angels to execute judgment on all the enemies of God, whether they be men or evil angels.

With these things before us, this chapter becomes exceedingly instructive. The first ten verses have to do with the prince of Tyre, the earthly ruler.

"The word of Jehovah came again unto me, saying, Son of man, say unto the prince of Tyre, Thus saith the Lord Jehovah: Because thy heart is lifted up, and thou hast said, I am a god, I sit in the seat of God, in the midst of the seas; yet thou art man, and not God, though thou didst set thy heart as the heart of God; behold, thou art wiser than Daniel; there is no secret that is hidden from thee; by thy wisdom and by thine understanding thou hast gotten thee riches, and hast gotten gold and silver into thy treasures; by thy great wisdom and by thy traffic hast thou increased thy riches, and thy heart is lifted up because of thy riches; therefore thus saith the Lord Jehovah: Because thou hast set thy heart as the heart of God, therefore, behold, I will bring strangers upon thee, the terrible of the nations; and they shall draw their swords against the beauty of thy wisdom, and they shall defile thy brightness. They shall bring thee down to the pit; and thou shalt die the death of them that are slain, in the heart of the seas. Wilt thou yet say before him that slayeth thee, I am God? But thou art man, and not God, in the hand of him that woundeth thee. Thou shalt die the death of the uncircumcised by the hand of strangers: for I have spoken it, saith the Lord Jehovah"—vers. 1-10.

This monarch is pictured as the very incarnation of pride and self-will. So haughty is he that he pro- claims himself to be a god sitting in the seat of Deity, and one, therefore, whose power no armies can destroy; but he was soon to learn that he was but man and not God, though he had set his heart as the heart of God. He gloried in his wisdom; in his own judgment he was wiser than Daniel and felt that no secret was hidden from him.

This, in itself, is intensely interesting, for it shows us how widespread was Daniel's reputation at this time as a man of probity and sagacity; his fame had gone far beyond the actual kingdom of Babylon, and this Tyrian prince compared himself with Daniel, and in his conceit considered himself wiser than the prophet whom God had raised up even in Babylon in order to make known His mind and will.

The prince of Tyre gave himself credit for the wealth and commercial standing of the city which he ruled. He was to learn that only by the will of God does any man hold authority, and when that authority is abused God wrests it from him. The army of the strangers whom the Tyrians despised, had come against the city and proven themselves to be the terrible of the nations. God was about to give Tyre into their hands. Its nobles would be brought down to the pit, and its prince was to have an ignominious death, not only unable to protect his city but also unable to save himself. This would be the end of the man who had said, "I am God." His doom was predicted by Jehovah and none could turn it aside.

In verses 11 to 19 the supernatural ruler of Tyre comes before us; though in the latter part of this section we may find it difficult to distinguish between the human and the supernatural, because the one was so completely dominated by the other that his doom was but a picture of that awaiting Satan himself.

"Moreover the word of Jehovah came unto me, saying, Son of man, take up a lamentation over the king of Tyre, and say unto him, Thus saith the Lord Jehovah: Thou sealest up the sum, full of wisdom, and perfect in beauty. Thou wast in Eden, the garden of God; every precious stone was thy covering, the sardius, the topaz, and the diamond, the beryl, the onyx, and the jasper, the sapphire, the emerald, and the carbuncle, and gold: the workmanship of thy tabrets and of thy pipes was in thee; in the day that thou wast created they were prepared. Thou wast the anointed cherub that covereth: and I set thee, so that thou wast upon the holy mountain of God; thou hast walked up and down in the midst of the stones of fire. Thou wast perfect in thy ways from the day that thou wast created, till unrighteousness was found in thee. By the abundance of thy traffic they filled the midst of thee with violence, and thou hast sinned: therefore have I cast thee as profane out of the mountain of God; and I have destroyed thee, O covering cherub, from the midst of the stones of fire. Thy heart was lifted up because of thy beauty; thou hast corrupted thy wisdom by reason of thy brightness: I have cast thee to the ground; I have laid thee before kings, that they may behold thee. By the multitude of thine iniquities, in the unrighteousness of thy traffic, thou hast profaned thy sanctuaries; therefore have I brought forth a fire from the midst of thee; it hath devoured thee, and I have turned thee to ashes upon the earth in the sight of all them that behold thee. All they that know thee among the peoples shall be astonished at thee: thou art become a terror, and thou shalt nevermore have any being"—vers.11-19.

It is very evident that of no earthly ruler could these words be spoken. Undoubtedly we have here the original condition and the fall of Satan himself. It was of him that God could say, "Thou sealest up the sum, full of wisdom, and perfect in beauty." Men often ask why God created the devil. The answer is He never created the devil; He created a pure spirit-being of great wisdom and glory, but this spirit dared to conspire against the throne of God, and so the greatest of all the angels became the arch-enemy of God and man.

The prophet says of this spirit leader, "Thou wast in Eden, the garden of God." This would seem to suggest that before man himself was created, this glorious being had charge of the lower creation. There is a mystery here that we may not be able to solve, but Jesus Himself says, "I beheld Satan as lightning fall from heaven" (Luke 10:18). He may have been the one appointed from the beginning to take charge of this world. We do not speak dogmatically, however, as to this, but these verses seem at least to suggest it. Every precious stone was his covering. These precious stones speak of the glories in which God's saints are yet to stand before Him, as we find in the book of Revelation; and here we see them all combined in the robes of this great angelic leader. It was his to lead the praises of the angelic host. The workmanship of his tabrets and of his pipes suggests this: in the day that he was created he was prepared to lead the heavenly choir. He is described as the "anointed cherub that covereth": that is, he was the angel that attended on the throne of God. It was Jehovah Himself who had set him there. He dwelt in the very presence of Deity, walking up and down in the midst of the stones of fire, for we read, "Our God is a consuming fire" (Heb. 12:29). He was created perfect, but how long this condition continued we are not told. The Word simply says, "Thou wast perfect in thy ways from the day that thou wast created, till unrighteousness was found in thee."

Verse 16 links the supernatural ruler very closely with the prince who sat on the throne; but God goes on to speak directly of the covering cherub in the following verse, and gives us the secret of his fall. He says, "Thy heart was lifted up because of thy beauty; thou hast corrupted thy wisdom by reason of thy brightness."

The Lord Jesus shows us that Satan is an apostate; he "abode not in the truth" (John 8:44). The Apostle Paul instructs Timothy not to put undue responsibility upon a novice, or one newly come to the faith, lest he be lifted up with pride and fall into the condemnation of the devil (1 Tim. 3:6). This passage is the key to both these other scriptures. It was pride that turned an archangel into a devil.

The closing verses, as we have mentioned, link this great being so intimately with the literal Tyrian ruler that one can hardly be distinguished from the other. Because of the way in which he dominated the heart of the last prince of Tyre, the judgments depicted were to fall.

The next section deals with the doom of Sidon, a city close to Tyre, which was destroyed by Nebuchadnezzar, but afterwards rebuilt.

"And the word of Jehovah came unto me, saying, Son of man, set thy face toward Sidon, and prophesy against it, and say, Thus saith the Lord Jehovah: Behold, I am against thee, O Sidon; and I will be glorified in the midst of thee; and they shall know that I am Jehovah, when I shall have executed judgments in her, and shall be sanctified in her. For I will send pestilence into her, and blood into her streets; and the wounded shall fall in the midst of her, with the sword upon her on every side; and they shall know that I am Jehovah. And there shall be no more a pricking brier unto the house of Israel, nor a hurting thorn of any that are round about them, that did despite unto them; and they shall know that I am the Lord Jehovah"—vers. 20-24.

This city is often linked with Tyre in the Scripture. Jesus said, "If the mighty works had been done in Tyre and Sidon, which have been done in you, they had a great while ago repented, sitting in sackcloth and ashes" (Luke 10:13). It was not for them to continue until Messiah came; they fell long before because of their pride and arrogance. While God's judgment as we have noticed before is His strange work, and He takes no delight in it, yet He is glorified even in the destruction of those cities or nations that dare to oppose themselves to His will. And so upon Sidon was to fall pestilence and bloody warfare; and this city, which had been for so long a pricking brier unto the house of Israel, a thorn in their side, was doomed to destruction. But God's power and might is not only shown in chastising His people when they would depart from Him, and in visiting judgment upon the wicked, but also in the recovery of those who return to Him; and so in the last verses of the chapter we have a promise of Israel's future restoration.

"Thus saith the Lord Jehovah: When I shall have gathered the house of Israel from the peoples among whom they are scattered, and shall be sanctified in them in the sight of the nations, then shall they dwell in their own land which I gave to My servant Jacob. And they shall dwell securely therein; yea, they shall build houses, and plant vineyards, and shall dwell securely, when I have executed judgements upon all those that do them despite round about them; and they shall know that I am Jehovah their God"—vers. 25, 26.

These verses are to be taken as literally as the many passages that speak of the desolations of Jerusalem and the scattering of the people of Israel among the nations. The day will come when a repentant remnant will ask the way to Zion, and the Lord will reveal Himself to them and eventually settle them again in their own land where they will dwell securely, building houses and planting vineyards. This is not a picture of the coming glory of the Church in its heavenly inheritance, but is very distinctly a prophecy of blessing upon the earth in the land of Palestine for the restored people of Israel.

They are going back now to their land in unbelief; going back, little as they realize it, to greater sorrows than they have ever known among the Gentiles, even to the days of the great tribulation. But when all that is passed and the Lord Jesus is revealed to them as the Messiah for whom they have waited so long, they will look upon him whom they have pierced, and bow in contrition at His feet, and thus be restored to Jehovah, and so settled in their land in perfect peace.

Chapter Twenty-nine Judgment On Egypt

From the days when the dynasty of the Pharaohs who were friendly to Joseph and his brethren ended, and another king arose who knew not Joseph: that is, a new dynasty which overthrew the former one and immediately began to take steps to enslave the people of Israel, Egypt had been an enemy of the Hebrew people, except for a very short time during the reign of King Solomon when it was otherwise, doubtless because of the alliance that Solomon had made with the daughter of Pharaoh. But, generally speaking, through many centuries Egypt was opposed to Israel, and either was allied with Israel's foes or seeking to subjugate and make that nation a mere vassal state under Egyptian domination.

Only a few years had elapsed prior to the prophecies recorded in this chapter, since Pharaoh-Necho had invaded Palestine, besieged and conquered Jerusalem, carrying away King Jehoahaz, and setting up as a puppet king, his brother Eliakim, whose name Pharaoh-Necho changed to Jehoiakim.

The rise of Nebuchadnezzar and the enlargement of the Chaldean empire was recognized as a menace to Egyptian supremacy. Pharaoh at first sought to thwart the ambitions of the Babylonian leader, but was soon put on the defensive.

Ezekiel uttered the present prophecy, we are told, in the tenth month of the tenth year of Jehoiachin's captivity.

"In the tenth year, in the tenth month, in the twelfth day of the month, the word of Jehovah came unto me, saying, Son of man, set thy face against Pharaoh king of Egypt, and prophesy against him, and against all Egypt; speak, and say, Thus saith the Lord Jehovah: Behold, I am against thee, Pharaoh king of Egypt, the great monster that lieth in the midst of his rivers, that hath said, My river is mine own, and I have made it for myself. And I will put hooks in thy jaws, and I will cause the fish of thy rivers to stick unto thy scales; and I will bring thee up out of the midst of thy rivers, with all the fish of thy rivers which stick unto thy scales. And I will cast thee forth into the wilderness, thee and all the fish of thy rivers: thou shalt fall upon the open field; thou shalt not be brought together, nor gathered; I have given thee for food to the beasts of the earth and to the birds of the heavens. And all the inhabitants of Egypt shall know that I am Jehovah, because they have been a staff of reed to the house of Israel. When they took hold of thee by thy hand, thou didst break, and didst rend all their shoulders; and when they leaned upon thee, thou brakest, and madest all their loins to be at a stand"—vers. 1-7.

In Tyre we have seen a picture of the world viewed as a great commercial system, acting independently of God. Egypt is a picture of the world in a different aspect, as the place of bondage out of which God delivers His people. Pharaoh was both its prince and its god, and therefore typifies Satan, the prince and the god of this age.

Situated along the sides of the Nile, whose annual overflow fertilized its fields and provided its people with sustenance, Egypt aptly sets forth the world as the home of unsaved men dependent upon the bounty of heaven and living in independence of God. Thus Pharaoh is described here as a great monster lying in the midst of his rivers and saying in his heart, "My river is mine own, and I have made it for myself." There was no realization of his direct dependence on the one true and living God who caused the waters of Ethiopia to fill the banks of the Nile and overflow unto the alluvial fields of Egypt. The people had become so accustomed to this phenomenon year after year that they took for granted that it would always be in the future as it had been in the past. If occasionally conditions at the upper Nile were such that the water did not flow down as in former years, they turned not to the true God but offered sacrifices to the river and to their idols, in order that they might procure the favor which they needed.

In the sight of God Pharaoh had become like a great crocodile lying in his rivers. The plural form is used because of the many streams of the Delta. In his pride and conceit Pharaoh defied all who dared to disregard him. But because of their independence of God, destruction was to come upon Pharaoh and all his land; so that all the inhabitants of Egypt would know that the Jehovah of Israel, from whom His own people had turned to lean upon a broken staff, when they tried to make a league with Egypt, was the only true God. They had entered into an alliance with Israel but had proven unfaithful and powerless to protect them against the Babylonian army. Judgment was, therefore, about to fall upon the entire land for a period of forty years.

"Therefore thus saith the Lord Jehovah: Behold, I mil bring a sword upon thee, and will cut off from thee man and beast. And the land of Egypt shall be a desolation and a waste; and they shall know that I am Jehovah. Because he hath said, The river is mine, and I have made it; therefore, behold, I am against thee, and against thy rivers, and I will make the land of Egypt an utter waste and desolation, from the tower of Seveneh even unto the border of Ethiopia. No foot of man shall pass through it, nor foot of beast shall pass through it, neither shall it be inhabited forty years. And I will make the land of Egypt a desolation in the midst of the countries that are desolate; and her cities among the cities that are laid waste shall be a desolation forty years; and I will scatter the Egyptians among the nations, and will disperse them through the countries"—vers. 8-12.

A sword was to be brought upon Egypt—that great land which had from time to time sent its armies out to battle against other nations, but had so seldom known anything in the way of an invasion on its own ground.

Only a short time before, Pharaoh-Hophra had endeavored to help the Israelites against Nebuchadnezzar, by marching an army up into the land to raise the siege of Jerusalem, but he had almost immediately returned when Nebuchadnezzar came again with an augmented host. Pharaoh-Hophra was powerless to help. The Egyptians were soon to know what it meant to have an invading army enter into their own cities, spreading ruin and desolation everywhere it went.

It was some seventeen years or more after this prophecy was given before it began to be fulfilled, but in God's due time this haughty power was made to feel the horrors of warfare such as in the past it had inflicted on other peoples. We may not be able to trace exactly the beginning and the end of that forty years' desolation spoken of in verses 12 and 13, but we may be certain of this: even though the monuments of the past do not tell us anything about this period, God's Word was fulfilled to the letter.

"For thus saith the Lord Jehovah: At the end of forty years will I gather the Egyptians from the peoples whither they were scattered; and I will bring back the captivity of Egypt, and will cause them to return into the land of Pathros, into the land of their birth; and they shall be there a base kingdom. It shall be the basest of the kingdoms; neither shall it any more lift itself up above the nations: and I will diminish them, that they shall no more rule over the nations. And it shall be no more the confidence of the house of Israel, bringing iniquity to remembrance, when they turn to look after them: and they shall know that I am the Lord Jehovah"—vers. 13-16.

When the forty years should expire Egypt once more was to lift up her head, and many of its people who had fled to surrounding nations for refuge would return to their own patrimony. But never again would Egypt be the great power it had been in the past. "They shall be a base kingdom," we are told; and verse 15 says, "It shall be the basest of the kingdoms," which should no more rule over the nations. The time soon came when Egypt had so deteriorated that it was dependent on the nations roundabout; and through all the centuries since the days of the Ptolemies, Egypt has been a land of wretchedness and distress. Some from Israel sought to find refuge there after the destruction of Jerusalem and the first temple; and at one time there were more Jews settled in Egypt than in Palestine; yet Egypt was never again in a position to warrant Israel's confidence.

We have seen something of a revival of Egyptian power in our own days, preparatory to the place its ruler is to take as the king of the south in the time of the end, but had it not been for Britain's help it is questionable if Egypt would have ever occupied a place of any prominence among the nations.

The closing verses of the chapter tell us definitely just how the prophecy would be fulfilled:

"And it came to pass in the seven and twentieth year, in the first month, in the first day of the month, the word of Jehovah came unto me, saying, Son of man, Nebuchadrezzar king of Babylon caused his army to serve a great service against Tyre: every head was made bald, and every shoulder was worn; yet had he no wages, nor his army, from Tyre, for the service that he had served against it. Therefore thus saith the Lord Jehovah: Behold, I will give the land of Egypt unto Nebuchadrezzar king of Babylon; and he shall carry off her multitude, and take her spoil, and take her prey; and it shall be the wages for his army. I have given him the land of Egypt as his recompense for which he served, because they wrought for Me, saith the Lord Jehovah. In that day will I cause a horn to bud forth unto the house of Israel, and I will give thee the opening of the mouth in the midst of them; and they shall know that I am Jehovah"—vers. 17-21.

As intimated above, seventeen years after the former prophecy was given, God caused Egypt to become the possession of Nebuchadnezzar, king of Babylon, as reward for the vengeance He had meted against Tyre. God Himself, as the Governor of the Universe, declared, as recorded in verse 20, "I have given him the land of Egypt as his recompense for which he served, because they wrought for Me, saith the Lord Jehovah." Little did the proud Chaldean monarch realize that his army was the sword of God executing what Jehovah had decreed upon Tyre, and later upon Egypt. But all was in accordance with the prophetic Word. And we may be certain that just as the prophecies that have to do with the past have been literally fulfilled, so will every prophecy that has to do with the future be fulfilled in due time.

While executing judgment on Egypt, God had not forgotten His promise to restore Israel in the future to Himself. The last verse reiterates this promise and assures us that the day will come when the house of Israel shall bud forth and the people of Jehovah will be recognized in the earth as those to whom has been committed the Word of the Lord.

Chapter Thirty Details Of Egypt's Judgment

In this chapter the prophet continues to declare the word of the Lord concerning the judgments which were to come upon Egypt, all of which were fulfilled in due time.

"The word of Jehovah came again unto me, saying, Son of man, prophesy, and say, Thus saith the Lord Jehovah: Wail ye, Alas for the day! For the day is near, even the day of Jehovah is near; it shall be a day of clouds, a time of the nations. And a sword shall come upon Egypt, and anguish shall be in Ethiopia, when the slain shall fall in Egypt; and they shall take away her multitude, and her foundations shall be broken down. Ethiopia, and Put, and Lud, and all the mingled people, and Cub, and the children of the land that is in league, shall fall with them by the sword"—vers. 1-5.

"Alas for the day!" The day referred to was the day in which Jehovah was to use Nebuchadnezzar and his armies to chastise the people of the land of Egypt for their idolatry and corruption. It was to be a day of clouds, and it was called specifically "a time of the nations." This expression is very much like the one used by our Lord in Luke 21:24, where He tells us that "Jerusalem shall be trodden down of the Gentiles, until the times of the Gentiles be fulfilled." While the two terms seem at first sight to be similar, the context in each instance shows that they have a very different application. The time of the nations here in Ezekiel was the time when judgment was to fall upon the nations surrounding the land of Palestine—the nations with which the people of Israel had trafficked for years, and from some of which they had suffered greatly. In Luke 21:24 the Lord uses the expression, "the times of the Gentiles," to cover the entire period during which Palestine, the city of Jerusalem, and the people of the Jews, are under Gentile domination. This began with the rise of Nebuchadnezzar, and is still in progress, and will continue until the day when the Lord Himself appears from heaven in His glorious second advent to execute judgment upon the nations and to set up His own heavenly kingdom over all this lower universe.

The sword of Nebuchadnezzar was to come upon Egypt, and not only upon Egypt, but also upon the lands contiguous to it, Ethiopia, Put, and all the mingled people, and Cub—these are all lands bordering upon Egypt according to their ancient names. Ethiopia alone still retains the name it had at that time. In addition, judgment was to fall upon the children of the land that is in league, or, as the margin of the Revised Version gives it, the children of "the land of the covenant." This undoubtedly refers to the Jews who had fled from Palestine and settled in the land of Egypt, hoping thereby to find relief from the troublesome times that had fallen upon their own country, but their hope was in vain. In looking to Egypt for help they trusted in a bruised reed.

"Thus saith Jehovah: They also that uphold Egypt shall fall; and the pride of her power shall come down: from the tower of Seveneh shall they fall in it by the sword, saith the Lord Jehovah. And they shall be desolate in the midst of the countries that are desolate; and her cities shall be in the midst of the cities that are wasted. And they shall know that I am Jehovah, when I have set a fire in Egypt, and all her helpers are destroyed. In that day shall messengers go forth from before Me in ships to make the careless Ethiopians afraid; and there shall be anguish upon them, as in the day of Egypt: for, lo, it cometh"—vers. 6-9.

The Lord now proceeds to mention definitely certain cities and sections of the land of Egypt against which His judgment was to be executed in order that the pride of her power might be destroyed. All the way from Migdol to Seveneh (from "the tower" to Seveneh) the people were to fall by the sword. These two places mentioned are at the northern and southern extremities of upper Egypt. This entire part of the land was to become desolate and her cities wasted; thus should the Egyptians know that they had to deal with the Eternal One, Jehovah, whom they had defied in years gone by. Messengers would go from them to the careless Ethiopians who were allies of Egypt at this time. Because of the almost inaccessible character of their country, they dwelt in utter indifference to the conflicts going on elsewhere, but the fall of Egypt would be to them a serious omen, foretelling the desolation coming upon their own land.

"Thus saith the Lord Jehovah: I will also make the multitude of Egypt to cease, by the hand of Nebuchadnezzar king of Babylon. He and his people with him, the terrible of the nations, shall be brought in to destroy the land; and they shall draw their swords against Egypt, and fill the land with the slain. And I will make the rivers dry, and will sell the land into the hand of evil men; and I will make the land desolate, and all that is therein, by the hand of strangers: I, Jehovah, have spoken it"—vers. 10-12.

By the overrunning of the armies of the King of Babylon, the multitude of Egypt would be made to cease. The terrible Chaldean conquerors would not draw their sword against Egypt in vain, but through them the land was to be filled with the slain. Moreover, providential judgments were to fall upon the country itself so that the rivers, that is, the streams of the Delta, would be made dry, and the land sold into the hands of evil men; thus should it become desolate and strangers inherit what once belonged to the Egyptians. There could be no way of escape, for Jehovah Himself had spoken it.

"Thus saith the Lord Jehovah: I will also destroy the idols, and I will cause the images to cease from Memphis; and there shall be no more a prince from the land of Egypt: and I will put a fear in the land of Egypt. And I will make Pathros desolate, and will set a fire in Zoan, and will execute judgments upon No. And I will pour My wrath upon Sin, the stronghold of Egypt; and I will cut off the multitude of No. And I will set a fire in Egypt: Sin shall be in great anguish, and No shall be broken up; and Memphis shall have adversaries in the daytime. The young men of Aven and of Pibeseth shall fall by the sword; and these cities shall go into captivity. At Tehaphnehes also the day shall withdraw itself, when I shall break there the yokes of Egypt, and the pride of her power shall cease in her: as for her, a cloud shall cover her, and her daughters shall go into captivity. Thus will I execute judgments upon Egypt; and they shall know that I am Jehovah"—vers. 13-19.

From early days Egypt had been a land of idolatry, and her great images have remained throughout the centuries as the memorials of her false religion. Against these idols, which really represented

179

demons as we know, God's heavy judgments were to be executed. Memphis, or Noph, was one of the leading cities devoted to such worship. Its vast temples and colossal images were among the greatest in the world, but God declared He would cause these things of nought to cease. And in that connection we are told, "There shall be no more a prince from the land of Egypt." This prophecy was soon literally fulfilled. When the dynasty then ruling Egypt died out there was never again a genuine Egyptian king ruling over the land. The Ptolemies who were strangers from the outside came in later, but even they were destroyed eventually; and through all the years since to the present day no prince of Egyptian blood has ever ruled that land. Egypt has a king, but King Fuad was not an Egyptian but an Albanian, and his son now reigning is not of real Egyptian blood.

Pathros, which is usually the name for upper Egypt in the prophetic writings, was to be made desolate, and a fire kindled in Zoan. Zoan is generally supposed to be identical with the land of Goshen where the people of Israel dwelt. Upon a portion of this land, in which was situated the capital of the shepherd kings of the Hyksos rulers, God's sore judgments fell in the days of His controversy with the king who knew not Joseph.

No is No-Amon or Thebes, another great center of idolatry. Upon this, too, God's judgment was to fall, so that Thebes was to become but an empty ruin. God declared, "I will cut off the multitude of No." His wrath was to be poured upon Sin, which is generally identified with Pelusium. All these cities were utterly ruined, and today men look with wonder on the evidences of their former greatness, and perhaps few realize that their present condition is the result of divine indignation against them.

The young men of Aven and of Pibeseth, or Bubastis, were also to fall by the sword, and the people in the cities to be carried into captivity. At Tehaphnehes where many of the Jews congregated, the power of Egypt was to be broken and a cloud cover her, and her daughters go into captivity. In this way was God to execute His judgments upon Egypt that men might know that He was Jehovah God.

In the last section of the chapter, from verse 20 to the end, the Lord makes it plain that whatever efforts Egypt might make to strengthen itself against Babylon, they would be in vain.

"And it came to pass in the eleventh year, in the first month, in the seventh day of the month, that the word of Jehovah came unto me, saying, Son of man, I have broken the arm of Pharaoh king of Egypt; and, lo, it hath not been bound up, to apply healing medicines, to put a bandage to bind it, that it be strong to hold the sword. Therefore thus saith the Lord Jehovah: Behold, I am against Pharaoh king of Egypt, and will break his arms, the strong arm, and that which was broken; and I will cause the sword to fall out of his hand. And I will scatter the Egyptians among the nations, and will disperse Lhem through the countries. And I will strengthen the arms of the king of Babylon, and put My sword in his hand: but I will break the arms of Pharaoh, and he shall groan before him with the groanings of a deadly wounded man. And I will hold up the arms of the king of Babylon; and the arms of Pharaoh shall fall down; and they shall know that I am Jehovah, when I shall put My sword into the hand of the king of Babylon, and he shall stretch it out upon the land of Egypt. And I will scatter the Egyptians among the nations, and disperse them through the countries; and they shall know that I am Jehovah"— vers. 20-26.

Pharaoh and his hosts had been completely defeated by the Chaldeans and retreated to Egypt. Pharaoh had endeavored to rebuild his army and to fit it for another trial of strength with the Babylonian leader, but God Himself declared that He was against Pharaoh, whom He likened to a man with a broken arm, endeavoring to stand against a powerful foe. Whatever efforts he might make to defend himself would prove abortive: his armies would be destroyed, and his people would be dispersed among the nations, for God who puts up one and puts down another, was at this time using the king of Babylon as a sword in order to judge the nations with whom He had a controversy. Through Nebuchadnezzar the armies of Pharaoh would be broken, and he would cry out as a deadly wounded man, but the arms of the king of Babylon were to be upheld by God Himself until He should have executed the judgments decreed upon Egypt and the nearby nations, for it was Jehovah who had put His sword into the hand of the Chaldean leader, and that sword was not to be sheathed until the predicted doom fell upon all the land of Egypt, and the Egyptians were Scattered among the nations and dispersed through the countries, to learn in abject captivity that it was a vain thing to fight against Jehovah.

Chapter Thirty-one Assyria's Pride And Fall

In this chapter God, through His prophet, in a message given about two months later than the previous predictions, directs the attention of Pharaoh and his people to the judgment that had already fallen upon Assyria in order that Egypt might learn therefrom the folly of self-exaltation and independence of God. Assyria and Egypt had been the two greatest dominions in the world of their day prior to the meteor-like rise of the Babylonian empire. At one time it seemed as though Assyria was destined to rule the world, but that was not God's plan. The day came when this great kingdom was utterly destroyed, and Chaldea became the outstanding Asiatic power, as Egypt was the outstanding African kingdom. The same God who had dealt with Assyria was now dealing with Egypt; and He called upon Pharaoh to learn a lesson from that which had taken place in Mesopotamia in order that he himself might be humbled before God ere the predicted judgment fell in all its fury upon him.

"And it came to pass in the eleventh year, in the third month, in the first day of the month, that the word of Jehovah came unto me, saying, Son of man, say unto Pharaoh king of Egypt, and to his multitude: Whom art thou like in thy greatness? Behold, the Assyrian was a cedar in Lebanon with fair branches, and with a forest-like shade, and of high stature; and its top was among the thick boughs. The waters nourished it, the deep made it to grow: the rivers thereof ran round about its plantation; and it sent out its channels unto all the trees of the field. Therefore its stature was exalted above all the trees of the field; and its boughs were multiplied, and its branches became long by reason of many waters, when it shot them forth. All the birds of the heavens made their nests in its boughs; and under its branches did all the beasts of the field bring forth their young; and under its shadow dwelt all great nations. Thus was it fair in its greatness, in the length of its branches; for its root was by many waters. The cedars in the garden of God could not hide it; the fir-trees were not like its boughs, and the plane-trees were not as its branches; nor was any tree in the garden of God like unto it in its beauty. I made it fair

183

by the multitude of its branches, so that all the trees of Eden, that were in the garden of God, envied it"—vers. 1-9.

The Assyrians were likened to a great cedar in Lebanon with outstretched branches and a forest-like shade under which the beasts of the field might find refuge, and in whose branches the birds of the heaven might build their nests. The same figure was afterwards used of Babylon as headed up in Nebuchadnezzar; and in a somewhat different way, a similar figure was used by our Lord Jesus Christ later on to depict the great world church which was to be developed as a result of the corruption of the Church by religious politics. This is seen in the parable of the mustard tree.

Assyria included that portion of Asia in which the garden of Eden originally had its place. It was a great oasis between the two rivers, the Euphrates and the Tigris, and just as Egypt was dependent upon the Nile so was Assyria dependent upon these mighty streams.

From a small beginning a vast empire had been built up in central Asia—an empire which one might have supposed would have stood for many centuries, but when it came to the height of its power its kings were so inflated with a sense of their own superiority and so carried away by their dependence upon their false gods that Jehovah dealt with them in judgment; and Nineveh and all the great cities of Assyria fell before vast floods and invading armies. Thus Babylon came to the front soon to assume world-dominion. Let Egypt learn from the fate of Assyria the folly of vaunting itself against God.

"Therefore thus said the Lord Jehovah: Because thou art exalted in stature, and he hath set his top among the thick boughs, and his heart is lifted up in his height; I will even deliver him into the hand of the mighty one of the nations; he shall surely deal with him; I have driven him out for his wickedness. And strangers, the terrible of the nations, have cut him off, and have left him: upon the mountains and in all the valleys his branches are fallen, and his boughs are broken by all the watercourses of the land; and all the peoples of the earth are gone down from his shadow, and have left him. Upon his ruin all the birds of the heavens shall dwell, and all the beasts of the field shall be upon his branches; to the end that none of all the trees by the waters exalt themselves in their stature, neither set their top among the thick boughs, nor that their mighty ones stand up in their height, even all that drink water: for they are all delivered unto death, to the nether parts of the earth, in the midst of the children of men, with them that go down to the pit"—vers. 10-16.

In this particular section God speaks retrospectively. Some have thought that these verses apply directly to Egypt inasmuch as Assyria had already fallen to rise no more until the coming day when this great kingdom will be revived under Messiah's reign to share with Israel and with Egypt in the glory of Christ's earthly kingdom. Of this we read in Isaiah 19:24. It seems clear that the prophet is still directing the attention of Pharaoh to that which God had wrought in connection with Assyria in order that he might learn a much-needed lesson as to his own utter inability to fight successfully against Jehovah. These verses depict the judgment that came on Assyria and carry us on to the doom of its leaders in the unseen world. We read, "They are all delivered unto death, to the nether parts of the earth, in the midst of the children of men, with them that go down to the pit."

God had declared in Psalm 9:17, "The wicked shall be turned into hell, and all the nations that forget God." Hell here is not the lake of fire, the final doom of the unsaved, but it is the same as Hades in the New Testament, the place of departed spirits awaiting the final day of judgment. In that dark abode can be found all who have fought against God and died unrepentant, and all who have lived in neglect of His Holy Word and forgotten their obligations to walk in obedience to the revelation He has given. There are those who insist that Sheol is but the grave; but it speaks of something deeper far than any tomb. Men may build sepulchers and possess them themselves, but Sheol is the abode of the spirits that have to do with God after the death of the body. Verses 15 to 17 confirm this.

"Thus saith the Lord Jehovah: in the day when he went down to Sheol I caused a mourning: I covered the deep for him, and I restrained the rivers thereof; and the great waters were stayed;

185

and I caused Lebanon to mourn for him, and all the trees of the field fainted for him. I made the nations to shake at the sound of his fall, when I cast him down to Sheol with them that descend into the pit; and all the trees of Eden, the choice and best of Lebanon, all that drink water, were comforted in the nether parts of the earth. They also went down into Sheol with him unto them that are slain by the sword; yea, they that were his arm, that dwelt under his shadow in the midst of the nations"—vers. 15-17.

The nations that had been in alliance with Assyria were struck dumb with astonishment and made to tremble in fear as those at the head of that mighty dominion were cut off with the sword and went down under divine judgment into Sheol—there to await the day when they would answer before God for their arrogant pride.

The reference to the trees of Eden has to do, as intimated, with the fact that the location of Eden as given in Genesis was the same as that of Assyria afterward. No people had been able to stand against Nebuchadnezzar. Destroyed by the triumphant Chaldean armies they, too, went down into Sheol with Assyria, unto those who before them had been slain by the sword. What hope then had Egypt to withstand the power of the Chaldeans when it was God Himself who had decreed that they should be used to visit judgment upon all nations!

"To whom art thou thus like in glory and in greatness among the trees of Eden? Yet shalt thou be brought down with the trees of Eden unto the nether parts of the earth: thou shalt lie in the midst of the uncircumcised, with them that are slain by the sword. This is Pharaoh and all his multitude, saith the Lord Jehovah"—ver. 18.

Let Pharaoh learn from what had taken place in Asia and understand that however he might seek to guard against destruction, so long as he lifted himself up against the God of Israel he but exposed himself to the same doom as that which had overtaken Assyria. This, says the prophet, is Pharaoh and all his multitude, for they, too, must suffer in the same way as their great sister kingdom.

Chapter Thirty-two Jehovah's Lamentations Over Egypt

God's judgments are reserved for individuals and nations which refuse to acknowledge His authority. As of old He sent message after message to Pharaoh through Moses, only to have the haughty monarch harden his heart against His entreaties, until at last judgment had to fall, so in the case that we have had before us in these last few chapters, God gave one warning after another through Ezekiel, which we may be certain were conveyed in some way to Pharaoh, the proud, insolent Egyptian ruler; but they brought forth no response, unless indeed, like his predecessor of so long ago, he became all the more set in his attitude of independence of God.

Finally, the last messages were given before the judgment fell; and these messages, it will be noted, take the form of lamentations because Pharaoh, like Israel in a later day, knew not the time of his visitation. Our Lord's lamentation over Jerusalem was the expression of the heart of God over an unrepentant people, and such lamentations come before us here.

"And it came to pass in the twelfth year, in the twelfth month, in the first day of the month, that the word of Jehovah came unto me, saying, Son of man, take tip a lamentation over Pharaoh king of Egypt, and say unto him, Thou wast likened unto a young lion of the nations: yet art thou as a monster in the seas; and thou didst "break forth with thy rivers, and troubledst the waters with thy feet, and fouledst their rivers. Thus saith the Lord Jehovah: I will spread out My net upon thee with a company of many peoples; and they shall bring thee up in My net. And I will leave thee upon the land, I will cast thee forth upon the open field, and will cause all the birds of the heavens to settle upon thee, and I will satisfy the beasts of the whole earth with thee. And I will lay thy flesh upon the mountains, and fill the valleys with thy height. I will also water with thy blood the land wherein thou swimmest, even to the mountains; and the watercourses shall be full of thee. And when I shall extinguish thee, I will cover the heavens, and make the stars thereof dark; I will cover the sun with a cloud, and the moon shall not give its light. All the bright lights of heaven will I make dark over thee, and set darkness upon thy land, saith the Lord Jehovah. I will also vex the hearts of many peoples, when I shall bring thy destruction among the nations, into the countries which thou hast not known. Yea, I will make many peoples amazed at thee, and their kings shall be horribly afraid for thee, when I shall brandish My sword before them; and they shall tremble at every moment, every man for his own life, in the day of thy fall"—vers. 1-10.

It is noticeable that the first message recorded in this chapter was given in the twelfth year and the twelfth month, considerably more than a year-and-a-half from the time of the last prophecy. Ezekiel was commanded to take up a lamentation over Pharaoh, in which he was likened now not to a crocodile in the river, as previously, but to a young lion rearing himself up in his savage independence of spirit, and seeking to destroy the nations that were leagued against him. He is also likened to a great sea monster, possibly a whale, which had entered into the Nile and was slashing about in its waters, troubling them so that they were foul and unfit for drink. Against him Jehovah was to spread out a net, thus rendering him helpless when the foe came upon him.

It is an interesting fact that even at this present time, various African tribes when hunting the lion, the leopard, and other savage creatures, try to get them into a den or hut of some kind where the hunters can surround them completely with a net; for they have a saying, "The beasts know not the wisdom of the net." The beasts become so bewildered and entangled that they are then dispatched easily. Thus it was with Pharaoh. All his efforts to recoup his fortunes were to prove vain; and in due time he was to be ignominiously defeated, and his people subjugated to his foe. The land should be watered with the blood of the slain in that day. God said He would cover the heavens and make the stars dark, veil the sun with a cloud, and so arrange it that the moon should not give its light. All the bright lights of heaven were to be darkened, and the whole land covered with gloom.

This prophecy is very interesting and helps us to understand similar prophecies concerning the judgments that are to fall upon the world in the last days. It is very evident that these words were not to be taken literally, but they indicated the destruction of delegated authority and the gloom that would settle down upon the hearts of men because of the ruin that was to fall upon the land.

Not only would judgment be visited upon the Egyptians, but upon many peoples who were allied with them, destruction was to come. While other nations standing afar off and hearing of the terrible defeat of Pharaoh and his hosts, would be amazed and horribly afraid as they realized the seeming impregnability of such power as Nebuchadnezzar's. That it was the power of Babylon which God had in view is evidenced from the definite way in which He speaks in the next section.

"For thus saith the Lord Jehovah: The sword of the king of Babylon shall come upon thee. By the swords of the mighty will I cause thy multitude to fall; the terrible of the nations are they all: and they shall bring to nought the pride of Egypt, and all the multitude thereof shall be destroyed. I will destroy also all the beasts thereof from beside many waters; neither shall the foot of man trouble them any more, nor the hoofs of beasts trouble them. Then will I make their waters clear, and cause their rivers to run like oil, saith the Lord Jehovah. When I shall make the land of Egypt desolate and waste, a land destitute of that whereof it was full, when I shall smite all them that dwell therein, then shall they know that I am Jehovah. This is the lamentation wherewith they shall lament; the daughters of the nations shall lament therewith; over Egypt, and over all her multitude, shall they lament therewith, saith the Lord Jehovah"—vers. 11-16.

The sword of the king of Babylon was the sword of Jehovah, for God Himself had commissioned Nebuchadnezzar to subjugate, not only Egypt but also every other nation of the civilized world of that day. Therefore the Babylonians are described as the terrible of the nations who are to bring to nought the pride of Egypt and all its multitude.

Destruction, too, would fall even upon the beasts beside the waters. These were undoubtedly the water-buffalo, the king of

Egypt, upon which the people were so dependent. God had decreed that the very means of livelihood should, temporarily at least, come to an end, so that all the nations would realize that He was dealing in judgment with them.

As He lamented over them because of their obdurate and misguided spirit, the voice of lamentation should be heard on all sides, weeping over Egypt and her multitude because God had destroyed them.

"It came to pass also in the twelfth year, in the fifteenth day of the month, that the word of Jehovah came unto me, saying, Son of man, wail for the multitude of Egypt, and cast them down, even her, and the daughters of the famous nations, unto the nether parts of the earth, with them that go down into the pit. Whom dost thou pass in beauty? Go down, and be thou laid with the uncircumcised. They shall fall in the midst of them that are slain by the sword: she is delivered to the sword; draw her away and all her multitudes. The strong among the mighty shall speak to him out of the midst of Sheol with them that help him: they are gone down, they lie still, even the uncircumcised, slain by the sword"—vers. 17-21.

Fifteen days elapsed ere this final message came through the prophet. In it he speaks specifically not only of Egypt but also of various other nations with whom God was dealing at this time. He was called upon to wail for the multitude of Egypt who were to be cast down unto the nether parts of the earth, with them that go down into the pit, as we have seen already. They had forgotten God, and therefore they were about to be turned into Sheol, their day of probation on earth having come to an end. The prophet sees them literally covering the ground as slain with the sword, but beholds the spirit going deeper down even into Sheol, there to lie with all who were unclean in the sight of God.

"Asshur is there and all her company; her graves are round about her; all of them slain, fallen by the sword: whose graves are set in the uttermost parts of the pit, and her company is round about her grave; all of them slain, fallen by the sword, who caused terror in the land of the living"—vers. 22, 23.

Upon Asshur, or Assyria, as previously noted, the judgment had fallen already. Her graves were openly manifest, and her people who once caused terror in the land of the living, had gone down into the pit. The God who had dealt with this great empire was about to exercise the fulness of His indignation against Egypt.

"There is Elam and all her multitude round about her grave; all of them slain, fallen by the sword, who are gone down uncircumcised into the nether parts of the earth, who caused their terror in the land of the living, and have borne their shame with them that go down to the pit. They have set her a bed in the midst of the slain with all her multitude; her graves are found about her; all of them uncircumcised, slain by the sword; for their terror was caused in the land of the living, and they have borne their shame with them that go down to the pit: he is put in the midst of them that are slain"—vers. 24, 25.

Elam is next mentioned, the ancient name of Persia. Nebuchadnezzar had already conquered this nation, destroyed its armies and slain vast multitudes who, with the others mentioned, had gone down into the lower parts of the earth; that is, into the pit, or Sheol. No longer would Elam be a terror to other nations. She was powerless before the might of Nebuchadnezzar's army.

"There is Meshech, Tubal, and all their multitude; their graves are round about them; all of them uncircumcised, slain by the sword; for they caused their terror in the land of the living. And they shall not lie with the mighty that are fallen of the uncircumcised, that are gone down to Sheol with their weapons of war, and have laid their swords under their heads, and their iniquities are upon their bones; for they were the terror of the mighty in the land of the living. But thou shalt be broken in the midst of the uncircumcised, and shalt lie with them that are slain by the sword"—vers. 26-28.

Meshech and Tubal, of whom we are to learn more later when we come to chapters 38 and 39, were the names of tribes that had descended from Japheth, as we learn in Genesis 10. According to the most ancient records that have come down to us, they dwelt in the region bordering on the Black Sea, and at one time evidently they were people of some renown, but their encampments had been destroyed, and the slain had gone down to Sheol with their weapons of war. They were buried with these weapons under their heads, as became mighty warriors. But all their might proved unavailing against the Babylonian armies. Those who escaped fled farther north, for later on we find them in history as a nomadic people dwelling north of the Black Sea, and ranging from there to the region of the Caspian Sea. Eventually they were absorbed into the great Russian empire. Some have thought even that the names Meshech and Tubal are practically preserved for us in the two great cities of Moscow in Europe, and Tobolsk in Siberia.

"There is Edom, her kings and all her princes, who in their might are laid with them that are slain by the sword: they shall lie with the uncircumcised, and with them that go down to the pit. There are the princes of the north, all of them, and all the Sidonians, who are gone down with the slain; in the terror which they caused by their might they are put to shame; and they lie uncircumcised with them that are slain by the sword, and bear their shame with them that go down to the pit"—vers. 29, 30.

Edom, related intimately to Israel as we have seen, descending from Jacob's twin brother Esau, had rejoiced when they saw the sons of Jacob in adversity, but God had punished them by means of the same power that was wreaking vengeance upon the Jews. The princes of Edom, on the southeast of Palestine, and the Sidonians, a Phoenician people on the north, had been destroyed also. Their might availed nothing; they were put to shame, and they lay dead with others who had refused to obey the voice of Jehovah.

"Pharaoh shall see them, and shall be comforted over all his multitude, even Pharaoh and all his army, slain by the sword, saith the Lord Jehovah. For I have put his terror in the land of the living; and he shall be laid in the midst of the uncircumcised, with them that are slain by the sword, even Pharaoh and all his multitude, saith the Lord Jehovah"—vers. 31, 32.

God brought these various nations before Pharaoh, indicating their doom, that he might know the day would soon come when he and his armies would join them in their utter defeat and destruction. They had simply gone into Sheol a little ahead; Pharaoh and his people would soon be with them there. Thus should the judgment of God be visited upon all the nations roundabout Palestine that had refused to heed the voice of His prophets.

With this chapter this particular section of the book of Ezekiel comes to a close.

Part III, The Moral Condition Of Israel Exposed, And The Promise Of A Future Restoration To God And To Their Land (chs 33-39)

Chapter Thirty-three
The Divine Government And Man's Responsibility

No attentive reader can fail to notice the similarity between this chapter and portions of chapter 3 and all of chapter 18. One might wonder why the duplication of instruction, but we may be very sure of this: when God repeats Himself it is in order that His truth may be impressed upon our hearts and minds. It is so easy to forget divine principles and to let slip the teaching of any portion of God's Holy Word. Repetition is recognized among pedagogues generally as an important process for impressing certain lessons upon the student's mind. And so when we find repetition in the Holy Scriptures we may well give the passages in question our most careful consideration, realizing that God had something very important to communicate, or He would not have duplicated it, as in the case of Pharaoh's dreams, and the visions of Daniel. When a thing is repeated it is in order to assure us of its great importance and absolute certainty.

We have already noticed, in considering chapter 18, that the principles set forth in these portions do not in any sense picture the grace of God as revealed in the gospel. They have to do definitely with man under the government of God, and particularly in the legal dispensation. God had given His holy law and declared that the man who walked in obedience to it should live long on the earth; whereas he who disobeyed would bring judgment upon himself, and his days on earth would be cut short. But even under law there was provision for repentance. If a man turned to God and abjured his evil ways and sought to walk carefully before Him,

God extended mercy and did not immediately execute judgment upon him.

These principles come out clearly in the present chapter.

"And the word of Jehovah came unto me, saying, Son of man, speak to the children of thy people, and say unto them, When I bring the sword upon a land, and the people of the land take a man from among them, and set him for their watchman; if, when he seeth the sword come upon the land, he blow the trumpet, and warn the people; then whosoever heareth the sound of the trumpet, and taketh not warning, if the sword come, and take him away, his blood shall be upon his own head. He heard the sound of the trumpet, and took not warning; his blood shall be upon him; whereas if he had taken warning, he would have delivered his soul. But if the watchman see the sword come, and blow not the trumpet, and the people be not warned, and the sword come, and take any person from among them; he is taken away in his iniquity, but his blood will I require at the watchman's hand. So thou, son of man, I have set thee a watchman unto the house of Israel; therefore hear the word at My mouth, and give them warning from Me. When I say unto the wicked, O wicked man, thou shalt surely die, and thou dost not speak to warn the wicked from his way; that wicked man shall die in his iniquity, but his blood will I require at thy hand. Nevertheless, if thou warn the wicked of his way to turn from it, and he turn not from his way; he shall die in his iniquity, but thou hast delivered thy soul"— vers. 1-9.

This first section is almost the same as chapter 3:16-21. Once more God emphasized the responsibility of the watchman placed upon the walls of a city in order that he might see the approach of any hostile army and blow the trumpet to warn the people that they might not be taken unawares by the foe. If the watch- man does his part and the people fail to take warning, he has delivered his own soul, and the people themselves will be responsible for their own destruction. But if he fails to give the warning and the people are taken unawares and destroyed by the enemy, the watchman will be held responsible. The blood of the inhabitants of that city will be upon him.

There is surely a very solemn lesson for all of us here who know the danger to which this poor godless world is exposed. We are called upon by God to seek to arouse men to flee from the wrath to come. If they refuse to take warning we have delivered our souls, but if, knowing that the judgment of God is against all who do evil, we fail to sound the trumpet of alarm and men and women are left to die in their sins, there will be a solemn accounting for us at the judgment-seat of Christ. Paul was able to say, in addressing the Ephesian elders, "I take you to record this day, that I am pure from the blood of all men" (Acts 20:26). So faithful had he been in giving the message that the responsibility was thrown entirely upon his hearers. We might well seek to emulate him.

Ezekiel himself had been set by God to be a watchman to the house of Israel. It was for him to hear the Word at the mouth of Jehovah and give the people warning. As he set forth the principles of the divine government, if men took heed, then God would turn away the sword of judgment; if they refused, as indeed had been the case in so many instances since Ezekiel began to prophesy, then they themselves were responsible for the loss of their own souls, but Ezekiel was free. He had carried out the will of God, and in doing this he had met the requirements of a faithful watchman.

"And thou, son of man, say unto the house of Israel: Thus ye speak, saying, Our transgressions and our sins are upon us, and we pine away in them; how then can we live? Say unto them, As I live, saith the Lord Jehovah, I have no pleasure in the death of the wicked; but that the wicked turn from his way and live: turn ye, turn ye from your evil ways; for why will ye die, O house of Israel? And thou, son of man, say unto the children of thy people, The righteousness of the righteous shall not deliver him in the day of his transgression; and as for the wickedness of the wicked, he shall not fall thereby in the day that he turneth from his wickedness; neither shall he that is righteous be able to live thereby in the day that he sinneth. When I say to the righteous, that he shall surely live; if he trust to his righteousness, and commit iniquity, none of his righteous deeds shall be remembered; but in his iniquity that he hath committed, therein shall he die. Again, when I say unto the wicked, Thou shalt surely die; if he turn from his sin, and do that which is lawful and right; if the wicked restore the pledge, give again that which he had taken by robbery, walk in the statutes of life, committing no iniquity; he shall surely live, he shall not die. None of his sins that he hath committed shall be remembered against him: he hath done that which is lawful and right; he shall surely live"—vers. 10-16.

Here, as in chapter 18, the principle is laid down that no man need consider himself in a hopeless condition because he has failed in the matter of obedience to the law of God. While he is rightly under condemnation because of sin, yet the Lord has no pleasure in the death of the wicked but desires that all men should turn from their evil ways and live. So He entreats those who have gone astray, saying, "Turn ye, turn ye from your evil ways; for why will ye die, O house of Israel?" If men thus turned, God would have mercy on them.

On the other hand, no one was entitled to glory in his own righteousness, or to become careless after a life of obedience to the law. His righteousness did not deliver him if he turned away from the law and took the path of transgression: he would fall in his own wickedness in the day that he sinned. He who trusted in his own past righteousness and congratulated himself on his good record, and so allowed himself to become careless in the future, would have to learn in bitterness of soul that he had to do with One who demanded of him continued obedience to the law that He had given. But if once more he recognized the error of his ways and turned back to God, seeking to walk obediently, the Lord declared he should not surely die, but because of his reformation of life the past would be remitted, and he would live before God here on the earth.

It should be clearly seen that this is not a question of the salvation of the soul; it is not a matter of redemption by the blood of Christ, such as we have in the New Testament. It sets forth God's dealings with men under law, in accordance with the principles of His government over the earth.

Many in Israel, failing to realize this, blamed God for the disasters that had come upon them, forgetting that He was judging them for their own sins. Notice how they dared to put the blame on the Lord rather than to acknowledge their own failures.

"Yet the children of thy people say, The way of the Lord is not equal: hut as for them, their way is not equal. When the righteous turneth from his righteousness, and committeth iniquity, he shall even die therein. And when the wicked turneth from his wickedness, and doeth that which is lawful and right, he shall live thereby. Yet ye say, The way of the Lord is not equal. O house of Israel, I will judge you every one after his ways"—vers. 17-20.

Man is always prone to try to find some excuse for his own failures and to make another responsible for the ills that come upon him. It was so with Adam in the very beginning. Instead of frankly acknowledging his own waywardness, he sought to put the blame upon God by declaring, "The woman whom *Thou* gavest to be with me, she gave me of the tree, and I did eat." Adam was not merely blaming his wife; the sin was far greater than that: it was impugning the wisdom of God in giving him that wife. So Israel, failing to recognize that their own iniquities had brought judgment upon them, impudently threw the blame back on God as they said, "The way of the Lord is not equal." God's ways are just and right; it was their way that was unequal, and this they needed to learn.

The remaining part of this chapter forms a distinct section in which we have the messages that came to Ezekiel when some of his prophecies were being fulfilled concerning the destruction of Jerusalem.

"And it came to pass in the twelfth year of our captivity, in the tenth month, in the fifth day of the month, that one that had escaped out of Jerusalem came unto me, saying, The city is smitten. Now the hand of Jehovah had been upon me in the evening, before he that was escaped came; and He had opened my mouth, until he came to me in the morning; and my mouth was opened, and I was no more dumb"—vers. 21, 22.

Year after year Ezekiel had been declaring that no human power would be able to protect Jerusalem against the onslaught of the Babylonians, nor would God Himself interfere to deliver the city where He of old had set His name. Its iniquities and manifold crimes had reached unto heaven, and judgment must ensue.

At last in the twelfth year of the captivity and the tenth month, word was brought by one who had escaped out of Jerusalem to bring the information, that the city had been smitten and all hope of its deliverance was at an end. This was sad news indeed to those who had dwelt in Chaldea. They had cherished the hope that, after all, Jerusalem might withstand the siege and that God would intervene to give His people victory over the invader, but now they knew that their hope had been in vain.

Before the messenger came, Ezekiel's spirit had been greatly disturbed, evidently as God was preparing him for the word he was to receive on the morrow. He sat as one dumb throughout the evening before the messenger reached him. When at last in the morning he was informed as to what had actually taken place, his mouth was opened, and he spoke again in the name of Jehovah, rebuking those who had self-confidently counted on being delivered soon from bondage and returning to take possession of the land.

"And the word of Jehovah came unto me, saying, Son of man, they that inhabit those waste places in the land of Israel speak, saying, Abraham was one, and he inherited the land: but we are many; the land is given us for inheritance. Wherefore say unto them, Thus saith the Lord Jehovah: Ye eat with the blood, and lift up your eyes unto your idols, and shed blood: and shall ye possess the land? Ye stand upon your sword, ye work abomination, and ye defile every one his neighbor's wife: and shall ye possess the land? Thus shalt thou say unto them, Thus saith the Lord Jehovah: As I live, surely they that are in the waste places shall fall by the sword; and him that is in the open field will I give to the beasts to be devoured; and they that are in the strongholds and in the caves shall die of the pestilence. And I will make the land a desolation and an astonishment; and the pride of her power shall cease; and the mountains of Israel shall be desolate, so that none shall pass through. Then shall they know that I am Jehovah, when I have made the land a desolation and an astonishment, because of all their abominations which they have committed"— vers. 23-29.

They had said Abraham was but a single person and yet to him God gave the land; they were many: surely the land should be theirs for an inheritance. But Ezekiel reproved them in the name of Jehovah for the sins they had committed. They violated the law by eating with the blood, and by idolatrous practices; innocent blood was shed and there was no repentance; corruption of life, such as characterized the heathen, marked them as those who had thrown off all allegiance to the law of God: therefore, the Lord gave them over to fall by the sword. Let them defend themselves if they could; He refuses to aid them. He had given their land up to become a desolation and an astonishment, and they were to be slain or to go into captivity.

"And as for thee, son of man, the children of thy people talk of thee by the walls and in the doors of the houses, and speak one to another, every one to his brother, saying, Come, I pray you, and hear what is the word that cometh forth from Jehovah. And they come unto thee as the people cometh, and they sit before thee as My people, and they hear thy words, but do them not; for with their mouth they show much love, but their heart goeth after their gain. And, lo, thou art unto them as a very lovely song of one that hath a pleasant voice, and can play well on an instrument; for they hear thy words, but they do them not. And when this cometh to pass (behold, it cometh), then shall they know that a prophet hath been among them"—vers. 30-33.

To Ezekiel God spoke as with His friend. He reminded him how the people to whom he ministered professed admiration for him and his messages, and yet secretly reviled him and spoke against him, having no intention of obeying the word that he proclaimed. They seemed interested in hearing his words, saying one to another, "Come, I pray you, and hear what is the word that cometh forth from Jehovah." But they had no intention of obeying that word. With their mouths they showed much love, but their hearts were set upon covetousness. Ezekiel was to them as one singing a very lovely song with a pleasant voice, and playing well upon an instrument. They delighted in his eloquence and the forceful way in which he presented his messages, but like so many today who can admire a preacher and revel in his utterances, and yet give no heed to his words, so the people of Israel went on in the path of disobedience and refused to take anything seriously that came from the lips of the prophet. When at last the judgments in all their horror fell upon them God declared that they should know a prophet had been among them, but then it would be too late to deliver their souls by heeding his words.

Chapter Thirty-four
The True Shepherd Of Israel Contrasted With The False

The present chapter contains Jehovah's invective against the unworthy and selfish shepherds of Israel, whose one great concern was to take advantage of every opportunity to enrich themselves at the expense of the flock. There is no date given for this particular prophecy; it may have followed immediately after those we have been considering. From early times kings and governors as well as ecclesiastical leaders, such as priests and prophets, were designated "shepherds." Our word "pastor" is just the Latin for shepherd. In all ages it has pleased God to place upon certain men the responsibility of ministering to and caring for the temporal and spiritual needs of their fellows. Where this service is performed in the fear of God and out of love for the people of his flock, it brings rich reward, as we see in 1 Peter 5:1-4, where the faithful pastor is promised a crown of glory at the appearing of Jesus Christ.

Jehovah Himself is pictured as the Shepherd of His people in many places in the Old Testament. We need hardly remind our readers of the beauty of the twenty-third Psalm, with its opening verse, "The Lord is my shepherd; I shall not want." Then again in Psalm 80:1, "Give ear, O Shepherd of Israel, Thou that leadest Joseph like a flock"; Isaiah uses the same figure in 40:11, "He shall feed His flock like a shep- herd"; and Jeremiah, in 31:10, tells how Jehovah will keep Israel "as a shepherd doth his flock." It is prophesied of Messiah that He will be a faithful Shepherd who will be raised up in the land of Palestine (Zech. 11:16). When our Lord actually appeared among men He announced Himself as the Good Shepherd that giveth His life for the sheep. All His hearers would understand that He meant thereby to declare Himself the promised Deliverer, the Messiah of Israel. Here Ezekiel is commissioned by God to give a solemn warning to the selfish shepherds.

"And the word of Jehovah came unto me, saying, Son of man, prophesy against the shepherds of Israel, prophesy, and say unto them, even to the shepherds, Thus saith the Lord Jehovah: Woe unto the shepherds of Israel that do feed themselves! Should not the shepherds feed the sheep? Ye eat the fat, and ye clothe you with the wool, ye kill the fatlings; but ye feed not the sheep. The diseased have ye not strengthened, neither have ye healed that which was sick, neither have ye bound up that which was broken, neither have ye brought back that which was driven away, neither have ye sought that which was lost; but with force and with rigor have ye ruled over them. And they were scattered, because there was no shepherd; and they became food to all the beasts of the field, and were scattered. My sheep wandered through all the mountains, and upon every high hill: yea, My sheep were scattered upon all the face of the earth; and there was none that did search or seek after them"—vers. 1-6.

The shepherds were the leaders of the people in things both civil and religious. Corruption was everywhere rife among them. They had no real concern for the sheep of the flock; they took advantage of every possible opportunity to enrich themselves, and cared nothing about those for whom they should have had deep concern: they did not minister to the diseased nor to those who were sick, neither did they care for any who were maimed or injured in other ways; nor did they seek after those who had gone astray, as the shepherd is pictured doing in the fifteenth of Luke. They ruled the people with force and rigor, and as a result when the enemy appeared the sheep were terrified and scattered abroad and soon became food to all the beasts of the field: that is, beast-like Gentile powers. How tender the expression used by the Lord in verse 6 where He bewails the sheep wandering through all the mountains and upon every high hill with none to seek after or care for them. Such has been the condition of Israel ever since the dispersion, and will be until in a coming day they return to the Shepherd and Bishop of their souls.

"Therefore, ye shepherds, hear the word of Jehovah: As I live, saith the Lord Jehovah, surely forasmuch as My sheep became a prey, and My sheep became food to all the beasts of the field, because there was no shepherd, neither did My shepherds search for My sheep, but the shepherds fed themselves, and fed not My sheep;

therefore, ye shepherds, hear the word of Jehovah: Thus saith the Lord Jehovah, Behold, I am against the shepherds; and I will require My sheep at their hand, and cause them to cease from feeding the sheep; neither shall the shepherds feed themselves any wore; and I will deliver My sheep from their mouth, that they may not be food for them"—vers. 7-10.

Since these shepherds had been so faithless to their trust the Lord Himself would deal with them. He had taken note of all their evil ways; He saw how they fed themselves and left the people to starve: therefore, He declared He was against these evil shepherds, and would require His sheep at their hand. What a solemn accounting it would be when they would have to answer before His judgment-bar for failing to fulfil the responsibilities He had laid upon them. He would deliver His sheep out of their hand, and deal with them for their perfidy. Surely such words as these may be well taken to heart by any who today are in the position of leaders among God's people and yet fail to feed the flock committed to them, or to seek after those who have gone astray. Nor need we think only of ecclesiastical leaders, for it is God who has given authority to magistrates, and He holds them responsible to consider themselves as having been entrusted with authority in order that they may exercise it for the good of the nation as a whole. Where it is otherwise His judgment is certain to fall.

But if these shepherds are faithless the Lord Himself abideth true, as we see in verses 11 to 16.

"For thus saith the Lord Jehovah: Behold, I Myself, even L will search for My sheep, and will seek them out. As a shepherd seeketh out his flock in the day that he is among his sheep that are scattered abroad, so will I seek out My sheep; and I will deliver them out of all places whither they have been scattered la the cloudy and dark day. And I will bring them out from the peoples, and gather them from the countries, and will bring them into their own land; and I will feed them upon the mountains of Israel, by the watercourses, and in all the inhabited places of the country. I will feed them with good pasture; and upon the mountains of the height of Israel shall their fold be: there shall they lie down in a good fold; and on fat pasture shall they feed upon the mountains of Israel. I Myself will be the Shepherd of My sheep, and I will cause them to lie down, saith the Lord Jehovah. I will seek that which was lost, and will bring back that which was driven away, and will bind up that which was broken, and will strengthen that which was sick: but the fat and the strong I will destroy; I will feed them in justice"—vers. 11-16.

Jehovah Himself will search for His sheep and seek them out. As a shepherd endeavoring to gather together his dispersed flock, He will seek for them individually and deliver them out of all places where they have been scattered in the dark and cloudy day. Then together He will bring them out from the nations and gather them from the various countries in which they have been oppressed, and will bring them as a renewed nation into their own land: that is, the land of Palestine, where He will shepherd them upon the mountains of Israel, and cause that land once more to bring forth abundantly for their blessing.

It is the height of folly to attempt to spiritualize such a passage as this and make it apply only to God's gracious dealings with His people today. It is clear that the same nation that has been scattered is the nation that will be gathered again when God's due time comes. Then, indeed, He will feed them with good pasture, and on the heights of Israel they will find their fold and rejoice in the goodness of the Lord.

Note the definiteness of His language, "I Myself will be the Shepherd of My sheep, and I will cause them to lie down." Charles H. Spurgeon has well said, "One would think even a poor silly sheep would have sense enough to lie down when weary, but alas, with the sheep of Christ's flock it is often otherwise." David declared, "He maketh me to lie down in green pastures"; and here Jehovah says, "I will cause them to lie down." He will seek after those that are lost, and will bring back those that have been driven away; He will bind up those that have been maimed, and will strengthen those that were sick; but the self-sufficient and the strong will be disappointed in that day when He shepherds His sheep in righteousness.

"And as for you, O My flock, thus saith the Lord Jehovah: Behold, I judge between sheep and sheep, the rams and the he-goats. Seemeth it a small thing unto you to have fed upon the good pasture, but ye must tread down with your feet the residue of your pasture? and to have drunk of the clear waters, but ye must foul the residue with your feet? And as for My sheep, they eat that which ye have trodden with your feet, and they drink that which ye have fouled with your feet"—vers. 17-19.

Not all who profess to be the Lord's sheep are actually numbered among His own; so He distinguishes between those who truly trust Him and those who do not. He will judge those who, instead of enjoying the still waters and the green pastures, tread down the latter and defile the former, thus making them unfit for the true people of Jehovah to eat and drink.

May we not see in the behavior of those who spurn the truth of God and ridicule the testimony of Holy Scripture, a sample of this very thing today: they befoul that which means so much to the hungry and thirsty people of Christ's flock. Because of such behavior judgment is sure to fall.

"Therefore thus saith the Lord Jehovah unto them: Behold, I, even I, will judge between the fat sheep and the lean sheep. Because ye thrust with side and with shoulder, and push all the diseased with your horns, till ye have scattered them abroad; therefore will I save My flock, and they shall no more be a prey; and I will judge between sheep and sheep. And I will set up one shepherd over them, and he shall feed them, even My servant David; he shall feed them, and he shall be their shepherd. And I, Jehovah, will be their God, and My servant David prince among them; I, Jehovah, have spoken it"—vers. 20-24.

In the day when everyone's work shall be made manifest, the Lord will judge between those who are genuine and those who are unreal; He will hold responsible those who have had anything to do with turning His own away from Himself, and will save the flock that they shall no more be a prey to their enemies. This refers undoubtedly to the time when the remnant of Israel will be gathered back to the land of Palestine, when they shall look on

Him whom they have pierced and shall mourn for Him "as one mourneth for his only son, and shall be in bitterness for him, as one that is in bitterness for his firstborn" (Zech. 12:10). Then the Lord shall set up one shepherd over them— His servant David: that is, great David's greater Son, our Lord Jesus Christ, the one true Shepherd of Israel. Then indeed they will know in reality that Jehovah is their God, and the Prince of David's house will be recognized as the promised Messiah.

"And I will make with them a covenant of peace, and will cause evil beasts to cease out of the land; and they shall dwell securely in the wilderness, and sleep in the woods. And I will make them and the places round about My hill a blessing; and I will cause the shower to come down in its season; there shall be showers of blessing. And the tree of the field shall yield its fruit, and the earth shall yield its increase, and they shall be secure in their land; and they shall know that I am Jehovah, when I have broken the bars of their yoke, and have delivered them out of the hand of those that made bondmen of them. And they shall no more be a prey to the nations, neither shall the beasts of the earth devour them; but they shall dwell securely, and none shall make them afraid. And I will raise up unto them a plantation for renown, and they shall be no more consumed with famine in the land, neither bear the shame of the nations any more. And they shall know that I, Jehovah their God, am with them, and that they, the house of Israel, are My people, saith the Lord Jehovah. And ye My sheep, the sheep of My pasture, are men, and I am your God, saith the Lord Jehovah"—vers. 25-31.

In the day of Israel's restoration to God and to the land, the Lord will recognize them as His covenant people, He Himself becoming their Protector, so that no harm will touch them in the future; evil beasts will cease out of the land, and they will dwell securely even in the wilderness or the forest; and He will order everything necessary for their welfare. No longer will the land suffer for lack of moisture: the former and the latter rains, as another prophet has told us, will be given in their season, and there shall be showers of blessing. These words have made an appeal to many hearts and spoken loudly of both spiritual and tem- poral mercies which God delights to send for the refreshment of His trusting people. We sing even today:

"There shall be showers of blessing:

This is the promise of love;

There shall be seasons refreshing,

Sent from the Saviour above."

We are thinking particularly of spiritual blessings. In that coming day God will vouchsafe blessing to Israel, both material and spiritual, which will give them to rejoice in His goodness and praise Him for His loving-kindness. All the blessings that were promised of old to those who kept His law will be given to them in that day because of the covenant of grace. The yoke of their enemies will be broken off their necks, and they will be delivered out of the hand of the Gentiles under whose bondage they have suffered for so long. No more will they be ruthlessly hunted down by haughty and contemptuous nations, but they shall dwell securely in their own land with none to make them afraid. The evils that they have had to meet throughout the centuries will trouble them no more, and Jehovah their God will be with them and will rejoice over them in that day of His power.

The last verse makes this perfectly clear, and explains fully the parable of the Shepherd and the sheep. Jehovah says, "Ye My sheep, the sheep of My pasture, are men, and I am your God."

Chapter Thirty-five
The Doom Of Edom

Under divine direction Ezekiel now turns to deliver a message against Mount Seir and the land of Edom. Mount Seir is definitely identified with Edom in Genesis 32:3. It was the inheritance of those who were descended from Esau (Genesis 36:8). As the Edomites were so closely related to Israel, God forbade His people to lift up the sword against them (Deut. 23:7) when they were on their way from Kadesh-Barnea to the east side of the Jordan. They were commanded definitely not to fight with the children of Esau but to ask permission to pass through their territory on the main highway. This permission the Edomites refused, and so the Israelites were obliged to take a much longer route compassing the land of Edom in order to obtain their goal. But while the Israelites sought carefully to obey the command of God in regard to their brethren, the Edomites, the latter manifested from the beginning a very different spirit toward their brethren. They not only joined at times with Israel's enemies in seeking to wreak havoc upon them, but even if they stood by and took no part in the border conflicts that prevailed so frequently, they nevertheless rejoiced in every setback that Israel had and gloried in the victories of their enemies. All this was under the eye of God, and stirred His heart to indignation: therefore, the prophets Isaiah, Jeremiah, Obadiah, and Ezekiel pronounced God's judgment upon Edom and the entire land of Idumea, as it was later known.

We turn then to consider the present chapter which pronounces judgment on this haughty and idolatrous people.

"Moreover the word of Jehovah came unto me, saying, Son of man, set thy face against mount Seir, and prophesy against it, and say unto it, Thus saith the Lord Jehovah: Behold, I am against thee, O mount Seir, and I will stretch out My hand against thee, and I will make thee a desolation and an astonishment. I will lay thy cities waste, and thou shalt be desolate; and thou shalt know that I am Jehovah. Because thou hast had a perpetual enmity, and hast given over the children of Israel to the power of the sword in the time of their calamity, in the time of the iniquity of the end;

therefore, as I live, saith the Lord Jehovah, I will prepare thee unto blood, and blood shall pursue thee: since thou hast not hated blood, therefore blood shall pursue thee. Thus will I make mount Seir an astonishment and a desolation; and I will cut off from it him that passeth through and him that returneth. And I will fill its mountains with its slain: in thy hills and in thy valleys and in all thy watercourses shall they fall that are slain with the sword. I will make thee a perpetual desolation, and thy cities shall not be inhabited; and ye shall know that I am Jehovah"—vers. 1-9.

Jehovah was against Mount Seir, the land which He had given to Esau, because of the attitude that its people had taken toward Israel. Therefore, He was about to stretch out His hand against the land and make it a desolation and an astonishment. The cities were to be laid waste and to become utterly desolate—a prophecy that has been literally fulfilled. As we have noticed, Edom had been a perpetual enemy against the children of Israel; not only had they themselves taken up the sword against their blood-brothers, but also they had joined with others in seeking to prevent their escape when attacked by cruel foes. In retributive judgment, the mountains, hills, and valleys of the land of Edom were to be filled with its slain by the sword. Their cities, of which Petra and Teman were the chief, were to be made desolate perpetually, and left uninhabited in order that Jehovah might be manifested as the One whose word cannot be turned aside. Students of history know how exactly this prophecy has been fulfilled.

For some centuries after Ezekiel uttered these words Edom continued as a subject country, dominated first by Babylon, then by Medo-Persia, and later, in 126 B. C, it was conquered by John Hycranus of the Maccabee family. He forced the Idumeans, who remained alive, to become Jews. When Jerusalem was destroyed by the Romans, and the Jews were scattered throughout the world, the remnant of Edom absolutely disappeared. It is impossible to find a person whose Edomite ancestry can be identified today; but their cities remain, as predicted by Obadiah (ver. 18), and Jeremiah (49:13). One may walk through the streets of these desolate Edomite cities, particularly Petra, and enter into the houses where the frescoes on the walls are as brilliant as if painted yesterday, but there are no inhabitants. God's word has been fulfilled to the letter. By and by when the Lord Jesus returns to reign as King and Israel will be restored to Himself, their land will include that of Edom, but the Edomites themselves will never again appear in history.

"Because thou hast said, These two nations and these two countries shall he mine, and we will possess it; whereas Jehovah was there: therefore, as I live, saith the Lord Jehovah, I will do according to thine anger, and according to thine envy which thou hast showed out of thy hatred against them; and I will make Myself known among them, when I shall judge thee. And thou Shalt know that I, Jehovah, have heard all thy revilings which thou hast spoken against the mountains of Israel, saying, They are laid desolate, they are given us to devour. And ye have magnified yourselves against Me with your mouth, and have multiplied your words against Me: I have heard it. Thus saith the Lord Jehovah: When the whole earth rejoiceth, I will make thee desolate. As thou didst rejoice over the inheritance of the house of Israel, because it was desolate, so will I do unto thee: thou shalt he desolate, O mount Seir, and all Edom, even all of it; and they shall know that I am Jehovah"—vers. 10-15.

It is evident that as Edom saw the plight into which Israel had fallen they considered it their opportunity to attempt to conquer the land of Palestine, and thus unite the two nations; and in a certain sense, this is exactly what occurred temporarily, although as we have seen it was Israel who conquered Edom, but it was an Edomite who reigned over the two nations. Because of this spirit of envy and hatred, Jehovah would make Himself known to Edom. They had gone far from Him and fallen into the vilest kind of idolatry. He would judge them for their wickedness and visit their sin upon them; thus they should know that Jehovah had spoken, and that He had heard all their revilings against the mountains of Israel. Edom rejoiced to see Israel made a desolation, and declared that they had been given to them to devour. They had magnified themselves against the Lord in thus speaking against the Jews. His ear had heard their boastings, and His heart was stirred on behalf of His people. He declared that when at last the whole earth should be made to rejoice: that is, when the kingdom of God should be set up in power, Edom would remain desolate. As they rejoiced over the inheritance of the house of Israel when it became desolate, so God will visit their iniquities upon them, and there should be another desolation—a desolation from which they should never recover.

There is surely a serious lesson for all who are guilty of what is commonly called anti-Semitism, as we contemplate this solemn prophecy. In spite of all their sins and mistakes the people of Israel are beloved for the fathers' sake, and God takes note of every hand lifted in opposition to them and of every voice that is raised in ridicule or contumely against the people whom He called out to be His peculiar treasure. Their failures do not warrant our joining with any people in helping to make conditions worse for them. Rather should we seek to do what we can to alleviate their grief and help to bring them to a saving knowledge of our Lord Jesus Christ. Otherwise we may depend upon it that He who judged Edom because of its attitude toward Israel, will not overlook similar conduct on the part of Gentiles today, even though they be professing Christians.

Chapter Thirty-six Born Of Water And Of The Spirit

We have seen already that Israel's glorious future as a nation settled in the land of Palestine under Messiah's beneficent and righteous rule, depends primarily upon the return of the remnant to God. Not until they are regenerated by the Spirit and the Word will they be prepared to enter into fulness of blessing. This comes out very clearly in the present chapter. Undoubtedly our blessed Lord had this portion of Scripture in mind when, after informing Nicodemus of the importance of new birth by water and the Spirit, He gently reproved him for his ignorance in not knowing these things; for had he but apprehended the teaching given here he would have understood what the Saviour meant when He spoke of the new birth of water and of the Spirit in order that one might enter into the kingdom of God.

The first part of our chapter has to do with the coming restoration of the people to the land—a restoration which, as we know, has begun even now, although in unbelief, and will never bring settled peace to Israel until they return in heart to the Lord Himself.

"And thou, son of man, prophesy unto the mountains of Israel, and say, Ye mountains of Israel, hear the word of Jehovah. Thus saith the Lord Jehovah: Because the enemy hath said against you, Aha! and, The ancient high places are ours in possession; therefore prophesy, and say, Thus saith the Lord Jehovah: Because, even because they have made you desolate, and swallowed you up on every side, that ye might be a possession unto the residue of the nations, and ye are taken up in the lips of talkers, and the evil report of the people; therefore, ye mountains of Israel, hear the word of the Lord Jehovah: Thus saith the Lord Jehovah to the mountains and to the hills, to the watercourses and to the valleys, to the desolate wastes and to the cities that are forsaken, which are become a prey and derision to the residue of the nations that are round about; therefore thus saith the Lord Jehovah: Surely in the fire of My jealousy have I spoken against the residue of the nations, and against all Edom, that have appointed My land unto themselves for a possession with the joy of all their heart, with despite of soul, to cast it out for a prey. Therefore prophesy concerning the land of Israel, and say unto the mountains and to the hills, to the watercourses and to the valleys, Thus saith the Lord Jehovah: Behold, I have spoken in My jealousy and in My wrath, because ye have borne the shame of the nations: therefore thus saith the Lord Jehovah: I have sworn, saying, Surely the nations that are round about you, they shall bear their shame"—vers. 1-7.

Observe that in this message the prophet is commanded to address himself directly to the mountains of Israel: that is, he speaks rather to the land itself than to the people, and this of course that the people may learn from his message what God has in store for Palestine in the latter days. In the light of what has happened within the last thirty years we can almost apply these words literally to the present time, but they will have a more complete fulfilment later on. Already has that land, which lay desolate so long, begun to answer to the description given in this chapter of what God is yet to do for it.

Throughout the long centuries of Gentile dominion Palestine has been made desolate; the enemies of Israel have swallowed her up on every side, and one great power after another has dominated the land of which Jehovah said so long ago, "The land shall not be sold for ever: for the land is Mine" (Lev. 25:23). Babylonian, Medo-Persian, Grecian, Egyptian, Syrian, Roman, Turk, and other powers have fought for possession of Palestine. God has taken note of all the bitter enmity that these nations have manifested toward Israel, and He will never overlook the manner in which they have made Palestine a prey. Their attitude toward the land of the people of Jehovah's choice has stirred the fire of His jealousy, so that He has declared His judgments against all nations that seek to take possession of that land and bring His people into bondage. He has sworn in His indignation and concern for Israel, that as they have borne the shame of the nations so the nations themselves, who have been the cause of Israel's distress, should be put to shame in the coming day of the Lord. At that time the land will be freed from the treading down of the Gentiles, and the remnant of Israel will return to it, a chastened and repentant people.

"But ye, O mountains of Israel, ye shall shoot forth your branches, and yield your fruit to My people Israel; for they are at hand to come. For, behold, I am for you, and I will turn unto you, and ye shall be tilled and sown; and I will multiply men upon you, all the house of Israel, even all of it; and the cities shall be inhabited, and the waste places shall be builded; and I will multiply upon you man and beast; and they shall increase and be fruitful; and I will cause you to be inhabited after your former estate, and will do better unto you than at your beginnings: and ye shall know that I am Jehovah. Yea, I will cause men to walk upon you, even My people Israel; and they shall possess thee, and thou shalt be their inheritance, and thou shalt no more henceforth bereave them of children. Thus saith the Lord Jehovah: Because they say unto you, Thou land art a devourer of men, and hast been a bereaver of thy nation; therefore thou shalt devour men no more, neither bereave thy nation any more, saith the Lord Jehovah; neither will I let thee hear any more the shame of the nations, neither shalt thou bear the reproach of the peoples any more, neither shalt thou cause thy nation to stumble any more, saith the Lord Jehovah"—vers. 8-15.

Still addressing the mountains of Israel, Ezekiel predicts that in God's due time great forests shall once more cover them and orchards yield their fruit to the people of Israel, for they are at hand to come.

For two millennia the mountains of Israel have to a great extent been denuded of their forests, only a few groves have remained of the once famous cedars of Lebanon, but during the past three decades, under the British mandate, a great movement has been set on foot for the reforestation of the mountains, and millions of trees have been planted—all this in preparation for the coming back to their own land of God's ancient people.

If we did not know that God has something more for Israel than simply her restoration as a nation, we might think that these verses are now having a complete fulfilment. That which we see is in perfect accord with what is presented here, but it is simply a beginning of that which God has in mind, and which will have complete fulfilment after the great tribulation is past and Messiah has appeared in glory. Then the city shall be inhabited, and the waste places shall be builded. That land which lay desolate, a great desert with just here and there a fruitful oasis, will increase in abundance with orchards, vineyards, dairy farms and other evidences of the divine pleasure. At the present time such renewed conditions are the wonder of the world, but we must remember that the time of Jacob's trouble is in the future. Much that is being done will be undone because .of the wars that are to ravage that land in the time of the end; but eventually all will be literally fulfilled as indicated here, and Israel shall possess their former inheritance and never again be bereaved of her children.

Because of the manifold conflicts in which Palestine has been involved, the nations have considered it a devourer of men, and it has seemed as though there was no possibility of Israel's rehabilitation, but God's Word is sure, and He will see that every prophecy is fulfilled to the letter. In the coming day of glory the land shall be able to sustain in abundant measure a great population who, through the entire kingdom age, will flourish in peace and happiness. The nations of the world will no longer reproach Israel nor cause them to stumble, but will recognize the fact that they are indeed the people of Jehovah.

All their past sufferings and those which they are yet to undergo in that awful hour of the great tribulation when the vials of the wrath of God will be poured out upon the earth, are the result of the sins to which they have given themselves.

"Moreover the word of Jehovah came unto me, saying, Son of man, when the house of Israel dwelt in their own land, they denied it by their way and by their doings: their way before Me was as the uncleanness of a woman in her impurity. Wherefore I poured out My wrath upon them for the blood which they had poured out upon the land, and because they had defiled it with their idols; and I scattered them among the nations, and they were dispersed through the countries: according to their way and according to their doings I judged them. And when they came unto the nations, whither they went, they profaned My holy name; in that men said of them, These are the people of Jehovah, and are gone forth out of his land. But I had regard for My holy name, which the house of Israel had profaned among the nations, whither they went"— vers. 16-21.

When God gave Palestine to Israel in the beginning, He warned them against following after the customs of the nations out of which He had delivered them, and of those nations that surrounded their territory, but they paid no heed to this, and so the land became defiled by their evil ways and their wicked actions. Because of this, God poured out His wrath upon them. Innocent blood had been shed in libation to their idols, thus defiling the land even more: therefore God gave them a baptism of blood in righteous retribution. He scattered them among the nations and dispersed them through the lands of the earth, judging them according to their evil ways. When thus scattered among the Gentiles, instead of returning in heart to Him, they profaned His holy name, even as the Apostle Paul tells us in the Epistle to the Romans, "The name of God is blasphemed among the Gentiles through you" (2:24). Though they had thus dishonored Him, He still preserved His watch over them and made it impossible for their enemies to destroy them utterly.

"Therefore say unto the house of Israel, Thus saith the Lord Jehovah: I do not this for your sake, O house of Israel, but for My holy name, which ye have profaned among the nations, whither ye went. And I will sanctify My great name, which hath been profaned among the nations, which ye have profaned in the midst of them; and the nations shall know that I am Jehovah, saith the Lord Jehovah, when I shall be sanctified in you before their eyes. For I will take you from among the nations, and gather you out of all the countries, and will bring you into your own land. And I will sprinkle clean water upon you, and ye shall be clean: from all your filthiness, and from all your idols, will I cleanse you. A new heart also will I give you, and a new spirit will I put within you; and I will take away the stony heart out of your flesh, and I will give you a heart of flesh. And I will put My Spirit within you, and cause you to walk in My statutes, and ye shall keep Mine ordinances, and do them. And ye shall dwell in the land that I gave to your fathers; and ye shall be My people, and I will be your God. And I will save you from all your uncleannesses: and I will call for the grain, and will multiply it, and lay no famine upon you. And I will multiply the fruit of the tree, and the increase of the field, that ye may receive no more the reproach of famine among the nations. Then shall ye remember your evil ways, and your doings that were not good; and ye shall loathe yourselves in your own sight for your iniquities and for your abominations"—vers. 22-31.

Not for their own sake was Jehovah to act but for the glory of His holy name which they had profaned. In order to sanctify that great name He pledged Himself to carry out the promise of restoration. When the day comes that His Word in this regard is fulfilled all nations will recognize the fact that Jehovah has kept His covenant, and thus His name will be sanctified before their eyes. Note the particularity of the promises in regard to their regeneration. The Lord has declared, "I will take you from among the nations, and gather you out of all the countries, and will bring you into your own land." Then in accordance with our Lord's words to Nicodemus, He declares, "I will sprinkle clean water upon you, and ye shall be clean: from all your filthiness, and from all your idols." We know from other scriptures that this refers to the washing of water by the Word. In Psalm 119:9 we read, "Wherewithal shall a young man cleanse his way? By taking heed thereto according to Thy word." When that Word is received by Israel and takes effect, it will result in the cleansing of their ways and thus fit them to enter again into fellowship with God.

"A new heart," He says, "will I give you," and "a new spirit will I put within you." This is the new birth of which Jesus spoke to Nicodemus. Had Nicodemus been as careful a student of the Prophets as his profession implied, being a doctor of the law, he would not have been bewildered when Jesus spoke of being born of water and of the Spirit. He would have understood that the Word of God was to be applied to the hearts and consciences of the people in the power of the Holy Spirit. The stony heart of unbelief would be taken from them, and God would give them a heart of flesh. Moreover, He promised to put His own Spirit within them and cause them to walk in His statutes and delight in His ordinances. Just as truly as Scripture teaches the second coming of Christ so it predicts the second coming of the Holy Spirit. He came at Pentecost to baptize believers into one Body and to dwell in the Church, empowering it for testimony. He will be poured out from on high in the day of Israel's restoration, and will indwell the regenerated people who will then be gathered back to their land, never more to be rooted out of it. In that day God will own them as His people, and He will be their God. The Lo-Ammi sentence of Hosea 1:9 will then be repealed, and those whom He refused to acknowledge as His own during the long dispersion will be recognized by Him again when they have come back to Him in confession of sin and recognition of His righteousness. Thus, they will be saved from all their uncleannesses, and it will be the delight of Jehovah to pour out upon them every temporal mercy as well as spiritual blessing: then they will look back over the years of their wanderings, and as they remember their evil ways and their doings, they will loathe themselves in their own sight because of these iniquities and abominations.

"Not for your sake do I this, saith the Lord Jehovah, be it known unto you: be ashamed and confounded for your -ways, O house of Israel. Thus saith the Lord Jehovah: In the day that I cleanse you from all your iniquities, I will cause the cities to be inhabited, and the waste places shall be builded. And the land that was desolate shall be tilled, whereas it was a desolation in the sight of all that passed by. And they shall say, This land that was desolate is become like the garden of Eden; and the waste and desolate and ruined cities are fortified and inhabited. Then the nations that are left round about you shall know that I, Jehovah, have builded the ruined places, and planted that which was desolate: I, Jehovah, have spoken it, and I will do it"—vers. 32-36.

All God's dealings in regard to Israel's future blessing will be in pure grace; nothing will be on the ground of merit, for they have merited only judgment. They will be ashamed and confounded as they reflect on their failures and His manifold mercies. The Lord will show by His care for them in temporal things how fully He has cleansed them from their iniquities and forgiven all their sins.

Their cities will be inhabited; their waste places will be built; their former desolate lands will be covered with fruitful farms and orchards; and the nations that once looked upon them with contempt will exclaim with amazement as they behold the land that was once desolate, and as they see formerly ruined cities rebuilt and inhabited, "It is become like the garden of Eden." It is an unimpeachable testimony to the power and the faithfulness of Jehovah the God of Israel, who never calls back His word, but who declares, "I, Jehovah, have spoken it, and I will do it."

"Thus saith the Lord Jehovah: For this, moreover, will I he inquired of by the house of Israel, to do it for them: I will increase them with men like a flock. As the flock for sacrifice, as the flock of Jerusalem in her appointed feasts, so shall the waste cities be filled with flocks of men; and they shall know that I am Jehovah"— vers. 37, 38.

In view of these manifold promises of future blessing, God would have His people Israel take all these things to heart and turn to Him even now, confessing their sin and looking to Him to hasten the fulfilment of His Word. This should ever be the effect of prophetic testimony upon the soul. It was never the thought of God simply to occupy the people with future events, what we might call the political aspect of prophetic fulfilment, but rather that the promises made might exercise the heart of those who read them and humble them before God, turning them to Him in contrition of heart and confession of sin, that thus they might enter even now into the reality of the blessedness of iniquities forgiven, and fellowship with God enjoyed.

Chapter Thirty-seven The Valley Of Dry Bones

This vision brings before us the spiritual condition of Israel nationally during all the long centuries of the dispersion. Having turned away from God they are characterized no longer, as a people, by divine life. Not only has blindness in part happened to them so that they find it difficult, even when reading their own Scriptures, to discern the mind of God, but also they are actually dead in trespasses and in sins, as are the Gentiles whom once they despised, because of their ignorance of the law and of the true God.

In vision Ezekiel found himself set down in a deep valley filled with dry bones. He says:

"The hand of Jehovah was upon me, and He brought me out in the Spirit of Jehovah, and set me down in the midst of the valley; and it was full of bones. And He caused me to pass by them round about: and, behold, there were very many in the open valley; and, lo, they were very dry. And He said unto me, Son of man, can these bones live? And I answered, O Lord Jehovah, Thou knowest. Again He said unto me, Prophesy over these bones, and say unto them, O ye dry bones, hear the word of Jehovah. Thus saith the Lord Jehovah unto these bones: Behold, I will cause breath to enter into you, and ye shall live. And I will lay sinews upon you, and will bring up flesh upon you, and cover you with skin, and put breath in you, and ye shall live; and ye shall know that I am Jehovah"—vers. 1-6.

Commanded by Jehovah to look all about him, he noticed that in every part of the valley these bones were seen, and they were very many and very dry; in other words, there was not the slightest evidence of spiritual life. Then came the question, asked by God Himself, "Son of man, can these bones live?" Surely none but He who asked the question could answer it. So far as human power is concerned it must have seemed impossible that they would ever be revived. As we come in contact with individual Israelites today we find that the most discouraging work in the world is that of trying to bring them to a saving knowledge of their own Messiah, our Lord Jesus Christ. So utterly dead are they to the great truths of their own Scriptures that it is only as the Spirit of God moves upon them that they can apprehend in any sense these tremendous verities. We are told in the New Testament, "It pleased God by the foolishness" (or the simplicity) "of preaching to save them that believe" (1 Cor. 1:21). And so Ezekiel was commanded to prophesy over these bones: that is, to proclaim the message of God, saying to them, "O ye dry bones, hear the word of Jehovah." He Himself declared that the day would come when He would cause breath to enter into them and they should live, for He would put sinews upon them and bring flesh upon them, and cover them with skin, and put breath in them, that they might once more respond to His love and know that He is Jehovah. We are reminded of the prayer of David in Psalm 119:25, "Quicken Thou me according to Thy word"; and the Lord Jesus has told us, "The words that I speak unto you, they are spirit, and they are life" (John 6:63). So when the life-giving Word goes forth in the energy of the Holy Spirit even poor, dead, dry Israelites will be revived and will know that God has spoken.

Immediately upon hearing the divine command Ezekiel began to prophesy or preach to the bones, and the results were manifest at once.

"So I prophesied as I was commanded: and as I prophesied, there was a noise, and, behold, an earthquake; and the hones came together, bone to its bone. And I beheld, and lo, there were sinews upon them, and flesh came up, and skin covered them above; but there was no breath in them. Then said he unto me, Prophesy unto the wind, prophesy, son of man, and say to the wind, Thus saith the Lord Jehovah: Come from the four winds, O breath, and breathe upon these slain, that they may live. So I prophesied as He commanded me, and the breath came into them, and they lived, and stood up upon their feet, an exceeding great army"— vers. 7-10.

As Ezekiel proclaimed the word there was a noise as of thunder and a tremendous shaking of the earth; and then, before the prophet's startled eyes, the bones came together, each one fitted to the other, until they formed complete human skeletons. In another moment sinews and flesh came upon them and skin covered them, and they became perfect human bodies, but there was no breath or life in them. Again the word of the Lord came to the prophet, saying, "Prophesy unto the wind, prophesy, son of man, and say to the wind, Thus saith the Lord Jehovah: Come from the four winds, O breath, and breathe upon these slain, that they may live." So far as I have been able to discern this is the only place in sacred Scripture where we have prayer addressed directly to the Holy Spirit. Ordinarily, as we see in Eph. 2:18, prayer is by or in the energy of the Spirit to the Father in the name of the Son; but here we have a definite case where one was commanded to speak directly to the Holy Spirit, for the term "wind" here can mean no other than He who is the blessed life-giving Spirit of God. It is He who quickens the dead; and in answer to this prayer, breath came into these resurrected bodies, and they stood up upon their feet an exceeding great army.

We need to remember that all this was in vision and is not to be taken as referring to a literal physical resurrection of the dead. That Scripture does teach such a resurrection—in fact, two resurrections: one of the just, and the other of the unjust—is perfectly clear; but that is not what is contemplated here. This is rather a fulfilment in vision of what is predicted in Daniel 12:2, "Many of them that sleep in the dust of the earth shall awake, some to everlasting life, and some to shame and everlasting contempt." These words might be applied to the two resurrections just referred to: the one before, and the other after the millennial reign of our Lord Jesus Christ, but the connection in which they are found in Daniel 12 makes it evident, in my judgment, that the resurrection there depicted is a national resuscitation, such as we have in our present chapter.

For long centuries Israel has been a dead nation, sleeping among the Gentiles. In the day of Jehovah's power, they will be brought out from their graves, gathered from the countries into which they have been dispersed, and appear as an exceeding great host: those in whose hearts faith is found entering into everlasting life, and those who refuse to believe the message of that day given over to shame and everlasting contempt.

The explanation of Ezekiel's vision is given very clearly in the next few verses:

"Then He said unto me, Son of man, these bones are the whole house of Israel: behold, they say, Our bones are dried up, and our hope is lost; we are clean cut off. Therefore prophesy, and say unto them, Thus saith the Lord Jehovah: Behold, I will open your graves, and cause you to come up out of your graves, O My people; and I will bring you into the land of Israel. And ye shall know that I am Jehovah, when I have opened your graves, and caused you to come up out of your graves, O My people. And I will put My Spirit in you, and ye shall live, and I will place you in your own land: and ye shall know that I, Jehovah, have spoken it and performed it, saith Jehovah"—vers. 11-14.

The identification is complete. These bones are the whole house of Israel. In their distress they have said, "Our bones are dried up, and our hope is lost; we are clean cut off." But they are yet to learn that Jehovah has better things in store for them: He is going to open their graves; that is, cause them to come up out of the condition in which they have been for so long as scattered over the world, suffering under the hand of the Gentiles, and He will bring them into the land of Israel. Then indeed they shall know that they have to do with Jehovah when He has renewed them as a nation and delivered them from the hopeless condition that has been theirs for so long. At that time, as we have seen in the previous chapter, they will be regenerated as a people. God will put His own Spirit within them, and they shall live, and He will place them securely in their own land, thus fulfilling all that He has spoken concerning them.

"The word of Jehovah came again unto me, saying, And thou, son of man, take thee one stick, and write upon it, For Judah, and for the children of Israel his companions: then take another stick and write upon it, For Joseph, the stick of Ephraim, and for all the house of Israel his companions: and join them for thee one to another into one stick, that they may become one in thy hand. And when the children of thy people shall speak unto thee, saying, Wilt thou not show us what thou meanest by these? say unto them, Thus saith the Lord Jehovah: Behold, I will take the stick of Joseph, which is in the hand of Ephraim, and the tribes of Israel his companions; and I will put them with it, even with the stick of Judah, and make them one stick, and they shall be one in My hand. And the sticks whereon thou writest shall be in thy hand before their eyes. And say unto them, Thus saith the Lord Jehovah: Behold, I will take the children of Israel from among the nations, whither they are gone, and will gather them on every side, and bring them into their own land: and I will make them one nation in the land, upon the mountains of Israel; and one king shall be king to them all; and they shall be no more two nations, neither shall they be divided into two kingdoms any more at all; neither shall they defile themselves any more with their idols, nor with their detestable things, nor with any of their transgressions; but I will save them out of all their dwelling-places, wherein they have sinned, and will cleanse them: so shall they be My people, and I will be their God"—vers. 15-23.

Following the death of Solomon the nation had been divided into two parts, the northern kingdom going by the name of Israel, and the southern kingdom by the name of Judah. That difference continued until the dispersion of both peoples, but when God restores them to Himself again the two houses of Israel will be united in one, nevermore to be separated. So the prophet was commanded to take sticks, or pilgrim rods, and to write upon one the name Judah, and upon the other the name Israel. These were to be joined one to another so that both could be held with a single hand; and in this way he was to picture the union of the two kingdoms in the coming day. When the people of the captivity inquired of him what was meant by his carrying the two sticks in one hand thus united to each other, he was to declare the truth that God had revealed to him, and tell them that Jehovah had said He would take the children of Israel from among the nations whither they had gone, and gather them on every side, and bring them into their own land, and make them one nation in that land upon the mountains of Israel, and set one king over them all. Moreover, they would be divided no more into two kingdoms; nor should they be denied by idolatry and other detestable things, but they would be saved in the Lord with an everlasting salvation, and cleansed from their sins, and openly acknowledged by God as His people, even as they would own Him as their God.

This is the glorious future which, according to the universal testimony of the Prophets, is yet in store for Israel. In that day Messiah, the Son of David, will be recognized as their King and Shepherd.

"And My servant David shall be king over them; and they all shall have one shepherd: they shall also walk in Mine ordinances, and observe My statutes, and do them. And they shall dwell in the land that I have given unto Jacob My servant, wherein your fathers dwelt; and they shall dwell therein, they, and their children, and their children's children, for ever: and David My servant shall be their prince for ever. Moreover I will make a covenant of peace with them; it shall be an everlasting covenant with them; and I will place them, and multiply them, and will set My sanctuary in the midst of them for evermore. My tabernacle also shall be with them; and I will be their God, and they shall be My people. And the nations shall know that I am Jehovah that sanctifieth Israel, when My sanctuary shall be in the midst of them for evermore"—vers. 24-28.

"My servant David," God says, "shall be king over them." I do not understand this to mean that David himself will be raised and caused to dwell on the earth as king. Some have thought this. It may be true, but it seems to me as one considers other scriptures, that the implication is that He who was David's Son, the Lord Jesus Christ Himself, is to be the King, and thus David's throne will be re-established. The Lord Jesus, when here on earth, declared Himself to be the Good Shepherd, and spoke of the gathering together of the children of God scattered abroad, and said there should be one flock. This is true now concerning Jews and Gentiles who put their trust in Him; it will be true also in millennial days when He will feed His flock like a shepherd, and those of Israel and those from among the Gentiles will together own His righteous sway and rejoice in His shepherd care. No man will then rebel against the law of God, but they will walk in obedience to His ordinances and observe His statutes, glorying in the fact that they belong to Him. Nor shall they ever again be driven out of the land which God gave by covenant to Abraham, Isaac, and Jacob. They shall dwell in the land with none to make them afraid, and under the benign sway of Messiah, the Son of David, who will be their Prince forever, they will delight in obedience to God. At that time a covenant of peace will be made with the people in accordance with God's promise through Jeremiah, to confirm a new covenant with Israel and Judah; this will be an everlasting covenant with no possibility of its ever being broken because of the fact that it will be a covenant of pure grace. The blood of that covenant has been shed already on Calvary's cross, but not until the time of the end will Israel come into the good of it. Then after restoration to God and to their land, Jehovah will set His sanctuary in the midst of them. When He brought them out of Egypt He put into their hearts the desire to make a dwelling-place for Him that He might live among them. The tabernacle in the wilderness was such a dwelling-place but only for a short time. Solomon's temple was owned of God in this way but soon became defiled. When the day of restoration comes the tabernacle of the Lord will again be set up in the midst of Israel, and He will be their God, and they shall be His people. Then they will understand that He is Jehovah the Sanctifier who shall set Israel apart for Himself and dwell in the sanctuary which will be rebuilt in Palestine, never to be destroyed so long as the world lasts.

Chapter Thirty-eight A Vast Northern Confederacy Of Israel's Enemies

Chapters 38 and 39 really form one complete prophecy and have to do with a vast confederation of nations from north of the Black and Caspian Seas, extending down to Persia on the east, and to North Africa on the southwest, who in the latter days will be leagued together in a great offensive against the Jewish nation after its return to the land of Palestine. There has been much attention directed to these chapters during recent years and many idle speculations as to the exact time when these northern powers will make an onslaught upon the land of Palestine. Some consider that the complete fulfilment of the prophecy may take place at any time, even while the Church is still here on earth and the Jews are gathering back to their ancient land in unbelief. Others who have a clearer conception of the prophetic plan and recognize the fact that many Old Testament predictions of judgment have not yet been fulfilled, believe these chapters have to do largely with conditions that will prevail during the last seventieth week of Daniel's great time-prophecy, as given in his ninth chapter. To these it seems unthinkable that this prophecy should have its fulfilment during the present age, in the great parenthesis between the sixty-ninth and seventieth weeks. Some indeed whose deep insight into the prophetic Word cannot be denied, have held and taught that it would be after the Lord had actually returned and set up His kingdom in Palestine, possibly between the close of the 1290 days and the end of the 1335 days of Daniel 12, that this onslaught would take place. This seems incongruous, as the words of the Holy Spirit, "Behold, He cometh with clouds; and every eye shall see Him" (Rev. 1:7), would seem to teach us very definitely that the Lord's second advent will be visible, not only in Palestine but also in some remarkable sense throughout the whole world: therefore, one can scarcely imagine vast populations unaware that He has actually returned and set up the throne of David in Jerusalem, and their venturing to attempt to subjugate Israel's land subsequent to this glorious event.

In Zech. 14:1-4 we are told of the gathering of all nations against Jerusalem, an event which certainly takes place just prior to the manifestation of Christ as King, when His feet shall stand upon the Mount of Olives. It would seem, therefore, that these northern and eastern hordes must be included among the armies that will then invade Palestine, and therefore the onslaught depicted in this chapter will take place toward the close of the great tribulation.

It is well to remember, however, that there are doubtless many details of unfulfilled prophecy concerning which we may not have an absolutely clear understanding at the present time, but which will all become plain after the Church has been caught away from this scene and God is dealing with the remnant of Israel, whose eyes will be opened to understand their own Scriptures in a way that we perhaps cannot.

"And the word of Jehovah came unto me, saying, Son of man, set thy face toward Gog, of the land of Magog, the prince of Bosh, Meshech, and Tubal, and prophesy against him, and say, Thus saith the Lord Jehovah: Eehold, I am against thee, O Gog, prince of Bosh, Meshech, and Tubal: and I will turn thee about, and put hooks into thy jaws, and I will bring thee forth, and all thine army, horses and horsemen, all of them clothed in full armor, a great company with buckler and shield, all of them handling swords: Persia, Cush, and Put with them, all of them with shield and helmet; Gomer, and all his hordes; the house of Togarmah in the uttermost parts of the north, and all his hordes; even many peoples with thee"—vers. 1-6.

Gog is said to mean "extension," and Magog "expansion." The two terms might well indicate the ruler of a vast territory, greater perhaps than that over which anyone else holds authority. Gog is designated as the prince of Rosh, Meshech, and Tubal.

The word "Rosh" admittedly is used again and again in Scripture for head or chief; but the construction of the text here has led the revisers as well as many other translators, even one so conservative in some respects as James Moffatt, to take the word "Rosh" as indicating a country. Remembering that there are no vowels in the Hebrew, it seems that Rosh then is really that land which we know as Russia. Meshech and Tubal—names found in the book of Genesis—have been identified as the progenitors of Scythian tribes located in the region of the Black and Caspian Seas. There seems to be little reason to doubt but that these tribes were the progenitors of the peoples in both Europe and Asia, who eventually were welded into the vast Russian empire.

Russia has been dominated in late years, as we know, by a thoroughly atheistic group of leaders opposed to everything in the way of divine revelation and the recognition of spiritual realities. While the Russian people are incurably religious even to superstition, yet their leaders have, ever since the Revolution, been committed to an anti-religious program.

In the last days the final head of the Russian people will look with covetous eyes upon the great developments going on in the land of Palestine, and will determine that Russia must have her part of the wealth there produced. Consequently, we have the picture which the prophet brings before us—that of a vast army augmented by warriors from Persia, Cush, and Put, marching down toward Palestine.

Cush seems to refer to Ethiopia, but there was also a Cush in the Arabian Peninsula; it may be impossible to identify the exact people referred to until the prophecy is actually being fulfilled.

Put, or *Phut,* as it is in the Hebrew, seems to be identical with Libya in North Africa. These allied nations with all the hordes of the Cimmerians—or as the Authorized Version renders it, *Gomer,* which is generally supposed to refer to the tribes that dwelt along the Danube and the Rhine, later forming the German empire—and with the house of Togarmah, or Armenia, will become a formidable host indeed as they move on toward the mountains of Israel. To them it will seem as though the taking of that land will be an easy accomplishment, but they are to know eventually that it is not the Jews with whom they have to do but the Eternal One, the God of Israel.

In verses 7 to 9 we note the spirit that actuates them.

"Be thou prepared, yea, prepare thyself, thou, and all thy companies that are assembled unto thee, and be thou a guard unto them. After many days thou shalt be visited: in the latter years thou shalt come into the land that is brought back from the sword, that is gathered out of many peoples, upon the mountains of Israel, which have been a continual waste; but it is brought forth out of the peoples, and they shall dwell securely, all of them. And thou shalt ascend, thou shalt come like a storm, thou shalt be like a cloud to cover the land, thou, and all thy hordes, and many peoples with thee"—vers. 7-9.

It is after many days that this great confederation will be formed, in the latter years after Israel returns to the land—that is, brought back from the sword. That country which has been so long a continual waste will become prosperous because of its productive or« chards, vineyards, and dairy farms, its chemical plants, on the shores of the Dead Sea, and great manufacturing concerns, which will be developed there through Jewish ingenuity. All this will stir the cupidity of Gog and his confederates so that they shall come down like a great cloud to cover the land, determined to subject it to their own authority, but they will find soon who it is with whom they have to do.

"Thus saith the Lord Jehovah: It shall come to pass in that day, that things shall come into thy mind, and thou shalt devise an evil device: and thou shalt say, I will go up to the land of un-walled villages; I will go to them that are at rest, that dwell securely, all of them dwelling without walls, and having neither "bars nor gates; to take the spoil and to take the prey; to turn thy hand against the waste places that are now inhabited, and against the people that are gathered out of the nations, that have gotten cattle and goods, that dwell in the middle of the earth. Sheba, and Dedan, and the merchants of Tarshish, with all the young lions thereof, shall say unto thee, Art thou come to take the spoil? Hast thou assembled thy company to take the prey? to carry away silver and gold, to take away cattle and goods, to take great spoil?"— vers. 10-13.

Thinking that it will be an easy thing to subdue a people practically unarmed and dwelling in a land of unwalled villages, this great army sets forth with boldness and self-assurance, determined to enrich themselves by the spoils of Israel: however, they are to find themselves antagonized by a group of peoples who have befriended the Jew. Sheba, Dedan, and the merchants of Tarshish will be aroused and alarmed, and will prepare to come to the defense of Israel.

Sheba and Dedan doubtless refer to Arab peoples, but Tarshish is generally identified with the lands of the far west of Europe, including perhaps a part of Spain but very definitely Great Britain. It was from Tarshish of old that the Phoenicians obtained tin, and the word *Britannia* means "the land of tin," as we have noted before. Britain has for many centuries been a friend of the Jews, and possibly with the help of other nations, she will prepare to defy the armies of Gog; but that help will not be needed, for God Himself is going to deal with this vast atheistic power.

In the verses that follow we see the hosts of Gog moving on in their might, knowing not that they are simply going to their doom.

"Therefore, son of man, prophesy, and say unto Gog, Thus saith the Lord Jehovah: In that day when My people Israel dwelleth securely, shalt thou not know it? And thou shalt come from thy place out of the uttermost parts of the north, thou, and many peoples with thee, all of them riding upon horses, a great company and a mighty army; and thou shalt come up against My people Israel, as a cloud to cover the land: it shall come to pass in the latter days, that I will bring thee against My land, that the nations may know Me, when I shall be sanctified in thee, O Gog, before their eyes"—vers. 14-16.

Having returned to Palestine the Jews will engage in building up their interests in that country. They will be alarmed as word reaches them concerning the many peoples and the mighty army coming against them: but their alarm will be needless, for they are to learn that it is God Himself who, in the latter days, will bring Gog against the land in order that He may deal with him in judgment, and thus be sanctified in the eyes of those who have boldly declared, "There is no God."

The form which that judgment will take comes out clearly in the closing section of the chapter.

"Thus saith the Lord Jehovah: Art thou he of whom I spake in old time by My servants the prophets of Israel, that prophesied in those days for many years that I would bring thee against them? And it shall come to pass in that day, when Gog shall come against the land of Israel, saith the Lord Jehovah, that My wrath shall come up into My nostrils. For in My jealousy and in the fire of My wrath have I spoken, Surely in that day there shall he a great shaking in the land of Israel; so that the fishes of the sea, and the birds of the heavens, and the beasts of the field, and all creeping things that creep upon the earth, and all the men that are upon the face of the earth, shall shake at My presence, and the mountains shall be thrown down, and the steep places shall fall, and every wall shall fall to the ground. And I will call for a sword against him unto all My mountains, saith the Lord Jehovah: every man's sword shall be against his brother. And with pestilence and with blood will I enter into judgment with him; and I will rain upon him, and upon his hordes, and upon the many peoples that are with him, an overflowing shower, and great hailstones, fire, and brimstone. And I will magnify Myself, and sanctify Myself, and I will make Myself known in the eyes of many nations; and they shall know that I am Jehovah"—vers. 17-23.

When it will seem as though Palestine's doom is sealed and Israel will be unable to escape the power of these selfish and vindictive enemies, Jehovah Himself will deal with them: He will speak in His indignation, and the nations shall learn that He is concerned about the deliverance of His people. First will come a mighty-earthquake that will wreak havoc upon the enemies of Israel, filling the hearts of their followers with fear and dread as well as destroying many of them. This will be followed by anarchy, and pestilence will break out among the hosts led by Gog, and great natural calamities, hailstones, fire, and brimstone falling from the skies, will literally annihilate the over-confident armies led by the prince of Kosh.

The details of their destruction are given us in the next chapter.

Chapter Thirty-nine The Doom Of Israel's Enemy

Doubtless when the leader of the northern confederacy orders his armies to press on to the land of Palestine in the last days he will have laid his plans very definitely for its complete subjugation, and will be counting on an easy victory because of the overwhelming number of men at his disposal. But he will learn, as many others have learned in the past, that he who rushes upon the thick bosses of the Almighty must be defeated. He who is Israel's all-powerful Protector will undertake to deliver His people by destroying their mighty foe. It is of this that we read in the following verses.

"And thou, son of man, prophesy against Gog, and say, Thus saith the Lord Jehovah: Behold, I am against thee, O Gog, prince of Bosh, Meshech, and Tubal: and I 'will turn thee about, and will lead thee on, and will cause thee to come up from the uttermost parts of the north; and I will bring thee upon the mountains of Israel; and I will smite thy bow out of thy left hand, and will cause thine arrows to fall out of thy right hand. Thou shalt fall upon the mountains of Israel, thou, and all thy hordes, and the peoples that are with thee: I will give thee unto the ravenous birds of every sort, and to the beasts of the field to be devoured. Thou shalt fall upon the open field; for I have spoken it, saith the Lord Jehovah. And I will send a fire on Magog, and on them that dwell securely in the isles; and they shall know that I am Jehovah. And My holy name will I make known in the midst of My people Israel; neither will I suffer My holy name to be profaned any more: and the nations shall know that I am Jehovah, the Holy One in Israel. Behold, it cometh, and it shall be done, saith the Lord Jehovah; this is the day whereof I have spoken. And they that dwell in the cities of Israel shall go forth, and shall make fires of the weapons and burn them, both the shields and the bucklers, the bows and the arrows, and the handstaves, and the spears, and they shall make fires of them seven years; so that they shall take no wood out of the field, neither cut down any out of the forests; for they shall make fires of the weapons; and they shall plunder those that plundered them, and rob those that robbed them, saith the Lord Jehovah"—vers. 1-10.

The mighty armies of Rosh, Meshech, and Tubal, when brought down from the far north to attack the highlands of Israel, will find themselves utterly unable to cope with the disasters that will face them.

Following the events described in the last section of the previous chapter, we are told here that their destruction will be so complete that their dead bodies will be left as food for all kinds of ravenous birds and wild beasts to devour. Israel will not be obliged to defend themselves, for the Lord will act for them. So terrible and all-embracing will be the destruction of the vast armies of these allied powers that the wood of their weapons will serve as fuel for the people of Israel for seven full years, during which time it will not be necessary to hew down any trees of the forest, because the plunder of those who had intended to plunder Israel will suffice for all purposes as far as fuel is concerned. Some have thought it strange in this age of metallic warfare that such a prophecy could ever be fulfilled literally, but undoubtedly in the coming day many weapons and vehicles of various sorts will be, to a large extent, composed of wood, at least in the area out of which the northern hordes will be gathered. We may not understand fully every detail of the prophecy, but we can be assured that in its own time it will be fulfilled to the letter.

"And it shall come to pass in that day, that I will give unto Gog a place for burial in Israel, the valley of them that pass through on the east of the sea; and it shall stop them that pass through: and there shall they bury Gog and all his multitude; and they shall call it The valley of Hamon-gog. And seven months shall the house of Israel be burying them, that they may cleanse the land. Yea, all the people of the land shall bury them; and it shall be to them a renown in the day that I shall be glorified, saith the Lord Jehovah. And they shall set apart men of continual employment, that shall pass through the land, and, with them that pass through, those that bury them that remain upon the face of the land, to cleanse it: after the end of seven months shall they search. And they that pass through the land shall pass through; and when any seeth a man's bone, then shall he set up a sign by it, till the buriers have buried it in the valley of Hamon-gog. And Hamonah shall also be the name of a city. Thus shall they cleanse the land"—vers. 11-16.

So suddenly will death claim the myriads who formed these armies that there will be no opportunity to bury their own dead. The blow will come as it were in a moment: the dead bodies will be strewn everywhere in the valley of Hamon-gog, which in all likelihood will be the same as the valley of Mageddo or Jezreel, where the different nations are to be destroyed by fire from heaven at the time of the end. These decayed corpses will poison the very air, and would be a source of grievous pestilence to the whole land if steps were not taken almost immediately to properly inter them: therefore, a great squad of grave-diggers will be formed whose business it will be to *go* throughout the entire section where Gog's army has been destroyed, and bury the bodies in order to cleanse the land. For seven months this work will continue before the last bodies will have been covered from human sight. Anyone passing through this region beholding bones or corpses will be required to set up a sign in order that the buriers may see it and so inter the body as soon as possible. In this way the land will be cleansed from its defilement and the air purified.

In the meantime, birds and beasts that feed upon carrion will assist in the work of clearing away the rotting corpses.

"And thou, son of man, thus saith the Lord Jehovah: Speak unto the birds of every sort, and to every beast of the field, Assemble yourselves, and come; gather yourselves on every side to My sacrifice that I do sacrifice for you, even a great sacrifice upon the mountains of Israel, that ye may eat flesh and drink blood. Ye shall eat the flesh of the mighty, and drink the blood of the princes of the earth, of rams, of lambs, and of goats, of bullocks, all of them fatlings of Bashan. And ye shall eat fat till ye be full, and drink blood till ye be drunken, of My sacrifice which I have sacrificed for you. And ye shall be filled at My table with horses and chariots, with mighty men, and with all men of war, saith the Lord Jehovah"—vers. 17-20.

236

One is reminded as he reads these words of that which we have in the nineteenth chapter of the Revelation, when the fowls of the air are called to the great supper of God to glut themselves on the flesh of kings, captains, and mighty men, of horses and those that sat thereon.

It is evident that the various powers to be destroyed in the last days will be dealt with similarly. God Himself will pour out His wrath upon those who have spurned His grace and have arrayed themselves in red-handed opposition to earth's rightful King, our Lord Jesus Christ.

The effect of this judgment upon the nations is given in the verses that follow:

"And I will set My glory among the nations; and all the nations shall see My judgment that I have executed, and My hand that I have laid upon them. So the house of Israel shall know that I am Jehovah their God, from that day and forward. And the nations shall know that the house of Israel went into captivity for their iniquity; because they trespassed against Me, and I hid My face from them: so I gave them into the hand of their adversaries, and they fell all of them by the sword. According to their unclean-ness and according to their transgressions did I unto them; and I hid My face from them"—vers. 21-24.

Jehovah's glory will be manifested among the nations when they see the judgment that shall be executed upon Gog. The house of Israel, too, will recognize then that Jehovah their God had intervened on their behalf, and they will turn to Him as in the days of their fathers when He brought them out of Egypt. The nations will understand then that all the sufferings that the house of Israel has endured through the many centuries of its captivity and the scattering among the Gentiles, was because of its iniquities. The people had trespassed against God, and therefore He had turned His face from them and given them over to the hand of their enemies; and so throughout all the centuries they had fallen by the sword, and because of their uncleanness and their manifold transgressions, God refused to intervene for them but turned away His face when they cried to Him. But in the coming day all this will be at an end, for they will turn back to Him in repentance, and He will turn His face upon them in blessing.

"Therefore thus saith the Lord Jehovah: Now will I bring back the captivity of Jacob, and have mercy upon the whole house of Israel; and I will be jealous for My holy name. And they shall bear their shame, and all their trespasses whereby they have trespassed against Me, when they shall dwell securely in their land, and none shall make them afraid; when I have brought them back from the peoples, and gathered them out of their enemies' lands, and am sanctified in them in the sight of many nations. And they shall know that I am Jehovah their God, in that I caused them to go into captivity among the nations, and have gathered them unto their own land; and I will leave none of them any more there; neither will I hide My face any more from them; for I have poured out My Spirit upon the house of Israel, saith the Lord Jehovah"—vers. 25-29.

It seems very clear from this portion of the prophecy that the full return of the captivity of Jacob will be after the onslaught and the defeat of Gog and his hosts. This seems to prove definitely that the events we have been considering as set forth in these two chapters, will take place during the time of the great tribulation and before the manifestation of the Lord Jesus Christ as King of kings and Lord of lords. Israel will understand then the reason for their suffering throughout the centuries, and will return in repentance to the God against whom they have sinned, who will in His infinite grace forgive their iniquities and restore them to Himself. Then they shall dwell safely in their own land with none to make them afraid. When He shall bring them back from the peoples, that is, from the Gentiles among whom they have been scattered for so long, and gather them out of all their enemies' lands, and be sanctified in them in the sight of many nations, then they shall know that Jehovah is indeed their God—Jehovah revealed—in that day, in the Person of the Lord Jesus Christ. He who caused them to go into captivity will re-gather them; He will leave none of them to wander longer among the nations, neither will He continue to hide His face from them, but will look upon them in infinite grace and loving-kindness. When they bow before

Him as a repentant, believing people, He will pour out His Spirit upon the house of Israel, and acknowledge them once more as His own.

This closes another section of Ezekiel's prophecy, in which God emphasized the sin of His people and their consequent suffering, but also revealed His purpose of grace to restore them when they have learned the important lesson that it is indeed an evil and a bitter thing to forsake the Lord their God. Humbled before Him, contrite and penitent, they will confess their sin and find restoration.

The chapters that follow are of quite a different character, and give an apocalyptic view of the restored nation worshiping in the land when Jehovah's Prince dwells among them.

Part IV, The Coming Glory (chapters 40-48)

Chapter Forty
The Vision From The Mountain-Top

A careful comparison of this new portion of our book with Rev. 21:9—22:5 will give us a better understanding of the true character of the chapter now before us. In the book of The Revelation the climax is reached when the holy city, the new Jerusalem, is seen coming down from God out of heaven. This is a symbolic picture of the future of the Church of this dispensation, of all who have died in Christ during past ages, and in the tribulation period —all these will have their part in the heavenly city. We read in Rev. 21:9, "There came one of the seven angels who had the seven bowls, who were laden with the seven last plagues; and he spake with me, saying, Come hither, I will show thee the bride, the wife of the Lamb." Then we are told, "He carried me away in the Spirit to a mountain great and high, and showed me the holy city Jerusalem, coming down out of heaven from God" (21:10). In Ezekiel 40 the prophet tells us that in the visions he was taken up into a very high mountain, and there he beheld the frame of a city on the south. This, it seems to me, should make it clear that we are not to take Ezekiel's vision too literally, but just as the vision of the heavenly Jerusalem is very largely symbolic, so is the vision of the earthly Jerusalem given in these chapters.

Our comments will be necessarily brief, for there is much in connection with the vision which we frankly admit we do not understand fully; nevertheless, there are certain outstanding things that demand our attention, and which were intended by God to speak to the hearts and consciences of His people of old as well as to us. We would remind ourselves again that all Scripture is given by inspiration of God and is profitable. Therefore, these chapters are not lacking in importance for us today even though we may not be able to trace all that is in them in the way that restored Israel will be able to do in the coming day.

240

"In the five and twentieth year of our captivity, in the beginning of the year, in the tenth day of the month, in the fourteenth year after that the city was smitten, in the selfsame day, the hand of Jehovah was upon me, and He brought me thither. In the visions of God brought He me into the land of Israel, and set me down upon a very high mountain, whereon was as it were the frame of a city on the south. And He brought me thither; and, behold, there was a man, whose appearance was like the appearance of brass, with a line of flax in his hand, and a measuring reed; and he stood in the gate. And the man said unto me, Son of man, behold with thine eyes, and hear with thine ears, and set thy heart upon all that I shall show thee; for, to the intent that I may show them unto thee, art thou brought hither: declare all that thou seest to the house of Israel"—vers. 1-4.

The last dated prophecy was that found in chapter 32:17, the twelfth year, in the fifteenth day of the twelfth month (ver. 1). The present prophecy was given thirteen years later, in the five-and-twentieth year of Israel's captivity, fourteen years after Jerusalem had fallen. Many stirring events had taken place in the meantime, and thousands who had heard the previous prophecies had now passed away; but Ezekiel was still preserved of God and once more called upon to give a message from the Lord. This time it was in connection with the coming glory when Jehovah's worship would be re-established in the land, and the Lord Himself would manifest His presence among His people. In the visions of God, Ezekiel, who was dwelling in Babylon, was brought into the land of Israel, and he found himself upon a very high mountain; possibly Mount Hermon is meant, though there is no definite identification. As Ezekiel looked down he saw the frame of a city on the south. A man of brilliant appearance like burnished brass, stood by with a line of flax and a measuring reed in his hand. This recalls the vision of Zechariah (2:1) where he saw a man with a measuring line in his hand about to measure Jerusalem, and also that of John (Rev. 11:1) where a reed was given to him like unto a rod that he might measure the temple of God and the altar and them that worship therein. Then in Rev. 21:15 John beheld an angel with a golden reed with which to measure the new Jerusalem, its gates and walls. The suggestion of course in each instance is the recognition of that which belongs to God, whether for earth or for heaven.

The man with the reed said to the prophet, "Son of man, behold with thine eyes, and hear with thine ears, and set thy heart upon all that I shall show thee; for, to the intent that I may show them unto thee, art thou brought hither." It is very evident, then, that there was something of great importance in the vision which he was to behold and which he was to declare to the house of Israel.

"And, behold, a wall on the outside of the house round about, and in the man's hand a measuring reed six cubits long, of a cubit and a handbreadth each: so he measured the thickness of the building, one reed; and the height, one reed. Then came he unto the gate which looketh toward the east, and went up the steps thereof: and he measured the threshold of the gate, one reed broad; and the other threshold, one reed broad. And every lodge was one reed long, and one reed broad; and the space between the lodges was five cubits; and the threshold of the gate by the porch of the gate toward the house was one reed. He measured also the porch of the gate toward the house, one reed. Then measured he the porch of the gate, eight cubits; and the posts thereof, two cubits; and the porch of the gate was toward the house. And the lodges of the gate eastward were three on this side, and three on that side; they three were of one measure: and the posts had one measure on this side and on that side. And he measured the breadth of the opening of the gate, ten cubits; and the length of the gate, thirteen cubits; and a border before the lodges, one cubit on this side, and a border, one cubit on that side; and the lodges, six cubits on this side, and six cubits on that side. And he measured the gate from the roof of the one lodge to the roof of the other, a breadth of five and twenty cubits; door against door. He made also posts, threescore cubits; and the court reached unto the posts, round about the gate. And from the forefront of the gate at the entrance unto the forefront of the inner porch of the gate were fifty cubits. And there were closed windows to the lodges, and to their posts within the gate round about, and likewise to the arches; and windows were round about inward; and upon each post were palm-trees"—vers. 5-16.

To the average reader all this detailed information in regard to the wall and gates of the temple of Jehovah is of very little interest no doubt; but when we remember that there is something significant in all the numbers of Scripture, and that God has not permitted anything to enter into His Bible which is not for edification, we shall realize that there is much here worthy of our careful study, even though we may not comprehend all its import.

Mr. John Bloore, an architect, has shown that everything here and in the chapters that follow can be reproduced according to scale in such a way that any architect or master-builder could follow every detail of it on a blueprint, and thus produce a magnificent building worthy of the object for which it would be erected: namely, a sanctuary for Jehovah. Whether or not the future temple in Jerusalem will be built according to these specifications we do not pretend to say, but if we think of it all as symbolic, still it must impress our hearts with the wonder and the glory of the temple that God has in mind for the future. As we study, remembering that Jehovah's sanctuary on earth is a type of the sanctuary above, we may get a better understanding of our Lord's words, "In My Father's house are many mansions" (John 14:2).

The various chambers mentioned here and in the following chapters were intended for the accommodation of the priests officiating at given periods in the temple service. It is of these our Lord speaks as typifying places of rest in the Father's house above. The ornamentation of palm-trees suggests victory over every evil force, for the vision looks on to the time when Jehovah will be supreme throughout all the earth, and all the world will recognize His matchless power.

"Then brought he me into the outer court; and, lo, there were chambers, and a pavement made for the court round about: thirty-chambers were upon the pavement. And the pavement was by the side of the gates, answerable unto the length of the gates, even the lower pavement. Then he measured the breadth from the forefront of the lower gate unto the forefront of the inner court without, a hundred cubits, both on the east and on the north"— vers. 17-19.

Comment on these verses is almost needless as they simply give forth information in regard to the thirty chambers for the priests, to which we have referred above. As we read on, however, we will find ourselves more and more impressed with the glory and the grandeur of the vision. As Ezekiel gazed upon it, it must have been to him a marvelous picture indeed of that which Jehovah had in store for His people.

"And the gate of the outer court whose prospect is toward the north, he measured the length thereof and the breadth thereof. And the lodges thereof were three on this side and three on that side; and the posts thereof and the arches thereof were after the measure of the first gate: the length thereof was fifty cubits, and the breadth five and twenty cubits. And the windows thereof, and the arches thereof, and the palm-trees thereof, were after the measure of the gate whose prospect is toward the east; and they went up unto it by seven steps; and the arches thereof were before them. And there was a gate to the inner court over against the other gate, both on the north and on the east; and he measured from gate to gate a hundred cubits"—vers. 20-23.

The prophet's gaze was directed to the gate of the outer court looking toward the north. As he looked upon it and meditated on its size and prospect he saw emphasized the windows and the palm-trees. Next, his attention was focused upon the gate whose prospect is toward the east, which is the place of the sunrising, from thence the glory was to appear and enter the temple, consecrating it to Jehovah.

"And he led me toward the south; and, behold, a gate toward the south: and he measured the posts thereof and the arches thereof according to these measures. And there were windows in it and in the arches thereof round about, like those windows: the length was fifty cubits, and the breadth five and twenty cubits. And there were seven steps to go up to it, and the arches thereof were before them; and it had palm-trees, one on this side, and another on that side, upon the posts thereof. And there was a gate to the inner court toward the south: and he measured from gate to gate toward the south a hundred cubits"—vers. 24-27.

Turning next toward the south, Ezekiel beheld another gate, and his guide measured the posts and the arches, directing his attention to the windows and the ascent, particularly noting again the palm-trees, symbol of victory, and thus impressed upon Ezekiel the spaciousness of the temple area, which was intended to signify the link yet to be established between Jehovah and the entire world. Further details are given in verses 28 to 31.

"Then he brought me to the inner court by the south gate: and he measured the south gate according to these measures; and the lodges thereof, and the posts thereof, and the arches thereof, according to these measures: and there were windows in it and in the arches thereof round about; it was fifty cubits long, and five and twenty cubits broad. And there were arches round about, five and twenty cubits long, and five cubits broad. And the arches thereof were toward the outer court; and palm-trees were upon the posts thereof: and the ascent to it had eight steps"—vers. 28-31.

As we ponder these words we are impressed with the magnificence of the cloisters in which we can almost see by sanctified imagination the white-robed priests of the Lord, walking about.

"And he brought me into the inner court toward the east: and he measured the gate according to these measures; and the lodges thereof, and the posts thereof, and the arches thereof, according to these measures: and there were windows therein and in the arches thereof round about; it was fifty cubits long, and five and twenty cubits broad. And the arches thereof were toward the outer court; and palm-trees were upon the posts thereof, on this side, and on that side: and the ascent to it had eight steps"—vers. 32-34.

It is now the inner court to the east which is before Ezekiel's eyes, and there, too, he beholds places for the lodging of the priests, spacious and adorned with palm-trees as in the other parts of the great building.

"And he brought me to the north gate: and he measured *it* according to these measures; the lodges thereof, the posts thereof, and the arches thereof: and there were windows therein round about; the length was fifty cubits, and the breadth five and twenty cubits. And the posts thereof were toward the outer court; and the palm-trees were upon the posts thereof, on this side, and on that side-and the ascent to it had eight steps"—vers. 35-37.

Again the guide turns to the north gate and takes the measurements of different parts of the building in that section. That all these measurements have a certain mystical significance I think is unquestionable, although it may not be easy to see always just what that significance is; but we cannot help but notice the frequent use of the number fifty, and of five and twenty. These numbers are connected with responsibility: fifty, of course, is the jubilee number; the fives and twenties that make it up point to the fulfilment of responsibility toward God—a responsibility which no one has ever completely been able to meet, but which has been met for us in all its fulness by our blessed Lord.

"And a chamber with the door thereof was by the posts at the gates; there they washed the burnt-offering. And in the porch of the gate were two tables on this side, and two tables on that side, to slay thereon the burnt-offering and the sin-offering and the trespass-offering. And on the one side without, as one goeth up to the entry of the gate toward the north, were two tables; and on the other side, which belongeth to the porch of the gate, were two tables. Four tables were on this side, and four tables on that side, by the side of the gate; eight tables, whereupon they slew the sacrifices. And there were four tables for the burnt-offering, of hewn stone, a cubit and a half long, and a cubit and a half broad, and one cubit high; whereupon they laid the instruments wherewith they slew the burnt-offering and the sacrifice. And the hooks, a handbreadth long, were fastened within round about: and upon the tables was the flesh of the oblation"—vers. 38-43.

These verses raise a question which has perplexed many, and which perhaps may never be satisfactorily settled until the day when the full meaning of the vision is made known. The question is, Are sacrifices and offerings to be reinstituted at Jerusalem in the coming day? That this will be the case during the great tribulation there can be, I think, no question; otherwise there would be no meaning to the words referring to the compact with the Beast, that "in the midst of the week he shall cause the sacrifice and the oblation to cease" (Dan. 9:27). But will these sacrifices be renewed in the millennial temple, and will they be carried on throughout the kingdom age? I cannot conceive of such a possibility. The truth revealed in the Epistle to the Hebrews will not be lost sight of in that age. The one offering of our Lord Jesus Christ has set aside completely all the offerings of the legal dispensation: therefore, may we not take it for granted that in this vision of Ezekiel, while it was necessary to picture spiritual realities in connection with the redemptive work of Christ by the sacrifices such as were still being offered at that time, yet when the fulfilment of all prophecy takes place Israel will understand for the first time the real meaning of the work of Christ and see how it answers antitypically to all the offerings that were prescribed under the law.

"And without the inner gate were chambers for the singers in the inner court, which was at the side of the north gate; and their prospect was toward the south; one at the side of the east gate having the prospect toward the north. And he said unto me, This chamber, whose prospect is toward the south, is for the priests, the keepers of the charge of the house; and the chamber whose prospect is toward the north is for the priests, the keepers of the charge of the altar: these are the sons of Zadok, who from among the sons of Levi come near to Jehovah to minister unto Him. And he measured the court, a hundred cubits long, and a hundred cubits broad, foursquare; and the altar was before the house"— vers. 44-47.

The outstanding thought in the present section is that in the day of Israel's future blessing there will be, as in the time when Solomon's temple was built, a special group who will be appointed to lead the praises of the people of God: therefore, we have certain cham- bers for the singers in the inner court. It is a blessed thing, even in this age, when the singers find their place of residence in the inner court. Alas, so often it is otherwise. People may sing like angels and yet know little of dwelling in the presence of the Lord.

The sons of Zadok, who are pictured as having charge of the altar, will be leaders in spiritual things in that coming age, in accordance with the promise that God made so long ago when He set aside the family of Eli and promised He would raise up a faithful priest whom He found among the sons of Zadok.

"Then he brought me to the porch of the house, and measured each post of the porch, five cubits on this side, and five cubits on that side: and the breadth of the gate was three cubits on this side, and three cubits on that side. The length of the porch was twenty cubits, and the breadth eleven cubits; even by the steps whereby they went up to it: and there were pillars by the posts, one on this side, and another on that side"—vers. 48, 49.

The last verses have to do with the porch of the house and its posts or pillars, also the stairway ascending to it. On this we have no special comment to make. A deeper understanding of divine things might lead us to expound more fully what the Spirit of God has hidden here, but we do not pretend to have that apprehension at present.

Chapter Forty-one The Sanctuary Of Jehovah

The man with the measuring reed now proceeds to direct the prophet's attention particularly to the sanctuary itself, which according to the description given would be a most magnificent building, and yet differing in many respects from the temple which Solomon erected of old to the glory of the God of Israel.

"And he brought me to the temple, and measured the posts, six cubits broad on the one side, and six cubits broad on the other side, which was the breadth of the tabernacle. And the breadth of the entrance was ten cubits; and the sides of the entrance were five cubits on the one side, and five cubits on the other side: and he measured the length thereof, forty cubits, and the breadth, twenty cubits. Then went he inward, and measured each post of the entrance, two cubits; and the entrance, six cubits; and the breadth of the entrance, seven cubits. And he measured the length thereof, twenty cubits, and the breadth, twenty cubits, before the temple: and he said unto me, This is the most holy place"—vers. 1-4.

It will be observed that the dimensions given for the inner sanctuary are the same as those of Solomon's temple and just double the size of the tabernacle in the wilderness. That all the numbers here have definite significance we do not question, but others have taken this up very fully, and it will not be my task to go into it in this place.

The sanctuary consists of two rooms as of old, the holy and the most holy places. It is noticeable that into the second the prophet apparently does not enter. The man with the measuring reed alone passes into this sacred enclosure while Ezekiel looks on.

Details as to the building itself are given in the verses that follow:

"Then he measured the wall of the house, six cubits; and the breadth of every side-chamber, four cubits, round about the house on every side. And the side-chambers were in three stories, one over another, and thirty in order; and they entered into the

249

wall which belonged to the house for the side-chambers round about, that they might have hold therein, and not have hold in the wall of the house. And the side-chambers were broader as they encompassed the house higher and higher; for the encompassing of the house went higher and higher round about the house: therefore the breadth of the house continued upward; and so one went up from the lowest chamber to the highest by the middle chamber. I saw also that the house had a raised basement round about: the foundations of the side-chambers were a full reed of six great cubits. The thickness of the wall, which was for the side-chambers, on the outside, was five cubits: and that which was left was the place of the side-chambers that belonged to the house. And between the chambers was a breadth of twenty cubits round about the house on every side. And the doors of the side-chambers were toward the place that was left, one door toward the north, and another door toward the south: and the breadth of the place that was left was five cubits round about"—vers. 5-11.

As we read this passage, whether or not our minds fully grasp the architectural arrangement, we cannot help but recognize a suggestion of hallowed fellowship between the priests of the Lord whose dwelling was to be in these side chambers and Jehovah Himself whose glory was to fill the house. God delights to have His people near Him. All His saints today are priests, and He would have them enter into the blessedness of intimate communion as those who abide constantly in the sanctuary. In Israel of old the priests were a separate family devoted especially to the things of the temple, and it would seem as though this will be the case again when the present dispensation comes to an end and millennial conditions are ushered in. While Israel as a whole will be a priestly nation, nevertheless a separated priesthood comes before us as those who are designated to represent the people before God and to carry on the service of the sanctuary. Anything like this in our dispensation is a reverting to Judaism and fails to take into account the present relation of the saints to Christ. In other words, there is no such distinction now made in Scripture as a clergy and laity such as we see in some of the great ecclesiastical organizations of our day. The idea of a distinctive priesthood apart from that of all believers is foreign to the genius of Christianity;

whereas it had its rightful place in Israel before the cross, and it will have a special place again when Israel shall be restored nationally to the Lord.

In addition to the temple itself it is evident that another great building was pictured as standing upon the mount of God's holiness. This is indicated in the following verses.

"And the building that was before the separate place at the side toward the west was seventy cubits broad; and the wall of the building was five cubits thick round about, and the length thereof ninety cubits. So he measured the house, a hundred cubits long; and the separate place, and the building, with the walls thereof, a hundred cubits long; also the breadth of the face of the house, and of the separate place toward the east, a hundred cubits"— vers. 12-14.

While it is difficult to follow the description of the house so as to visualize each part distinctly, our minds are impressed with the fact that it is of magnificent dimensions and wondrous beauty, lined with cedar which speaks of the incorruptible Humanity of our Lord, and adorned with cherubim and palm-trees, emphasizing the victory of righteousness and the blessings to be enjoyed under the divine government when the once-rejected Jesus reigns as King over all the earth.

"And he measured the length of the building before the separate place which was at the back thereof, and the galleries thereof on the one side and on the other side, a hundred cubits; and the inner temple, and the porches of the court; the thresholds, and the closed windows, and the galleries round about on their three stories, over against the threshold, ceiled with wood round about, and from the ground up to the windows (now the windows were covered), to the space above the door, even unto the inner house, and without, and by all the wall round about within and without, by measure. And it was made with cherubim and palm-trees; and a palm-tree was between cherub and cherub, and every cherub had two faces; so that there was the face of a man toward the palm-tree on the one side, and the face of a young lion toward the palm-tree on the other side. Thus was it made through all the house round about: from the ground unto above the door were cherubim and palm-trees made; thus was the wall of the temple"—vers. 15-20.

The cherubim, as we have seen in our consideration of the earlier chapters of this book, symbolized the divine government—God's ways with men and particularly with His people Israel. The palm-tree is the recognized symbol both of righteousness and of victory, as indicated in the 92nd Psalm where the righteous are said to flourish as the palm-tree, and in the last book of the Bible where we see the triumphant overcomers who have won the victory over the beast and his satellite, standing before God with palms in their hands.

As we read this description of the house, therefore, we are impressed with the fact that the day will come when in Jehovah's righteous government, all iniquity will be put down, and a King shall reign in righteousness, triumphant over all the powers of evil.

We turn again to consider the temple as indicated in vers. 21 to 26.

"As for the temple, the doorposts were squared; and as for the face of the sanctuary, the appearance thereof was as the appearance of the temple. The altar was of wood, three cubits high, and the length thereof two cubits; and the corners thereof, and the length thereof, and the walls thereof, were of wood: and he said unto me, This is the table that is before Jehovah. And the temple and the sanctuary had two doors. And the doors had two leaves apiece, two turning leaves: two leaves for the one door, and two leaves for the other. And there were made on them, on the doors of the temple, cherubim and palm-trees, like as were made upon the walls; and there was a threshold of wood upon the face of the porch without. And there were closed windows and palm-trees on the one side and on the other side, on the sides of the porch: thus were the Side-chambers of the house, and the thresholds"—vers. 21-26.

The altar referred to here is the altar inside the sanctuary, the altar of incense, and is not to be confounded with the great altar upon which sacrifices were offered outside in the court. This altar was of wood, speaking of the Humanity of our Lord Jesus Christ, and is called "the table that is before Jehovah," for in Christ, God finds His satisfaction. As to His people, He it is who presents their prayers and praises before God, taking from them all imperfection and adding to them His own gracious intercession.

We forbear attempting any further comment on these verses as we dread mere human speculation in regard to divine things, and we confess to a lack of understanding as to the marvelous details here given.

NOTE: For a much fuller and more satisfactory exposition of this great vision as a whole, it is a pleasure to refer the inquiring student to John Bloore's comments in *The Numerical Bible*. One complete volume is occupied with the book of Ezekiel. The late F. W. Grant was called home to be with Christ after he had written the comments on Ezekiel as far as chapter 37. The manuscript lay unpublished for some years, when it was taken up and edited by Mr. Bloore, who wrote on chapters 38 to 48 in a most illuminating and satisfactory manner. This volume can be had from the same publishers, and we are glad to commend it to those who are anxious for a better understanding of these chapters.

Chapter Forty-two The Many Mansions Of The Father's House

This chapter takes up, more particularly, the arrangements for the comfort of the priests of the Lord, the chambers or abodes where those who served might find accommodations during their stay at the temple. These, as we have seen, are the many mansions in the Father's house, depicting the places of rest in heaven, of which Jesus spoke in His last discourse to His disciples (John 14:1-3).

"Then he brought me forth into the outer court, the way toward the north: and he brought me into the chamber that was over against the separate place, and which was over against the building toward the north. Before the length of a hundred cubits was the north door, and the breadth was fifty cubits. Over against the twenty cubits which belonged to the inner court, and over against the pavement which belonged to the outer court, was gallery against gallery in the third story. And before the chambers was a walk of ten cubits' breadth inward, a way of one cubit; and their doors were toward the north. Now the upper chambers were shorter; for the galleries took away from these, more than from the lower and the middlemost, in the building. For they were in three stories, and they had not pillars as the pillars of the courts: therefore the uppermost was straitened more than the lowest and the middlemost from the ground. And the wall that was without by the side of the chambers, toward the outer court before the chambers, the length thereof was fifty cubits. For the length of the chambers that were in the outer court was fifty cubits: and, lo, before the temple were a hundred cubits. And from under these chambers was the entry on the east side, as one goeth into them from the outer court. In the thickness of the wall of the court toward the east, before the separate place, and before the building, there were chambers. And the way before them was like the appearance of the way of the chambers which were toward the north; according to their length so was their breadth: and all their egresses were both according to their fashions, and according to their doors. And according to the doors of the chambers that were toward the south was a door at the head of the way, even the way directly before the wall toward the east, as one entereth into them"—vers. 1-12.

On three sides of the temple proper and facing on the court itself there were three-story apartments, suitable as dwelling-places for the priests. It was as though God would have His worshippers close to Himself, according to the word, "Blessed are they that dwell in Thy house: they will be still praising Thee" (Psalm 84:4). He delights to abide amid the praises of His people.

"Then said he unto me, The north chambers and the south chambers, which are before the separate place, they are the holy chambers, where the priests that are near unto Jehovah shall eat the most holy things: there shall they lay the most holy things, and the meal-offering, and the sin-offering, and the trespass-offering; for the place is holy. When the priests enter in, then shall they not go out of the holy place into the outer court, but there they shall lay their garments wherein they minister; for they are holy: and they shall put on other garments, and shall approach to that which pertaineth to the people"—vers. 13-14.

The priests were to eat of the holy things within the temple enclosure in the chambers, or rooms prepared for them. In this they picture God's priestly house today feeding by meditation upon Christ who is the satisfying portion of His people's hearts. He has said, "He that eateth Me, even he shall live by Me" (John 6:57). All the offerings spoke of Him, and the priests fed upon these.

"Now when he had made an end of measuring the inner house, he brought me forth by the way of the gate whose prospect is toward the east, and measured it round about. He measured on the east side with the measuring reed five hundred reeds, with the measuring reed round about. He measured on the north side five hundred reeds with the measuring reed round about. He measured on the south side five hundred reeds with the measuring reed. He turned about to the west side, and measured five hundred reeds with the measuring reed. He measured it on the four sides: it had a wall round about, the length five hundred, and the breadth five hundred, to make a separation between that which was holy and that which was common"—vers. 15-20.

In this section we have the final measurements completing Ezekiel's tour of the temple area, as seen in the vision. There are certain difficulties and perplexities as to these measures which are not easily explained, but we may be sure the original text was without fault, and if in later manuscripts discrepancies appeared they were the result of copyists' mistakes.

The entire temple area is what is here before us—a spacious courtyard surrounded by a great wall with gates on the four sides. The entire space, according to the specifications given here, is far too large for the top of Mount Moriah on which the temple of Solomon, and the temple of Zerubbabel, and that of Herod, stood. So if all is to be taken literally we must understand some great convulsions of nature in the Jerusalem area that will alter considerably the topography of the land. If all is symbolic there need be no difficulty. In God's due time He will make everything plain.

Even the seeming vagueness of some of the details regarding the court, the sanctuary and the priests' apartments, might well remind us that God's ways are not our ways nor are His thoughts our thoughts. Much that He has in store for both His earthly and His heavenly people is far beyond our present understanding, but in due time all will be made clear. Till then it is ours to trust and wait patiently for the glory yet to be revealed.

As the wise-hearted in Israel meditated on the description and dimensions of this vast temple and its environs they must have been impressed with the greatness of God's plan for their future blessing and the meticulous care which He will take in the working out of all His counsels.

Chapter Forty-three The Return Of The Glory

In earlier chapters we have seen how the Shekinah Glory, the uncreated light that rested above the mercy-seat, moved slowly from the temple of Solomon, rising from its place between the cherubim, passing on to the door of the temple, then on to the gate in the east and thence to the Mount of Olives, from which the prophet saw it ascending to heaven; all of which is distinctly typical of our blessed Lord's giving up of Israel when they knew not the time of their visitation. But that glory which departed is yet to return when Israel shall be restored to the Lord, and it is of this the present chapter treats.

In vision the prophet sees the divine chariot, the glory which he had beheld by the river Chebar, now returning to take its place in the magnificent structure which he saw spread before him as he looked down from the top of the mountain.

"Afterward he brought me to the gate, even the gate that looketh toward the east. And, behold, the glory of the God of Israel came from the way of the east: and His voice was like the sound of many waters; and the earth shined with His glory. And it was according to the appearance of the vision which I saw, even according to the vision that I saw when I came to destroy the city; and the visions were like the vision that I saw by the river Chebar; and I fell upon my face. And the glory of Jehovah came into the house by the way of the gate whose prospect is toward the East. And the Spirit took me up, and brought me into the inner court; and, behold, the glory of Jehovah filled the house"—vers. 1-5.

Ezekiel was brought by the man with the measuring rod to the east gate, and there as he looked up he beheld the glory of the God of Israel coming from the way of the sunrising, and he heard a voice like the sound of many waters. So marvelous was the sight that the earth shone with the brilliance of the Shekinah. The prophet recognized it at once as the same glory which he had seen departing when God announced that the destruction of the city was near at hand. Reverently Ezekiel fell upon his face as a worshipper as he beheld the glory enter by way of the east gate, and then as he looked up he saw that it filled the entire house.

"And I heard one speaking unto me out of the house; and a Man stood by me. And He said unto me, Son of man, this is the place of My throne, and the place of the soles of My feet, where I will dwell in the midst of the children of Israel for ever. And the house of Israel shall no more defile My holy name, neither they, nor their kings, by their whoredom, and by the dead bodies of their kings in their high places; in their setting of their threshold by My threshold, and their door-post beside My door-post, and there was but the wall between Me and them; and they have defiled My holy name by their abominations which they have committed: wherefore I have consumed them in Mine anger. Now let them put away their whoredom, and the dead bodies of their kings, far from Me; and I will dwell in the midst of them for ever"—vers. 6-9.

A voice came from out of the house, and a Man hitherto unseen stood by Ezekiel. The voice announced, "Son of man, this is the place of My throne, and the place of the soles of My feet, where I will dwell in the midst of the children of Israel for ever." When the glory returns it will not be a question of whether the people themselves are deserving of blessing, but it will be a manifestation of the grace of God as set forth in the new covenant. The Lord Himself will see to it that the house of Israel shall never again defile His holy name nor bring dishonor upon His sanctuary by departing from Him and taking up with unclean and unholy practices. In that day His law will be written upon the hearts of His people so that they will delight to do His will. Idolatry will never again rear its hateful head in all the land of Palestine. No more will the priests of Baal and kindred systems set their thresholds by that of Jehovah as in the past when His house was often rendered unclean by the setting up of their images in or near to its courts. All this will be forever past, and God Himself will dwell in the midst of His people.

"Thou, son of man, show the house to the house of Israel, that they may be ashamed of their iniquities; and let them measure the pattern. And if they be ashamed of all that they have done, make known unto them the form of the house, and the fashion thereof, and the egresses thereof, and the entrances thereof, and all the forms thereof, and all the ordinances thereof, and all the forms thereof, and all the laws thereof; and write it in their sight; that they may keep the whole form thereof, and all the ordinances thereof, and do them. This is the law of the house: upon the top of the mountain the whole limit thereof round about shall be most holy. Behold, this is the law of the house"—vers. 10-12.

The tenth verse gives the real key to the entire vision, the reason for which God gave it. He said to Ezekiel, "Thou, son of man, show the house to the house of Israel, that they may be ashamed of their iniquities; and let them measure the pattern." As they thus dwelt upon the glory they might be moved for the time being, and they would loathe themselves as they realized that their iniquities had separated between them and their God. If conscience were inactive, of course, all this would have no effect upon them. But. Jehovah said that if they were ashamed of all they had done, then the prophet was to make known the form of the house, and the fashion thereof, the exits and the entrances, and everything connected with the service and its laws, in order that they might yield glad-hearted obedience to all that God asked of them.

It is noticeable that the law of the house was really the way of holiness, for we are told in ver. 12, "This is the law of the house: upon the top of the mountain the whole limit thereof round about shall be most holy. Behold, this is the law of the house." God makes Himself known to those who walk before Him in holiness and righteousness. We do not learn truth simply through the intellect; we learn it through the conscience. When the conscience is tender and responsive to the Word of God, then His truth is opened up to us in the power of the Holy Spirit, and we are enabled to understand His mind and find our delight in doing His will. So will it be with Israel when the many prophecies concerning their future regeneration shall have been fulfilled.

The measures of the altar are given in the verses that follow:

"And these are the measures of the altar by cubits (the cubit is a cubit and a handbreadth): the bottom shall be a cubit, and the breadth a cubit, and the border thereof by the edge thereof round about a span; and this shall be the base of the altar. And from the bottom upon the ground to the lower ledge shall be two cubits, and the breadth one cubit; and from the lesser ledge to the greater ledge shall be four cubits, and the breadth a cubit. And the upper altar shall be four cubits; and from the altar hearth and upward there shall be four horns. And the altar hearth shall be twelve cubits long by twelve broad, square in the four sides thereof. And the ledge shall be fourteen cubits long by fourteen broad in the four sides thereof; and the border about it shall be half a cubit; and the bottom thereof shall be a cubit round about; and the steps thereof shall look toward the east"—vers. 13-17.

It is noticeable here that the altar is measured not by ordinary cubits but by a cubit and a span. The ordinary cubit was approximately the measure from a man's elbow to the tip of his fingers, about eighteen inches; the span added to it would make it about twenty-one or twenty-two inches. It is by this longer cubit that the altar is measured, as though to remind us that the work of the cross is not to be measured by man's standards but by those that God Himself appoints. The altar here is, of course, the altar of sacrifice; and it speaks of the work of the cross.

It might seem as we read on in the chapter that sacrifices and offerings are to be presented to the Lord on this altar in millennial days, and, as we have mentioned previously, there have been many who have believed this in the past, and there are still numbers of very godly teachers who consider that the sacrifices will be reinstituted, but as memorials not as actually having any atoning value. It seems clear, however, that prior to the work of the cross there could be no other way of presenting that work prophetically than by directing attention to such offerings as the people understood, but when Christ fulfilled all the types on the cross and exclaimed, "It is finished," these sacrifices were done away forever, so that the ordinances of the altar which are spoken of in the closing verses of the chapter, all picture, I have no doubt, the way in which the people will enter into and appreciate the work of our Lord Jesus Christ when at last He is revealed to them.

"And he said unto me, Son of man, thus saith the Lord Jehovah: These are the ordinances of the altar in the day when they shall make it, to offer burnt-offerings thereon, and to sprinkle blood thereon. Thou shalt give to the priests the Levites that are of the seed of Zadok, who are near unto Me, to minister unto Me, saith the Lord Jehovah, a young bullock for a sin-offering. And thou shalt take of the blood thereof, and put on the four horns of it, and on the four corners of the ledge, and upon the border round about: thus shalt thou cleanse it and make atonement for it. Thou shalt also take the bullock of the sin-offering, and it shall be burnt in the appointed place of the house, without the sanctuary. And on the second day thou shalt offer a he-goat without blemish for a sin-offering; and they shall cleanse the altar, as they did cleanse it with the bullock. When thou hast made an end of cleansing it, thou shalt offer a young bullock without blemish, and a ram out of the flock without blemish. And thou shalt bring them near before Jehovah, and the priests shall cast salt upon them, and they shall offer them up for a burnt-offering unto Jehovah. Seven days shalt thou prepare every day a goat for a sin-offering: they shall also prepare a young bullock, and a ram out of the flock, without blemish. Seven days shall they make atonement for the altar and purify it; so shall they consecrate it. And when they have accomplished the days, it shall be that upon the eighth day, and forward, the priests shall make your burnt-offerings upon the altar, and your peace-offerings; and I will accept you, saith the Lord Jehovah"—vers. 18-27.

Everything here speaks of Christ as the burnt offering, who offered Himself without spot unto God, a sacrifice of a sweet-smelling savor. He is the true sin offering, who, though He was sinless, was made sin for us that we might become the righteousness of God in Him. Israel has never yet entered into the reality of this, but in that coming day they will see how Christ is the fulfilment of all these types, and so they will reach the place where, in holy fellowship with the Lord, they will enjoy Christ as the peace offering, who has brought God and man together, and made them as He has made those of us, both Jew and Gentile, who believe, to be accepted in the Beloved.

Chapter Forty-four Ordinances For The Priests

The chief theme of this chapter is that of the regulations under which the priests of Jehovah were to serve in His temple. In these we may see, in the main, a repetition of instruction given by Moses long before, as recorded in the book of Leviticus particularly, much of which had been ignored and even definitely disobeyed after idolatry came in and rulers, priests, and people drifted farther and farther from God. The reiteration of these commandments as given here tells us, in veiled form, of the unhindered worship that will be offered to the Lord in the coming glorious day of Israel's cleansing and regeneration.

First, however, we read of a prince who is to occupy a place of special privilege and authority in that day.

"Then he brought me back by the way of the outer gate of the sanctuary, which looketh toward the east; and it was shut. And Jehovah said unto me, This gate shall be shut; it shall not be opened, neither shall any man enter in by it; for Jehovah, the God of Israel, hath entered in by it; therefore it shall be shut. As for the prince, he shall sit therein as prince to eat bread before Jehovah; he shall enter by the way of the porch of the gate, and shall go out by the way of the same"—vers. 1-3.

Many have thought they saw in the "Golden Gate" so-called, on the east of the temple-area, the fulfilment of this prophetic vision. But the east gate here is clearly that of the temple seen by the prophet. By way of that gate the glory returned to fill the house: this was Jehovah's entrance into His sanctuary. Henceforth, the gate was to be closed to all men, no matter how exalted in rank or conspicuous for piety.

The prince, who will be in all probability a lineal descendant of David, hence his son, enters the court by way of the porch of the gate but not through the gate itself. But he eats bread within the entryway of the gate, inside the court, thus enjoying a special place of communion and fellowship.

The prophet proceeds to tell of the privileges and responsibilities of the priests.

"Then he brought me by the way of the north gate before the house; and I looked, and, behold, the glory of Jehovah filled the house of Jehovah: and I fell upon my face. And Jehovah said unto me, Son of man, mark well, and behold with thine eyes, and hear with thine ears all that I say unto thee concerning all the ordinances of the house of Jehovah, and all the laws thereof; and mark well the entrance of the house, with every egress of the sanctuary. And thou shalt say to the rebellious, even to the house of Israel, Thus saith the Lord Jehovah: O ye house of Israel, let it suffice you of all your abominations, in that ye have brought in foreigners, uncircumcised in heart and uncircumcised in flesh, to be in My sanctuary, to profane it, even My house, when ye offer My bread, the fat and the blood, and they have broken My convenant, to add unto all your abominations. And ye have not kept the charge of My holy things; but ye have set keepers of My charge in My sanctuary for yourselves. Thus saith the Lord Jehovah, No foreigner, uncircumcised in heart and uncircumcised in flesh, shall enter into My sanctuary, of any foreigners that are among the children of Israel. But the Levites that went far from Me, when Israel went astray, that went astray from Me after their idols, they shall bear their iniquity. Yet they shall be ministers in My sanctuary, having oversight at the gates of the house, and ministering in the house: they shall slay the burnt-offering and the sacrifice for the people, and they shall stand before them to minister unto them. Because they ministered unto them before their idols, and became a stumblingblock of iniquity unto the house of Israel; therefore have I lifted up My hand against them, saith the Lord Jehovah, and they shall bear their iniquity. And they shall not come near unto Me, to execute the office of priest unto Me, nor to come near to any of My holy things, unto the things that are most holy: but they shall bear their shame, and their abominations which they have committed. Yet will I make them keepers of the charge of the house, for all the service thereof, and for all that shall be done therein"—vers. 4-14.

In that house, so resplendent with the manifest presence of Jehovah, the glory which of old filled Solomon's temple on the occasion of its dedication but which was never seen in the later temple, the priests of the Lord will have free access, but their behavior and habiliments must be in accordance with the law of the house. All idolatry is to be forever abolished: no more will Jehovah's house be defiled or His priests contaminated by pagan practices. He alone is to be exalted in that day. Heretofore, self-will and disobedience had prevailed: henceforth the statutes of Jehovah were to be kept in truth and faithfulness, and His priests were to remember they were separated to Himself.

No stranger to the divine covenant was to enter those sacred precincts. They who worshipped there were to be circumcised in heart, not only in the flesh. All filthiness of flesh and spirit were to be put away. We may see the full meaning of this in the instructions given to the church at Corinth in 2 Cor. 6:14—7:1. The same standard was set forth as expressing God's will for the priests who should minister in this glorious sanctuary.

Neglect of these requirements had brought judgment upon both priests and Levites. Adherence to them would be the precursor to blessing, and would insure God's continued delight in His people. Again we would be reminded that every offering spoke of Christ and some special aspect of His work: therefore, we need have no difficulty when we read once more of sacrifices and offerings such as were commanded under the legal dispensation.

"But the priests the Levites, the sons of Zadok, that kept the charge of My sanctuary when the children of Israel went astray from Me, they shall come near to Me to minister unto Me; and they shall stand before Me to offer unto Me the fat and the blood, saith the Lord Jehovah: they shall enter into My sanctuary, and they shall come near to My table, to minister unto Me, and they shall keep My charge. And it shall be that, when they enter in at the gates of the inner court, they shall be clothed with linen garments; and no wool shall come upon them, while they minister in the gates of the inner court, and within. They shall have linen tires upon their heads, and shall have linen breeches upon their loins; they shall not gird themselves with anything that causeth sweat.

And when they go forth into the outer court, even into the outer court to the people, they shall put off their garments wherein they minister, and lay them in the holy chambers; and they shall put on other garments, that they sanctify not the people with their garments. Neither shall they shave their heads, nor suffer their locks to grow long; they shall only cut off the hair of their heads. Neither shall any of the priests drink wine, when they enter into the inner court. Neither shall they take for their wives a widow, nor her that is put away; but they shall take virgins of the seed of the house of Israel, or a widow that is the widow of a priest. And they shall teach My people the difference between the holy and the common, and cause them to discern between the unclean and the clean. And in a controversy they shall stand to judge; according to Mine ordinances shall they judge it: and they shall keep My laws and My statutes in all My appointed feasts; and they shall hallow My sabbaths. And they shall go in to no dead person to defile themselves; but for father, or for mother, or for son, or for daughter, for brother, or for sister that hath had no husband, they may defile themselves. And after he is cleansed, they shall reckon unto him seven days. And in the day that he goeth into the sanctuary, into the inner court, to minister in the sanctuary, he shall offer his sin-offering, saith the Lord Jehovah. And they shall have an inheritance: I am their inheritance; and ye shall give them no possession in Israel; I am their possession. They shall eat the meal-offering, and the sin-offering, and the trespass-offering; and every devoted thing in Israel shall be theirs. And the first of all the first-fruits of everything, and every oblation of everything, of all your oblations, shall be for the priest: ye shall also give unto the priests the first of your dough, to cause a bless- ing to rest on thy house. The priests shall not eat of anything that dieth of itself, or is torn, whether it be bird or beast"—vers. 15-31.

By consulting 1 Sam. 2:35; 2 Sam. 15:24; 1 Kings 2:27-35 we will understand what is said here of the sons of Zadok. These alone are given a true priestly place in this temple. All others of the sons of Levi are given positions of authority and service, but it is not theirs to present the offerings of the people on the altar. The priesthood failed almost from the beginning, and God set the other sons of Aaron aside in favor of the descendants of Zadok who was faithful in a day of declension and apostasy.

As we think of the typical character of the priesthood in Israel we may gain much for ourselves by a careful consideration of all these statutes and ordinances. "No word of God shall be void of power"; *all Scripture* is for our learning, and we cannot afford to neglect or pass lightly over any of it as though it contained nothing for our edification.

The priest is the worshiper; all believers are such, or should be, today—therefore the importance of keeping ourselves free from every defiling thing that we may worship the Lord in the beauty of holiness.

Chapter Forty-five Jehovah's Appointments

This chapter deals particularly with the apportionment of the land for the Lord, His priests the Levites and the people, all in connection with the site of the sanctuary and its court. It is an ideal picture of Jehovah dwelling in the midst of His saints.

"Moreover, when ye shall divide by lot the land for inheritance, ye shall offer an oblation unto Jehovah, a holy portion of the land; the length shall be the length of five and twenty thousand reeds, and the breadth shall be ten thousand: it shall be holy in all the border thereof round about. Of this there shall be for the holy place five hundred in length by five hundred in breadth, square round about; and fifty cubits for the suburbs thereof round about. And of this measure shalt thou measure a length of five and twenty thousand, and a breadth of ten thousand: and in it shall be the sanctuary, which is most holy. It is a holy portion of the land; it shall be for the priests, the ministers of the sanctuary, that come near to minister unto Jehovah; and it shall be a place for their houses, and a holy place for the sanctuary. And five and twenty thousand in length, and ten thousand in breadth, shall be unto the Levites, the ministers of the house, for a possession unto themselves, for twenty chambers. And ye shall appoint the possession of the city five thousand broad, and five and twenty thousand long, side by side with the oblation of the holy portion: it shall be for the whole house of Israel. And whatsoever is for the prince shall be on the one side and on the other side of the holy oblation and of the possession of the city, in front of the holy oblation and in front of the possession of the city, on the west side westward, and on the east side eastward; and in length answerable unto one of the portions, from the west border unto the east border. In the land it shall be to him for a possession in Israel: and My princes shall no more oppress My people; but they shall give the land to the house of Israel according to their tribes"—vers. 1-8.

Of old the land of Palestine was divided by lot among the children of Israel. The lot was an Old Testament way of determining the mind of God, "The lot is cast into the lap; but the whole disposing thereof is of the Lord" (Prov. 16:33). The last use of this method was that in connection with the choice of one to take the place of Judas, as recorded in Acts 1:26. This was before Pentecost. Since then God guides and directs His people by the Spirit and the Word.

As one reads the dimensions given which are somewhat indefinite owing to the fact that we are not told whether cubits or reeds are intended, the impression left on the mind is one of spaciousness, as though God would indicate that He has large things in store for His people in the coming day. The divisions for the tribes are given in chapter 48 and are altogether different from those of old. The portion for the prince has been before us already in the previous chapter but is enlarged upon here. All shall be holy unto the Lord.

"Thus saith the Lord Jehovah: Let it suffice you, O princes of Israel: remove violence and spoil, and execute justice and righteousness; take away your exactions from My people, saith the Lord Jehovah. Ye shall have just balances, and a just ephah, and a just bath. The ephah and the bath shall be of one measure, that the bath may contain the tenth part of a homer, and the ephah the tenth part of a homer: the measure thereof shall be after the homer. And the shekel shall be twenty gerahs; twenty shekels, five and twenty shekels, fifteen shekels, shall be your maneh"—vers. 9-12.

Government was established by God. It is He who puts men in places of authority. But all down through the centuries princes and rulers have been prone to misuse their God-given privileges and to forget their responsibilities. The later kings of Judah were fla- grantly recreant to their duty, and God judged them for it.

Here principles are laid down which all in positions of authority should heed, and which will characterize those who are associated with Christ in ruling in Israel, and over the entire world in the kingdom age.

"This is the oblation that ye shall offer: the sixth part of an ephah from a homer of wheat; and ye shall give the sixth part of an ephah from a homer of barley; and the set portion of oil, of the bath of oil, the tenth part of a bath out of the cor, which is ten baths, even a homer (for ten baths are a homer); and one lamb of the flock, out of two hundred, from the well-watered pastures of Israel;—for a meal-offering, and for a burnt-offering, and for peace-offerings, to make atonement for them, saith the Lord Jehovah. All the people of the land shall give unto this oblation for the prince of Israel. And it shall be the prince's part to give the burnt-offerings, and the meal-offerings, and the drink-offerings, in the feasts, and on the new moons, and on the sabbaths, in all the appointed feasts of the house of Israel: he shall prepare the sin-offering, and the meal-offering, and the burnt-offering, and the peace-offerings, to make atonement for the house of Israel"—vers. 13-17.

As before we may see in the instruction given here a picture of the worship in which princes and people shall participate in the day of the Lord's manifested authority. Christ Himself as set forth typically in these offerings, will be the joy of the hearts of His people. The perfection of His work will be remembered forever by those who have been brought into fellowship with Him on the basis of the blood of the cross.

"Thus saith the Lord Jehovah: In the first month, in the first day of the month, thou shalt take a young bullock without blemish; and thou shalt cleanse the sanctuary. And the priest shall take of the blood of the sin-offering, and put it upon the door-posts of the house, and upon the four corners of the ledge of the altar, and upon the posts of the gate of the inner court. And so thou shalt do on the seventh, day of the month for every one that erreth, and for him that is simple: so shall ye make atonement for the house"—vers. 18-20.

In Lev. 23 we have the feasts or appointed seasons of the Lord. Here our attention is directed to these set times, some of which will no doubt be observed in millennial days. The feast of Pentecost is omitted however. It has had its complete fulfilment in the Church, of which it was the type. The new moons, the passover, and the tabernacles or feast of ingathering, all have their place telling us that all Israel's future blessing rests upon and is the result of the work of the cross. Christ died as the paschal lamb, not for the Church of this age alone but for Israel and the nations as a whole. All who are ever saved in any age or in accordance with any dispensation will owe everything for eternity to the blood of the Lamb of God.

"In the first month, in the fourteenth day of the month, ye shall have the passover, a feast of seven days; unleavened bread shall be eaten. And upon that day shall the prince prepare for himself and for all the people of the land a bullock for a sin-offering. And the seven days of the feast he shall prepare a burnt-offering to Jehovah, seven bullocks and seven rams without blemish daily the seven days; and a he-goat daily for a sin-offering. And he shall prepare a meal-offering, an ephah for a bullock, and an ephah for a ram, and a hin of oil to an ephah. In the seventh month, in the fifteenth day of the month, in the feast, shall he do the like the seven days; according to the sin-offering, according to the burnt-offering, and according to the meal-offering, and according to the oil"—vers. 21-25.

The feast of tabernacles or booths, celebrated after the harvest was gathered in, very aptly typifies full millennial blessing, as we see here and in Zech. 14.

These appointed seasons will be observed as memorials of what God has wrought through the work of His Son, but it is not necessary to think of the sacrifices and offerings as being reinstituted; rather that of which they speak will be the joy of the hearts of the people of God forever.

Chapter Forty-six Regulations For Special Offerings

As we come to this chapter that deals with the sanctuary itself and the offerings which the prophet saw in vision as re-established, we note the special place given to the day of the new moon and the Sabbath.

"Thus saith the Lord Jehovah: The gate of the inner court that looketh toward the east shall be shut the six working days; but on the sabbath day it shall be opened, and on the day of the new moon it shall be opened. And the prince shall enter by the way of the porch of the gate without, and shall stand by the post of the gate; and the priests shall prepare his burnt-offering, and his peace-offerings, and he shall worship at the threshold of the gate: then he shall go forth; but the gate shall not be shut until the evening. And the people of the land shall worship at the door of that gate before Jehovah on the sabbaths and on the new moons. And the burnt-offering that the prince shall offer unto Jehovah shall be on the sabbath day six lambs without blemish and a ram without blemish; and the meal-offering shall be an ephah for the ram, and the meal-offering for the lambs as he is able to give, and a bin of oil to an ephah. And on the day of the new moon it shall be a young bullock without blemish, and six lambs, and a ram; they shall be without blemish: and he shall prepare a meal-offering, an ephah for the bullock, and an ephah for the ram, and for the lambs according as he is able, and a hin of oil to an ephah. And when the prince shall enter, he shall go in by the way of the porch of the gate, and he shall go forth by the way thereof"—vers. 1-8.

The fact that so much stress is laid upon the special observance of the Sabbath day shows the very distinctive Jewish character of the entire vision. It is not a picture of Christianity, except in the sense that the temple of old and also the temple seen in vision typify, in measure at least, God's present temple composed of all those who have been builded by the Spirit into the house of God. For us the Sabbath is found in our blessed Lord Himself who is the fulfilment of that typical day as well as of all else in the Old

Testament economy. But it is very evident from this and other scriptures that when the church period has come to an end and God will take up Israel again, the Sabbath of the law will once more be observed, and so we have it set before us here as an appointed day when special offerings are to be presented before God. We need have no difficulty here in regard to the possible literalness of these offerings, but as we have seen already they all speak of our Lord Jesus Christ, and the presentation of them before God on the Sabbath day would indicate the deep appreciation which the people of God in the coming kingdom age will have of the Person and work of Him who is our Saviour now, and will be recognized as their Saviour then. It is noticeable that there was to be no undue compulsion in regard to the offerings; they are to be presented voluntarily before the Lord, each one as he is able to give.

The day of the new moon is specially emphasized because it indicates from month to month a new beginning, even as the Sabbath sets forth a weekly ending; and each return of the moon speaks anew of the goodness of God to His people in watching over them through another month and pledging His grace for the month to come.

"But when the people of the land shall come before Jehovah in the appointed feasts, he that entereth by the way of the north gate to worship shall go forth by the way of the south gate; and he that entereth by the way of the south gate shall go forth by the way of the north gate: he shall not return by the way of the gate whereby he came in, but shall go forth straight before him. And the prince, when they go in, shall go in in the midst of them; and when they go forth, they shall go forth together. And in the feasts and in the solemnities the meal-offering shall be an ephah for a bullock, and an ephah for a ram, and for the lambs as he is able to give, and a bin of oil to an ephah. And when the prince shall prepare a freewill-offering, a burnt-offering or peace-offerings as a freewill-offering unto Jehovah, one shall open for him the gate that looketh toward the east; and he shall prepare his burnt-offering and his peace-offerings, as he doth on the sabbath day: then he shall go forth; and after his going forth one shall shut the gate"—vers. 9-12.

We are impressed as we read these words of the happy relationship that will exist between the prince and the people. While special recognition is given to the prince because of his office, yet all stand on one common ground before God and in His sanctuary; there is no room for worldly honors or human pride. All stand together upon redemption ground, the only basis of acceptance with God; and of this the sacrifices and offerings all speak.

There may be something suggestive here too in the instruction given as to entering in at one gate and passing on through the court and leaving by another portal. May not this speak to everyone of us, reminding us that we shall never pass over the same route again? We cannot retrace our steps as we go through this scene. It should be our happy privilege to go on with God from glory to glory as led by His Spirit.

There may be very much here that a more spiritual mind would enter into, but I hesitate to try to apply types beyond their clear, evident meaning.

"And thou shalt prepare a lamb a year old without blemish for a burnt-offering unto Jehovah daily: morning by morning shalt thou prepare it. And thou shalt prepare a meal-offering with it morning by morning, the sixth part of an ephah, and the third part of a hin of oil, to moisten the fine flour; a meal-offering unto Jehovah continually by a perpetual ordinance. Thus shall they prepare the lamb, and the meal-offering, and the oil, morning by morning, for a continual burnt-offering"—vers. 13-15.

Of old in the tabernacle service and also in that connected with the temple of Solomon, the burnt offering was present before God both morning and evening. Here we are told, "Thou shalt prepare a lamb a year old without blemish for a burnt-offering unto Jehovah daily: morning by morning shalt thou prepare it." There is no mention of the evening offering besides, because everything here is connected with the glorious day when the Lord Himself will be the light of His people and the morning of gladness will not be succeeded by an evening of sorrow or distress. How precious it is even now for those of us who know the Lord, to wait upon Him morning by morning, presenting a continual burnt offering before God as we meditate upon the preciousness and the effective work of our Lord Jesus Christ. It is of this indeed that the burnt offering really speaks. With it the meal offering was connected, and that, as we know, speaks of the perfection of Christ's Person rather than emphasizing the work which He accomplished on the cross. It is the incarnate Christ—God and Man in one Person— that is represented by the meal offering of fine flour mingled with oil, never to be separated again.

"Thus saith the Lord Jehovah: If the prince give a gift unto any of his sons, it is his inheritance, it shall belong to his sons; it is their possession by inheritance. But if he give of his inheritance a gift to one of his servants, it shall be his to the year of liberty; then it shall return to the prince; but as for his inheritance, it shall be for his sons. Moreover the prince shall not take of the people's inheritance, to thrust them out of their possession; he shall give inheritance to his sons out of his own possession, that My people be not scattered every man from his possession"—vers. 16-18.

In the coming great day of Israel's restoration they will enter fully into the meaning of the year of Jubilee, the year of liberty. All down through the centuries, had these Jubilees been properly observed, they would have been a constant reminder that God has in view both for Israel and the world something far better than they have ever known. A time is coming when liberty will be proclaimed to the captives, and the house of Israel shall return to their own possessions and enter fully into the enjoyment of them, never to be separated from them any more. The ancient law of the Jubilee, it seems, will prevail in millennial days: thus the family of Israel will not forfeit their lands, and the strangers will be permitted to enjoy, at least for a season, a portion with them; but God said of the land of Palestine, "The land shall not be sold for ever: for the land is Mine" (Lev. 25:23). He has given it by covenant to Abraham's literal seed so that no future arrangement will be permitted that will alienate it from them, however much others may be permitted to enjoy it with Israel.

"Then he brought me through the entry, which was at the side of the gate, into the holy chambers for the priests, which looked toward the north: and, behold, there was a place on the hinder part westward. And he said unto me, This is the place where the priests shall boil the trespass-offering and the sin-offering, and where they shall bake the meal-offering; that they bring them not forth into the outer court, to sanctify the people. Then he brought me forth into the outer court, and caused me to pass by the four corners of the court; and, behold, in every corner of the court there was a court. In the four corners of the court there were courts inclosed, forty cubits long and thirty broad: these four in the corners were of one measure. And there was a wall round about in them, round about the four, and boiling-places were made under the walls round about. Then said he unto me, These are the boiling-houses, where the ministers of the house shall boil the sacrifice of the people"—vers. 19-24.

Ezekiel saw in the vision adequate provision made for the nourishment of the priests. In the book of Exodus (29:33) we read, "They shall eat those things wherewith the atonement was made." The priests dwelling in the courts of the Lord's house, feasting upon the burnt offerings and the meal offerings, speak to us of God's family today who are privileged to feed their souls on what God has revealed concerning His Son and the work of the cross. And so in that coming day the priests of Jehovah will enter in a way they have never done in the past into the meaning of all these sacrifices; and in the quiet precincts of the chambers of the priests, shut away from the observance of the multitude, they will prepare their food and enjoy it in the presence of the Lord. How good it would be if we only knew more of this today—dwelling quietly in the secret place where the eye of God alone is upon us as we meditate upon what Scripture reveals concerning the Deity and Humanity of our Lord Jesus, His eternal fellowship, and His perfection as Man here on earth, His obedience unto death, and the effect of His work both as to the glorifying of the Father and the salvation of those who put their trust in Him! Here is rich food indeed on which we do well to nourish our souls that we may become strong in the Lord and in the power of His might.

Chapter Forty-Seven The Life-Giving River

"And he brought me back unto the door of the house; and, behold, waters issued out from under the threshold of the house eastward (for the forefront of the house was toward the east); and the waters came down from under, from the right side of the house, on the south of the altar. Then he brought me out by the way of the gate northward, and led me round by the way without unto the outer gate, by the way of the gate that looketh toward the east; and, behold, there ran out waters on the right side"—vers. 1, 2.

Back of all our meditations upon these last chapters of Ezekiel, from 40 to 48, the question has been kept ever in mind, Are we to take this vision literally as indicating something which will be fulfilled to the letter in millennial days, or are we to understand it as symbolic of wondrous blessing which God has in store for His ancient people and for the world, but which He has presented in this form in order that the poor finite minds of His people may get some conception of the wondrous things reserved for them which are utterly beyond human imagination? We cannot help contrasting and comparing the closing chapters of the Apocalypse with what we have here. In considering this vision of the river our attention necessarily will be directed to that pure river of water of life proceeding out of the throne of God and of the Lamb, which John saw in vision as he found himself in spirit on a great and high mountain beholding the holy city, New Jerusalem, coming down from God out of heaven. We are told definitely in the first verse of the Revelation that God sent and signified these things to His servant John; and we have observed that the word *signified* really means *symbolized*. There are very few indeed who would attempt to literalize the great visions of this remarkable book. No one expects to see a sevenfold-sealed roll in heaven broken by one who has the appearance of a lamb. The roll we know is the title-deed to this world, and the Lamb is the Man Christ Jesus seated on the throne of God. Neither do we expect an actual savage brute with seven heads and ten horns to come bodily up from the bottomless pit and dominate the world.

We see in this vision the symbol of human government in its last degenerate and atheistic condition; and so when it comes to the vision of the heavenly city we understand that God is using symbols of wondrous beauty and glory to set forth the magnificence and marvelous character of the eternal home of the saints. The river there is clearly the Holy Spirit's testimony to the risen Christ, which brings refreshment and blessing everywhere it goes; and we see on either side of the river the tree of life with its marvelous fruits, speaking of the message of the gospel which brings spiritual healing to all who receive it.

Now as we consider Ezekiel's vision it would seem to be but slavish adherence to literality which would deny the symbolic character of much that is here unfolded. For many, the river in this chapter is a literal stream which will break forth from underneath the temple in millennial days and will divide into two parts, according to Joel 3:18 and Zech. 14:8; thus linking the Mediterranean Sea with the Dead Sea and giving the city of Jerusalem itself a water-harbor. All this may indeed be true, but that this passage in Ezekiel refers to the same thing does not seem to the present writer either to be reasonable or in accordance with what we learn elsewhere in Scripture. What is the river that proceeds from under the threshold of the sanctuary of Jehovah? Can it be other than that same glorious stream which we have mentioned already, as brought before us in the twenty-second chapter of the Revelation? Of such a river Scripture speaks in many places. Wherever God rests we find a river flowing. There was one in Eden, a literal river flowing forth from the garden and dividing into four great streams; but elsewhere we find the river spoken of in a spiritual sense. In Ps. 36:8 we read, "Thou shall make them drink of the river of Thy pleasures"; and in Ps. 46:4 we are told, "There is a river, the streams whereof shall make glad the city of God." Observe, this is not a prophecy of some literal river to break forth from the floor of the temple in the future, but at the time the Psalmist wrote, it was a blessed fact, and it is a fact still, that there is such a river of refreshment of which all may drink who are willing to stoop down in repentance and receive that which God so graciously offers. This accords with what we have in the New Testament, "Whosoever will, let him take the water of life freely" (Rev. 22:17).

Our blessed Lord, using the same figure, said, "If any man thirst, let him come unto Me, and drink. He that be-lieveth on Me, as the scripture hath said, from within him shall flow rivers of living water" (John 7:37, 38). He has promised to bless and refresh the dry places like a river (Ps. 105:41); and Isaiah twice speaks of peace as a river (48:18; 66:12); while both the Psalmist and Jeremiah tell us of the righteous man who is like a tree planted by the rivers of water (Ps. 1:3; Jer. 17:8). Speaking prophetically of our Lord Jesus Christ, Isaiah says, "A man shall be as an hiding place from the wind, and a covert from the tempest; as rivers of water in a dry place, as the shadow of a great rock in a weary land" (32:2). "A man shall be...as rivers"—what a remarkable picture! But when we realize that this river speaks of life and refreshment we at once see that all this is centered in our Lord Jesus who gives life and rest of heart and conscience to all who come to Him and drink.

There are numerous passages to which we might turn, but these are sufficient to show how frequently the Holy Scriptures use the symbol of a river as referring to the grace of God in Christ ministered to the soul in the power of the Holy Spirit.

Whether, therefore, Ezekiel's vision of a river will be fulfilled literally or not we do not know. Of this we may be sure: it does speak to us today of that same glorious river which is brought before us in so many other places in the Word of God.

The prophet was led by his guide to the door of the house, and he beheld water issuing from under the threshold of the house toward the east. He had seen nothing like this before; though in vision he had been led through that court. It is as though now all is seen as completed, and God has found His rest in the sanctuary ; His glory has filled the house, and waters spread forth for the refreshment and blessing of His people.

These waters are pictured as running down from the court through the outer gate that looks toward the east and descending on the right side, going on down to the Jordan valley.

"When the man went forth eastward with the line in his hand, he measured a thousand cubits, and he caused me to pass through the waters, waters that were to the ankles. Again he measured a thousand, and caused me to pass through the waters, waters that were to the knees. Again he measured a thousand, and caused me to pass through the waters, waters that were to the loins. Afterward he measured a thousand; and it was a river that I could not pass through; for the waters were risen, waters to swim in, a river that could not be passed through"—vers. 3-5.

There is something here that is absolutely inexplicable if we think of a literal river. Rivers widen and deepen as the volume of water increases through tributaries pouring into them; but of such tributaries we have no mention here, and yet this river becomes deeper and broader the farther it flows from its source. Is not this true of the river of God's grace? How small the apparent beginnings on Pentecost when the glory of God filled all the place where the disciples were sitting, and immediately the testimony to the risen Christ began, and the river has been flowing on ever since until it has become a mighty stream encompassing the whole world.

Ezekiel's guide measured a thousand cubits—that is, fifteen hundred feet, and he caused the prophet to enter into the waters: they were up to his ankles. May this not suggest the very beginning of a life in fellowship with God? "If we live in the Spirit, let us also walk in the Spirit" (Gal. 5:25). The feet were in the river, and the waters covered them. But the guide measured another thousand cubits and caused Ezekiel to pass through the waters, and they were up to his knees. Who will think it fanciful if we say that the waters up to the knees suggest praying in the Holy Spirit? But the guide measured another thousand and caused the prophet to pass through the waters, and now they were up to his loins, suggesting the complete control of every fleshly lust in the power of the Spirit of God. He measured another thousand, and that which had begun as a small stream was a river so that Ezekiel could not pass through, for the waters were risen, waters to swim in. Surely this is to live in the fulness of the Spirit to which every child of God should aspire.

"And he said unto me, Son of man, hast thou seen this? Then he brought me, and caused me to return to the bank of the river. Now "when I had returned, behold, upon the bank of the river were very many trees on the one side and on the other. Then said he unto me, These waters issue forth toward the eastern region, and shall go down into the Arab ah; and they shall go toward the sea; into the sea shall the waters go which were made to issue forth; and the waters shall be healed. And it shall come to pass, that every living creature which swarmeth, in every place whither the rivers come, shall live; and there shall be a very great multitude of fish; for these waters are come thither, and the waters of the sea shall be healed, and everything shall live whithersoever the river cometh. And it shall come to pass, that fishers shall stand by it: from En-gedi even unto En-eglaim shall be a place for the spreading of nets; their fish shall be after their kinds, as the fish of the great sea, exceeding many. But the miry places thereof, and the marshes thereof, shall not be healed; they shall be given up to salt. And by the river upon the bank thereof, on this side and on that side, shall grow every tree for food, whose leaf shall not wither, neither shall the fruit thereof fail: it shall bring forth new fruit every month, because the waters thereof issue out of the sanctuary; and the fruit thereof shall be for food, and the leaf thereof for healing"—vers. 6-12.

Having brought the prophet back in vision to the bank of the river, the guide bade him to consider what he had seen and experienced. Then as Ezekiel continued to gaze he saw that upon the bank of the river many trees appeared on both sides. The guide explained that these waters issued forth toward the eastern region and should go down unto the Arabah—that is, the plain of the Jordan, and thence on to the Dead Sea—that sea which for four millennia has become more and more salty as time has gone by, and yet ever receiving millions of gallons of fresh water from the Jordan; but because of no outlet its brininess has increased rather than diminished, so that no fish can live in it. But as Ezekiel looked he saw that when the waters of this river poured into the sea they brought life and healing; a multitude of living things swarmed into the sea and great schools of fish were seen where before there had been only death and desolation, and all this because "these waters are come thither." We are told that, "everything shall live whithersoever the river cometh"; and because of this fishers shall stand by it, from the north and to the southern extremity of what had been a sea of death, spreading their nets, taking fish of every kind, furnishing abundant food for untold thousands of people. The miry places and the marshes were not to be healed but given up to salt. This is not yet the eternal condition; it speaks of millennial blessing, for salt tells of the preservative power of righteousness. Not until the eternal state do we read, "There was no more sea."

The beauty of the picture stirs the heart as we read of trees for food "whose leaf shall not wither, neither shall the fruit thereof fail. It shall bring forth new fruit every month," as in the case of the tree of life as seen in the Apocalypse. Who can measure the blessing that will come to this world and to mankind as a whole because of the stream of testimony that shall yet flow forth from the throne of Jehovah, when set up on earth!

The remaining part of the chapter might have been better linked with chapter 48 to which it is really an introduction.

"Thus saith the Lord Jehovah: This shall be the border, whereby ye shall divide the land for inheritance according to the twelve tribes of Israel: Joseph shall have two portions. And ye shall inherit it, one as well as another; for I sware to give it unto your fathers: and this land shall fall unto you for inheritance. And this shall be the border of the land: On the north side, from the great sea, by the way of Hethlon, unto the entrance of Zedad; Hamath, Berothah, Sibraim, which is between the border of Damascus and the border of Hamath; Hazerhatticon, which is by the border of Hauran. And the border from the sea, shall be Hazarenon at the border of Damascus; and on the north northward is the border of Hamath. This is the north side. And the east side, between Hauran and Damascus and Gilead and the land of Israel, shall be the Jordan; from the north border, unto the east sea shall ye measure. This is the east side. And the south side southward shall be from Tamar as far as the waters of Meriboth-kadesh, to the brook of Egypt, unto the great sea. This is the south side southward. And the west side shall be the great sea, from the south border as far as over against the entrance of Hamath. This is the west side. So shall ye divide this land unto you according to the tribes of Israel. And it shall come to pass, that ye shall divide it by lot for an inheritance unto you and to the strangers that sojourn among you, who shall beget children among you; and they shall be unto you as the home-born among the children of Israel; they shall have inheritance with you among the tribes of Israel. And it shall come to pass, that in what tribe the stranger sojourneth, there shall ye give him his inheritance, saith the Lord Jehovah"—vers. 13-23.

One can mark out these boundaries by the aid of an Atlas as the pencil moves on from city to city and district to district. It speaks of an enlarged Canaan where there will be abundant room for all who desire to dwell there in millennial days. It is to be divided among the twelve tribes, many of which though lost to man's vision are still known to God; but the strangers will be welcomed and will be permitted to share in the inheritance which God is to give to Israel in that day.

Chapter Forty-eight Jehovah Shammah

Ere the wondrous vision faded away our prophet saw the land far extended, as Isaiah 33:17 tells us, "Thine eyes shall see the King in His beauty: they shall behold the land of far distances" (A. V., *margin*).

"Now these are the names of the tribes: From the north end, beside the way of Hethlon to the entrance of Hamath, Hazarenan at the border of Damascus, northward beside Hamath (and they shall have their sides east and west), Dan, one portion. And by the border of Dan, from the east side unto the west side, Asher, one portion. And by the border of Asher, from the east side even unto the west side, Naphtali, one portion. And by the border of Naphtali, from the east side unto the west side, Manasseh, one portion. And by the border of Manasseh, from the east side unto the west side, Ephraim, one portion. And by the border of Ephraim, from the east side even unto the west side, Reuben, one portion. And by the border of Reuben, from the east side unto the west side, Judah, one portion"—vers. 1-7.

The inheritance of seven tribes is depicted in broad belts running from west to east across the entire land promised to the earthly seed of Abraham (Gen. 15:7, 18-21; 17:8). That covenant has never been rescinded, so remains inviolate, for it was based not upon man's faithfulness but upon pure grace. The universal testimony of the prophets is that when Israel returns to God they will be re-established in their land, never to be rooted out again.

Seven tribes are listed here who will possess the northern part of Canaan and the land east of the Jordan.

"And by the border of Judah, from the east side unto the west side, shall be the oblation which ye shall offer, five and twenty thousand reeds in breadth, and in length as one of the portions, from the east side unto the west side: and the sanctuary shall be in the midst of it. The oblation that ye shall offer unto Jehovah shall be five and twenty thousand reeds in length, and ten thousand in breadth. And for these, even for the priests, shall be the holy oblation; toward the north five and twenty thousand in length, and toward the west ten thousand in breadth, and toward the east ten thousand in breadth, and toward the south five and twenty thousand in length: and the sanctuary of Jehovah shall be in the midst thereof. It shall be for the priests that are sanctified of the sons of Zadok, that have kept My charge, that went not astray when the children of Israel went astray, as the Levites went astray. And it shall be unto them an oblation from the oblation of the land, a thing most holy, by the border of the Levites"—vers. 8-12.

Immediately south of the portion of Judah was the oblation set apart for the priests with the sanctuary in the midst. There the glory of God was seen. It is His delight to dwell amid the praises of His people. As a tender loving Father He would have all His children gathered about Him, enjoying happy fellowship and uninterrupted communion.

It is interesting to note how often this expression *in the midst* is used in connection with Jehovah's place among His chosen ones. Of old the tabernacle, God's dwelling-place, was in the midst of the camp (Num. 2:17; 5:3). God Himself walked in the midst of the camp (Deut. 23:14). He dwelt in the midst of Jerusalem (Ps. 46:5); the Holy One of Israel dwelt in the midst of the nations (Isa. 12:6; Hos. 11:9); Zephaniah who, like Ezekiel, looked forward to future blessing, saw the Lord again in the midst as of old (Zeph. 3:5, 15). It is this that Ezekiel saw in vision: the tribes resting in peace after all their long centuries of distress and wandering among the nations, and Jehovah dwelling in His sanctuary in the midst of His redeemed ones.

"And answerable unto the border of the priests, the Levites shall have five and twenty thousand in length, and ten thousand in breadth: all the length shall be five and twenty thousand, and the breadth ten thousand. And they shall sell none of it, nor exchange it, nor shall the first-fruits of the land be alienated; for it is holy unto Jehovah"—vers. 13, 14.

That which is dedicated to the Lord must not be alienated for any cause or used for any other purpose. As the first-fruits belonged to Him so with the oblation for His sanctuary. The holy must not be confounded with the secular, but the title of Jehovah is to be ever acknowledged.

"And the five thousand that are left in the breadth, in front of the five and twenty thousand, shall be for common use, for the city, for dwelling and for suburbs; and the city shall be in the midst thereof. And these shall be the measures thereof: the north side four thousand and five hundred, and the south side four thousand and five hundred, and on the east side four thousand and five hundred, and the west side four thousand and five hundred. And the city shall have suburbs: toward the north two hundred and fifty, and toward the south two hundred and fifty, and toward the east two hundred and fifty, and toward the west two hundred and fifty. And the residue in the length, answerable unto the holy oblation, shall be ten thousand eastward, and ten thousand westward; and it shall be answerable unto the holy oblation; and the increase thereof shall be for food unto them that labor in the city. And they that labor in the city, out of all the tribes of Israel, shall till it. All the oblation shall be five and twenty thousand by five and twenty thousand: ye shall offer the holy oblation foursquare, with the possession of the city"—vers. 15-20.

The city and its suburbs occupied a wide and a broad space surrounding the Lord's portion. Here the people were to dwell comfortably housed and enjoying the fruit of their labor as they tilled the open land surrounding the city itself, thus enjoying the fruits that it would bring forth. When God gets His rightful place His people may be sure that their interests will be well looked after.

"And the residue shall be for the prince, on the one side and on the other of the holy oblation and of the possession of the city; in front of the five and twenty thousand of the oblation toward the east border, and westward in front of the five and twenty thousand toward the west border, answerable unto the portions, it shall be for the prince: and the holy oblation and the sanctuary of the house shall be in the midst thereof. Moreover from the possession of the Levites, and from the possession of the city, being in the midst of that which is the prince's, between the border of Judah and the border of Benjamin, it shall be for the prince"—vers. 21, 22.

The inheritance of the prince was in close connection with that of the priests and the Levites, near to the sanctuary; thus everyone would have his allotted place according to the plan of God, with whom there is no disorder or confusion.

"And as for the rest of the tribes: from the east side unto the west side, Benjamin, one portion. And by the border of Benjamin, from the east side unto the west side, Simeon, one portion. And by the border of Simeor, from the east side unto the west side, Issachar, one portion. And by the border of Issachar, from the east side unto the west side, Zebulun, one portion. And by the border of Zebulun, from the east side unto the west side, Gad, one portion. And by the border of Gad, at the south side southward, the border shall be even from Tamar unto the waters of Meribath-kadesh, to the brook of Egypt, unto the great sea. This is the land which ye shall divide by lot unto the tribes of Israel for inheritance, and these are their several portions, saith the Lord Jehovah"—vers. 23-29.

Five tribes were seen as located on broad strips of land south of the city, even as seven had been depicted north of it. It is noticeable that the Levites, as of old, were not numbered among the tribes receiving an inheritance in the land because the Lord is their portion, but Joseph is divided into Ephraim and Manasseh, as when they took possession of Palestine of old. The Levites, as we have seen, had their place in the sacred oblation, in the vicinity of the temple.

"And these are the egresses of the city: On the north side four thousand and five hundred reeds by measure; and the gates of the city shall be after the names of the tribes of Israel, three gates northward: the gate of Reuben, one; the gate of Judah, one; the gate of Levi, one. And at the east side four thousand and five hundred reeds, and three gates: even the gate of Joseph, one; the gate of Benjamin, one; the gate of Dan, one. And at the south side four thousand and five hundred reeds by measure, and three gates: the gate of Simeon, one; the gate of Issachar, one; the gate of Zebulun, one. At the west side four thousand and five hundred reeds, with their three gates: the gate of Gad, one; the gate of Asher, one; the gate of Naphtali, one. It shall be eighteen thousand reeds round about: and the name of the city from that day shall be, Jehovah is there"—vers. 30-35.

Ezekiel saw twelve gates to the city of his vision, and on each gate the name of one of the tribes of Israel. In this case Levi was listed as one of the tribes, and Joseph as another, so that the distinction between Ephraim and Manasseh is not recognized here. The heavenly Jerusalem as seen by John also had twelve gates, and on these too the names of the twelve tribes were inscribed. But the one scene is earthly and the other heavenly. Abraham's literal seed will be partly in heaven and partly on earth. All Old Testament saints will be raised and have their place in Jerusalem which is above. Those living on the earth at the second advent will possess the land as promised to Abraham, Isaac, and Jacob, which is Israel.

The account of the vision closes with the declara- tion that the restored earthly city will bear the name of *Jehovah Shammah*— that is, *The Lord is there,* for He will, as we have seen, return in glory to His sanctuary and will dwell in the midst of His people throughout the kingdom age.

Made in the USA
Columbia, SC
16 January 2018